History in primary schools

Frontispiece   Lord Cobham and his family at table (reproduced courtesy of the Marquess of Bath)

History in primary schools

A practical approach for teachers of
5- to 11-year-old children

JOAN BLYTH

Open University Press
Milton Keynes · Philadelphia

Open University Press
12 Cofferidge Close
Stony Stratford
Milton Keynes MK11 1BY

and

242 Cherry Street
Philadelphia, PA 19106, USA

First Published 1989

British Library Cataloguing in Publication Data

Blyth, Joan
  History in primary schools : a practical
  approach for teachers of 5–11 year old
  children.
  1. England. Primary schools. Curriculum
  subjects : History. Teaching
  I. Title
  372.8′9044′0942

  ISBN 0–335–15830–7
  ISBN 0–335–15829–3 Pbk

Typeset by Inforum Ltd., Portsmouth
Printed in Great Britain by Redwood Burn Ltd., Trowbridge, Wiltshire

To the memory of my parents
Clare and Edward Guest

Contents

List of illustrations

Preface

Since the first edition of this book was published in 1982, much heartsearching has taken place as to the place of History in the primary curriculum, particularly with the impending introduction of a government sponsored national curriculum supporting History as a 'foundation subject'. The first edition proved helpful both to students in training and to experienced teachers and I am glad that the Open University Press has given me the opportunity to revise the text, particularly updating Chapter 2 on schemes of work and Chapter 4 on resources.

My thanks go to the many professional friends and colleagues who have offered advice about how to improve the first edition and especially to my husband, Alan Blyth, who has rewritten his adaptation of the Schools Council *Place, Time and Society Project* for the 7–11 age span, and given advice and support on many other parts of the book. Once again I want to thank teachers who have written of their experiences with children: Jayne Woodhouse, Viv Wilson, Anne Joyce, Shirley Makin, Margaret West, Claire Parker, John West, J.M. Salt, Carol Wilson, Kenneth May, Susan Lynn and Cottia Howard.

Joan Blyth

Acknowledgements

The author wishes to credit the following sources for material used in this book: Cover illustration of the portrait of Arabella Stuart is reproduced by permission of the National Trust Photographic Library; the frontispiece of Baron Cobham and his family is reproduced by permission of the Marquess of Bath, Longleat House, Warminster, Wiltshire; Moray House College of Education for figures 2.1 and 2.10; University of Sidney for figure 2.2; Controller of Her Majesty's Stationery Office for figures 2.6 and 5.3; Tom Holder for figure 2.7; Collins Educational for figure 2.8; Macdonald & Co. (Publishers) Ltd for figure 2.9; Anne Joyce for figure 2.13; the Chatsworth Settlement Trustees and Courtauld Institute of Art for figure 3.2; Liverpool Education Committee for figure 3.3; Southampton City Council for figure 3.4; Longman Group for figure 3.7; Unwin Hyman Ltd for figure 3.8; Liverpool Corporation for figure 3.9; Pat Raper at Cholsey Infants' School for figure 4.4; Liverpool City Libraries for figures 4.6, 4.8, 4.9 and 4.11; the Postmaster General for figure 4.7; Phillimore & Co. Ltd for figure 4.13 and *Educational Review* for permission to use work that formed the basis for an article in Vol. 39, No. 2, 1987, including figures 4.14, 4.15 and 4.16.

1 History in the primary school curriculum

In thinking about the place of history – if it has a place – in the curriculum of the primary school, we have to clarify the purpose of teaching and learning the subject in the years of 5 to 11. Cognitive psychologists emphasize the crucial importance of those years for subsequent academic achievement, an issue which is still too frequently ignored by teachers of older children. In addition, they are years of tremendous physical and emotional development for children. Primary teachers are certainly aware of the vital importance of their work and view their role as being involved in the welfare of all sides of the child's life.

Class teacher organization has emphasized concentration on general concerns, and especially on the linguistic and mathematical side of a child's development since communication, literacy, and numeracy are essential to all human beings. The child below the age of 13 also needs to be taught the basic methodology to understand science and the social subjects, and to appreciate the arts as well as to develop his physical powers. Within social subjects I include morality as well as history, geography and social science. Therefore, the primary school child needs a 'whole curriculum' which at certain times delves more deeply and technically into specific disciplines. In the time at the teacher's disposal this task is a formidable one. Faced with strident demands for other kinds of curricular content, she feels obliged to question the need to include much study of the past or development of the skills of the young historian. The past appears to be only a small part of the social subjects. Yet it is a part of much greater importance than some teachers appreciate. Teachers in the secondary school are educating the 'whole child' in a different way through more structural disciplines but the basic foundations for these disciplines need to have been laid in the primary school.

1.1   The nature of history

Before discussing the aims and purposes of studying history in the primary school it is wise to look at the essential nature of the discipline and find out how children of 5 to 11 will react to it. Many definitions have been made since the institution of Honours degrees in history in the late nineteenth century and they all vary, but from this mine of information five elements become apparent.

In the first place, history is about real people and real events interacting upon each other in the past. The age-old problem of how people and events impinge upon each other is a basic essential of history. Second, history must be concerned with sequence, time, and chronology. This is unique to the discipline and the most difficult concept to teach and understand. But it is the very essence of history. One well-known modern historian has recently said: 'Freedom to move through time and space is one of the greatest opportunities the historian has'.[1] A third element is the evidence which enables us to know what actually happened in the past. This comes not only from books written by historians (secondary sources) but also from documents written in the past, buildings, landscapes, archaeological remains, reminiscences of older people (oral history), pictures, photographs and films. These primary and secondary sources are the basic material of history but can be difficult to find. The time taken to find the much sought-after recent book in the library, to decipher the faded palaeography (handwriting) of an early document, to travel a distance to look at the relevant building, and to tape record the memories of old people are awe-inspiring tasks for the busy teacher in any school. If and when even some of this information seeking has been done, understanding and interpretation pose their problems. Understanding the meaning of technical terms and seeking advice require diligence and courage. Interpretation will probably involve reading several books (or articles) on the same subject. A fourth element is the communication of the past to others through talking and writing. Historians using the same sources often interpret them in different ways and from different standpoints, resulting in conflicts of opinion. These conflicts are often only resolved after the discovery of more primary evidence; sometimes, being dependent on irreconcilable approaches to history itself, they are never resolved and we have to be content to accept differing views. Yet controversy and discussion are of the essence of the discipline and help us to a truer view of the subject. The last element of the discipline of history is the way in which the past affects the present. A knowledge of the past, of individuals and institutions, can help to explain how these people and institutions react and how a chain of events has influenced them.

Primary school children will not be able to understand all these elements, nor for that matter are secondary school pupils or adults able to do so. But they can certainly learn about and try to understand many people in the past, especially children and relatively unsophisticated adults, and can begin to handle simple primary evidence (especially artefacts of the past) and to appreciate that all people and events happen in time, however short a time ago.

Beyond all these separate claims on behalf of history, there is the contention of some philosophers of education such as Paul Hirst, that history is a 'form of knowledge', logically distinct from others such as scientific or mathematical knowledge. If this is so, then the case for including history as such in the curriculum for younger children in an appropriate manner is greatly strengthened. The 'forms of knowledge' approach has itself been subjected to considerable crticism but it is noteworthy that one of the most important studies in the teaching of history, by P. J. Rogers, appears to give powerful empirical support to Hirst's assertion that children do encounter history as a form of knowledge.[2]

But the views of historians and philosophers are not the only relevant considerations. Nowadays, when considering the place of any subject or activity in the primary school curriculum, teachers are accustomed to hearing how the work of Piaget and his collaborators has thrown light on children's learning. In the case of history, this is less obviously the case. Piaget himself did make a specific study of children's understanding of time, and of their moral development, but it has been left to others to delineate the sequence of development in ideas about society, about historical inference, or indeed about person perception. Writers such as Roy Hallam[3] and Rogers have broken important new ground, but much of it has been at the post-primary level and so in the teaching of younger children it is still substantially necessary to rely on general notions of development, enlivened by the accumulated experience of teachers.

In common with Piaget, the work of Douglas Barnes on language in the curriculum is familiar to teachers. This type of research has been extended to the teaching of history through the work of A. D. Edwards.[4] He warns teachers of the danger of thinking that the language of history used in the classroom should be 'everyday' because the people being studied were 'ordinary' people. He says, 'There is an obvious risk of confusion between the "common sense" of then and now.' The language and concepts of past ages need to be taught specifically. A further consideration is the need to be aware of the generalizations made in historical writing; these generalizations are not always clarified by specific factual examples and are often too abstract in concept for both teacher and pupils.

Most primary teachers do not feel secure and happy in including historical material in their curriculum unless they are assured of specific assistance. If this is not forthcoming, it is only natural that teachers will despair and resort to well-tried areas of the curriculum in which help has been clear, practical, and easily-assessed.

1.2 History teaching in the English primary school

The beginnings of history teaching in elementary schools are notoriously difficult to trace. Some light has been thrown on local developments through the very extensive studies carried out by advanced students of education but it is rarely that these have been systematically brought together except by writers such as R. D. Bramwell and, more recently, Peter Gordon. The picture which we can now discern is one in which here and there, from surprisingly early in the nineteenth century, some schools touched upon the mainstream of English history, or on the local environment or both. Historical facts were included, too, in the compendia of information used in middle-class homes and in some of the monitorial and other schools. Some history percolated from the early training colleges down into the elementary school until the introduction of the Revised Code in 1861 virtually exting-uished any form of teaching outside the austere grant-earning minimum. Thus, although Victorian England was a culture which became increasingly aware of its past, and set history firmly in the pattern of its early adult education, the place of history in the elementary, or indeed in the secon-dary, schools was a variable and insecure one.

It is to be hoped that the present official emphasis on 'benchmarks' and tests at 7 and 11 will not once more drive real History as distinct from test History from the state system of schooling. Writing of social studies in the nineteenth and twentieth centuries, Peter Gordon and Denis Lawton say, 'In this area of the curriculum schools have shown themselves to be highly resistant to change throughout the century,' and again, 'Social studies and science . . . have very strong claims but have never been given the promin-ence they deserve'.[5]

Meanwhile, one celebrated source of information as to how at least the upper classes taught their children is the famous *Little Arthur's History of England* by Lady Callcott, first published in 1835 and addressed 'To Mother'. Lady Callcott presumed that every mother had the time, desire and ability to read to her children the story of Britain's heritage told in terms of 'heroes' and 'tyrants' (such as William the Conqueror – 'tyrant' rather than king). These stories are exciting, heroic, and heavily biased. They aim to teach morality and greatness.

In 1871, following Forster's Education Act, the New Code allowed an expansion of the elementary curriculum and an opportunity arose to include 'class subjects'. By coincidence, in 1871 and 1873 Oxford and Cambridge universities agreed to introduce Honours history degrees into their cur-ricula. But the gap between the elementary school and the older universities was vast and the new degrees had no direct effect on the training of teachers. History teaching, for most children, thus depended upon the combination of academic content and 'method' prevalent in training college courses. The universities joined in this training after the foundation of day training colleges towards the end of the nineteenth century, but it was not until the beginning of the present century that any official notice was taken of history in elementary schools. The *Suggestions for the Consideration of Teachers and Others Concerned in the Work of Public Elementary Schools* of 1905 saw history as difficult to teach but a subject that should be taught. It should be taught for reasons of morality (compare Lady Callcott); children must know their rights and duties, Britain's heritage must be compared with other nations and the example of 'good men' should be held up to them. Thus, as earlier, history was to be studied for the virtues it *might* develop, not for enjoyment or interest and certainly not for essential, practical reasons.

In 1923 the Board of Education published its first specific suggestions about the teaching of history. It recommended the reading of the good history story books that were being published, as a means of children knowing 'our own national story' and gave an 'alphabet' of 32 dates, events in English history which all children should learn. These ranged from 100 BC to the 1914–18 war. Thus history teaching was for national propaganda and was essentially factual and content based. In his thesis *Elementary School Work 1900–1925* (Institute of Education, University of Durham, 1961), R. D. Bramwell summarizes the aims of history teaching in the first quarter of the twentieth century as being a school of citizenship involving Britain's heritage from the beginning to the present day and thus encouraging teachers to show pupils historic buildings on their expeditions out of school. In 1927 a *Handbook of Suggestions for Teachers* viewed history as above all an instrument of moral training learnt through good and evil personalities. So by 1927 Lady Callcott's view of over a hundred years earlier still held good.

Confidence in the efficacy of history to transform children and make them 'good citizens' was evaporating by the 1930s. However, the substantial introduction of separate junior schools, 7–11, afforded a new opportunity and in 1931 the Hadow Report proclaimed the belief that a child up to the age of 11 could be expected to be able to read a simple story and to understand how history affected 'his everyday life and environment' (vague terms). Although individuals researched and wrote books on the teaching of history in primary schools, few teachers in elementary schools benefited from this work as the training colleges did not consider the subject to be as important as many other subjects for beginner teachers. Yet Sir Fred Clarke's *Foundations of History Teaching* remains a classic for all time, a philosophical and at the same time practical and easily understood basis for all teaching of the past up to the age of 12. This gem of methodology, first published in 1929, contains the arguments of what Rogers and others now call the 'new' history. In criticizing the abortive memorization of facts and dates which are not fully comprehended, Clarke speaks of 'children's minds strewn with the debris of a card-catalogue, which they piece together painfully in most unhappy families'. In discussing the difficulties of teaching chronology and time Clarke writes, 'For change, not time, is the historic idea', and goes on to warn of the danger of dates becoming mere telephone numbers. The general ignorance or disregard of little masterpieces such as Fred Clarke's book allowed initiative to come mainly from the Board of Education, through its reports. Yet this was an age when official direction of the curriculum was becoming less acceptable and it is doubtful whether these reports had any effect on headteachers or the majority of children.

After the Second World War and until the cutback of teacher training numbers in the 1970s, considerable interest was taken in history for the 5- to 11-year-olds. This came mainly from enthusiastic individuals but the Ministry of Education did publish a pamphlet in 1952 – *Teaching of History* – the cover consisting of small portraits of the sovereigns of England from the beginning to Elizabeth II. As the cover intimates, no very original ideas are voiced for the primary school child. Stories are to be the staple diet, with integration of the past into other areas of the curriculum. Shades of Sir Fred Clarke appear with the emphasis on change rather than time. Yet the use of artefacts as evidence and the building up of a class museum point forward to more recent literature.

The 1959 *Handbook* of the Ministry of Education also emphasized the difficulty of teaching history to younger pupils and suggested the 'magic of a well told story' (copied from the words of the 1952 pamphlet!) as the cure for all ills. Yet in addition the *Handbook* grasped the nettle of 'time' and suggested the value of the 'simple illustrated time chart' as a framework into which stories could fit. It is interesting that John West, in his research in Dudley Schools (from 1976–80), found this use of stories, interrelated with time charts, most effective for the clear understanding of time. The writers of the relevant chapter in the 1967 Plowden Report believed that history should be taught as part of the integrated approach with geography and might be studied topically at intervals instead of chronologically and systematically. Time charts were again recommended. From this time onward the emphasis was on the incidental use of the past as the tool of other more essential disciplines.

The 1960s were marked by the establishment of the Schools Council, in 1964, and the publication of the Plowden Report in 1967. Neither gave particular attention to primary history, though both recognized it either as a separate subject or as a component of Humanities.

The Schools Council's relevant contributions are listed in Chapter 2 (section 6) where their continuing significance is discussed. Meanwhile the Plowden Report, despite its subsequent image as a model of reckless innovation, said little that was new about History teaching. However, the general reformist climate associated with the Schools Council and Plowden did give rise to innovations, some of which were impressive, while others tended to substitute enthusiasm for scholarly rigour, and speculative links across the curriculum for sustained continuity and progression in learning.

When in 1978 the Department of Education and Science issued the survey by HMI entitled *Primary education in England*, it revealed that in a sample of classes in the 7–11 age-range the learning of history was sometimes superficial and insufficiently strenuous for the majority of children. Subsequent surveys of first and middle schools confirmed this impression.

Since 1978, the need for continuity and progression has been increasingly recognized, though the proposals for improvement have been far from uniform in their recommendations. Of particular significance is the treatment of primary history in the Inspectorate's own publication *History in the primary and secondary years: an HMI view*[6] in which the need for sequential development of historical understanding, rather than factual content, is recognized throughout the infant and junior years. More recently, faced with demands for a national curriculum, the Historical Association has also turned its attention to the primary years though perhaps with less understanding of young children's learning than might have been hoped.[7] In recent years, too, history has figured in demands for explicitly multicultural education. Some of the recent developments, as they affect syllabus-construction, are considered in Chapter 2.

Clearly, the time has come for a synthesis in primary history of the good in these ideas, new and not so new, and also for stricter guide-lines in aims, teaching methods, and syllabus-construction. It is to be hoped that this essential outcome will be encouraged, and not frustrated, within a national curriculum; and that some discretion about curriculum and assessment will be reserved to those who know the circumstances and strengths, as well as weaknesses, of individual schools.

1.3   The past at the infant stage

The professional definition of an 'infant' is a child aged between 4+ and 7. During these formative and crucial years teachers are concerned to socialize their pupils and help them to develop language, number, and physical skills. They have tended to favour an informal, friendly, perhaps unstructured approach, and work beyond the basic number and language tends to be 'one-off' experiences and activities enabling the child to take advantage of content and information in the 7–11 years. Therefore, for most infant teachers the past as 'history' has no place. Authors of books on history teaching and Government reports have also purposely overlooked the place of knowledge of the past in the infant curriculum. It is only recently that work has been done in this area showing that certain topics in the past can play a vital part in the development of young children. Family history, local history and field work, study of artefacts, and dramatization of the past have been found to be suitable topics for this age group to study. All these topics can easily be integrated into the normal infant day and taken up for shorter or longer periods. In her book *Children's Minds* (Fontana, 1978), a psychologist, Margaret Donaldson, suggested that the intellectual ability of young children has been underestimated, and that thinking about people and events beyond their immediate selves helps them to 'decentre' and 'move beyond the bounds of human sense'. This will form a stronger basis for future intellectual development than heretofore. Therefore, as far as the infant school is concerned history as a discipline is not to be justified, but certain parts of the past, both recent and long ago, have a real part to play in some sort of structured way at certain times in the infant curriculum. How this is to be done will be considered in more detail later.

1.4   Young juniors and history

Having tasted the joys of experiencing the past sporadically in the infant years, the young junior of 7 years, or the older pupil in the first school, is in a good position to develop this work on more continuous lines. As already mentioned, one overriding justification for studying the past between 7 and 11 is that by 14 in most secondary schools at least half of the pupils drop history or opt for other subjects if they are candidates for any public examination. Therefore, primary schools are very much justified in giving considerable space in the curriculum to subjects such as history in some form or other. This is even more true than before 7, since many children have begun to master the skills of writing and reading and need new material on which to exercise their new-found talents. History is fortunately a subject which attracts good writers of stories and novels; therefore there are plenty of short and well-illustrated reading books for all levels of ability. Children of 7 and 8 might as well read and write history stories as other stories and their imaginative writing about the past can be as creative as, and more realistic than, much other writing. The retentive memory of most seven-year-olds makes possible the teaching of continuous interrelated parts of the past. The recording of information in simple diagrams and time charts becomes a growing possibility. Therefore the keeping of a notebook, well illustrated by pupils in one way or another, gives coherence to the past and provides easy reference for discussion in the class. Although history should not be thought of as a 'body of knowledge' to be learnt and memorized for tests, the keeping of a notebook gives the subject a status and importance similar to mathematics and could also form an interest to be shared with parents. In addition, stories of the past can more easily be dramatized at the ages of 7 and 8 than earlier and the subject matter stimulates imagination and active participation. During these early junior years children tend to be less self-conscious than later and eager to participate in acting straightforward roles which can nevertheless involve the stimulation of critical-thinking.

Another justification for teaching history during these years is that children of this age range are able physically to participate in field work without becoming too tired. They are beginning to know how to look after themselves and their property without a fuss and to handle clip board, pencils, lunch packs, and mackintoshes a little more effectively. Thus the participation in field work as a usual part of the curriculum is excellent training.

1.5   Older juniors and history

Children of 9 years old are entering a new phase of their career. In some cases they go to middle schools, in others to preparatory boarding schools away from home, and a few may transfer to a local independent school with a junior department. But the majority remain in their primary school and need a more varied diet than previously. By this time, even if streaming is not the norm in a school, it has become apparent to both teachers and pupils which children are quick, slow, able intellectually, or particularly endowed with practical skills. History can provide opportunities for all abilities and interests, and all pupils enjoy a well-told story. During these two years more demanding history can easily be introduced. Group work is an excellent social and intellectual experience and 9- to 11-year-olds like it and are good at it. With so many suitable reading books on the market, history is an excellent means for providing this type of experience. Group work on an historical topic also allows leadership to the more able and those with initiative, while others work at collecting information. In addition the children can help each other and take pride as a group in competing with other small groups in the class.

Children of this age range also gain much satisfaction from individual projects in which they choose their own particular topic within the syllabus and refer to many books and other sources of the past. This may be the only time that pupils can enjoy so much time and so much choice in what they do.

Finally, in the later years of the primary school it is possible to begin to introduce written sources of evidence of the past. Children of 6 years can handle artefacts as evidence and talk about them, but by the age of 9 to 11 they can often take pleasure in, for example, the detective pursuit of deciphering seventeenth-century palaeography and coming to conclusions after discussion as to its point of view. The selection of the original material is most important and a dose of too much source material of the wrong sort can discourage the keenest 10-year-old. At this age, also, pupils can undertake quite extensive field work including a residential period. Castles, monasteries, churches, mansions, graveyards, and archaeological remains all provide extensive practical work and use the past, linking class work on books and documents to practical work on a site. Thus it is easy to see that the past has a crucial role to play in the primary years and that this work can be tackled in the way that professional historians undertake it: that is by finding out, observation, reading, and discussion without the anxiety and pressure of an examination at the end of the year.

Teaching history with enjoyment and success depends on conditions in schools, teachers willing to re-think and re-learn and children wanting to be stretched intellectually in the way the past can do it. Conditions in schools are not likely to be improved in the present economic climate but teachers and children can be helped. The purpose of this book in the remaining chapters is to suggest ways in which this can be done.

Notes

1. Lord Briggs, in a lecture at the National Association of Teachers in Further and Higher Education, History Section Conference at St. Mary's College, Twickenham, July 1978.
2. P.J. Rogers, *The New History*, T.H. 44, Historical Association, 1978.
3. R.H. Hallam, 'Piaget and Thinking in History' in M. Ballard (ed), *New Movements in the Study and Teaching of History*. Temple Smith, 1970.
4. A.D. Edwards, ' "The Language of History" and the Communication of Knowledge', in A.K. Dickenson and P.J. Lee (eds.), *History Teaching and Historical Understanding*, Heinemann, 1978, p. 58.
5. P. Gordon and D. Lawton, *Curriculum Change in the Nineteenth and Twentieth Centuries*, Hodder and Stoughton, 1978, p. 120.
6. D.E.S., *History in the Primary and Secondary Years – An H.M.I. View*, H.M.S.O. 1985.
7. *History for Life* and *Proposals for a Core Curriculum in History*, Historical Association, 1986.

2 Planning a scheme of work

2.1 Introduction

Any book which attempts to help teachers to teach history well must treat three basic issues: schemes of work, methods, and resources. The next three chapters of this book are devoted to these three issues. Those facing a class of thirty children or more, all day and every day, are more concerned with what history to teach, how to teach it, and what resources can help them, than why it is taught and how it is assessed.

Of these three important areas this chapter on schemes of work is the most 'sensitive' one. Most experienced teachers know which approaches work for them with their particular children. Most teachers have access to only limited resources and have limited time and energy to accumulate more materials. But the last twenty years in curriculum development have influenced, perhaps unduly, teachers' views of what children can understand and enjoy. Teachers' training 'dies hard', especially with so little opportunity to retrain and many of those in responsible positions have been trained between 1967 and 1977 (i.e., the Plowden era). Some of these teachers view historical content as unimportant and use what suits their chosen 'topic' or 'centre of interest'. In this way, history has been interrelated with geography, literature, R.E., and sometimes science. The DES Primary School Report of 1978 challenged this usual viewpoint and much discussion has since taken place on what to teach. Two extracts from the 1978 Report show this concern:

5.127. Taken as a whole in four out of five of all the classes which studied history the work was superficial.

5.128. A factor contributing to this situation was undoubtedly a lack of planning in the work. Few schools had schemes of work in history, or teachers who were responsible for the planning and implementation of work in this field . . . A framework is required to provide some ordering of the content to be taught. This may be a single path through a chronological sequence or a more complex series of historical topics, which, while not necessarily taught in chronological order, should give a perspective in terms of the ordering of events or by means of comparison with the present day.

I shall analyse some basic 'fundamental truths' about content before separate and integrated (or interrelated) frameworks are discussed. The infant years of 5–7 have been considered separately as a preparation for the junior and middle years in the same local area.

Exceptional teachers have experimented most successfully with their own schemes and written of their experiences in books and journals. Such enthusiasts as Don Steel and Lawrence Taylor have built up amazing work on family history in selected schools staffed by able teachers. Brendan Murphy of Wigan did similar work in family history with 10- to 11-year-olds, using family trees and family artefacts to learn history backwards. Eric Newton of Everton, Liverpool, used municipal sources to build up a local history scheme based on models made by children. Pat Raper, then of Cholsey Infants' School near Wallingford, organized the whole school in celebrating the school's centenary in 1976. John West stimulated fifteen schools to work on his schemes of stories, pictures, and patches of the past, helping teachers to plan their own frameworks for history. Henry Pluckrose used his expertise as an artist and craftsman to bring to life whatever part of the past he touched, particularly by his use of the environment. These are only a few examples of very able teachers with a flair for teaching the past and a high motivation in preparing scholarly material. My advice is not intended for such people but for the non-specialist young or older teacher emerging from college having spent too little time on history teaching and with many pressures upon her in the early years of her career. These teachers can only depend upon snippets of their own knowledge, a few 'tips for teachers' on teaching practice (sometimes long ago in schools of 'long ago') and on any textbooks and reading books they can muster. It is for these colleagues, keen to do their best for their children but not necessarily 'sold' on history, that this chapter is really intended. They must be helped to know that they can teach well without spending too much time in preparation.

2.2   Basic principles

In spite of the incongruous situation of teachers feeling strongly about the content of the curriculum, yet knowing in their hearts that *how* they teach the material is really more important, headteachers and advisers are looking for some guiding principles to be considered, even if not taken up, in the construction of the history scheme. Much discussion has taken place in the last ten years and a certain consensus of opinion has resulted: a framework is required. The present emphasis on a national curriculum for the 5–16 years of schooling has hastened the need for teachers to take the initiative to avoid too specific direction. Consideration of the following basic principles should go some way to help provide this framework.

- There must be *some sort of scheme* for all teachers – and children – to read; this should be related to the needs of the particular school and therefore reached by common agreement with the staff. Thus history could be treated as a separate discipline at one stage and be used to help an interrelated topic at another in the six years, or it could be entirely separate, or interrelated.
- *Chronology* should be the aim as far as possible; an understanding of ordering of events, the place of personalities, and sequence may be learnt from the constant use of time charts both around the classroom and in pupils' notebooks. 'History offers organization of material by time': this is how it was expressed by one historian interested in how younger children learn about the past.
- Content should be *national history* but closely related to *local* and *world history* where possible. Modern world history from about 1900 should only be studied in the later years of the primary school since it involves many countries, difficult names, and facility with the changing map of the world.
- *The history of everyday life* should form the basis of the work but important political events, simple economic trends, and far-reaching cultural changes should be included.
- The scheme should have room for *varying approaches* so that the patch of history, the line of development, and the important events are introduced at regular intervals. 'In teaching young children . . . it seems clear where the main emphasis should fall – upon the unique event'; this is the view of an historian who has researched on how children learn about the past.

With these basic, though not inflexible, principles in mind they may be applied in more detail to the 5–11 age-range on the understanding that most infant (First) schools feed into one junior school, therefore some continuity of approach can be maintained if there is co-operative consultation.

2.3   Trends in syllabus making 1950—87[1]

Those of us who have been interested in books on the teaching of history for many years are pleased with recent developments in this field, particularly in the secondary school area. One favourable sign which points to greater respect for each other among scholars is the open criticism levelled in a friendly manner by one writer towards another. This openness to different interpretations will eventually help teachers to get nearer to the truth in their teaching of history.

There are whispers of this wholesale questioning in the publications from which I am seeking guidance about scheme construction for 7- to 11-year-old children. My selection of books is limited to those specifically concerned with the primary school and to those which courageously address themselves to the question of content. Many valuable books which will be mentioned later are mainly concerned with method and resources, not with schemes of work. I am treating those that I have selected according to date of publication and this is to some extent an influence on their message. The books fall into three date spans and range from 1950 to 1987. The first, in the 1950s, are structured and didactic, laying down *one* scheme for recommendation and, on the whole, adopting the chronological/English history content. During the 1960s the movement towards the integrated curriculum gained momentum. During this period the tendency of the books selected was to favour local history and the study of the environment, with or without geography. Towards the end of the 1960s, the 'topic' approach, popular following the Plowden Report of 1967, took the form of authors offering various approaches and not favouring any one exclusively. With this open-ended approach, which may have led to no history being taught in some schools with the headteacher's agreement and even at her instigation, the late 1970s were reached with the need for a more structured framework. The years of 1980 to 1987 represent a greater interest in the historical understanding in the 5–7 years of schooling and more high level research being done on concepts, artefacts and sequence as well as many other methods of teaching, but there was no generally accepted resolution of the content dilemma.

During the 1930s and 1940s few 'method' books in history were published for the primary age range, an interruption strengthened by the Second World War and lack of paper for printing, as well as lack of time and interest. Three books appeared in the early 1950s all generally advocating the chronological treatment of English history. C.F. Strong's *History in the Primary School* (1950) and R.J. Unstead's *Teaching History in the Junior School* (1956) are seen now by some experts to put the primary syllabus in a straitjacket. In his chapter called 'The four year course', Strong deals with the general framework of 'increasing specialization', the 7–9 years being broad topics, mainly biographical, into which other disciplines may be integrated – 'suitable Projects based on centres of interest, which involve other subjects in the curriculum besides History'. The 9–11 age-range should study English history 'in neighbourhood, Homeland and Commonwealth' in topics arranged chronologically. When the author refers to his full scheme as 'the bare bones of a possible syllabus' one wonders what the detailed implementation would be like! He does agree with the introduction of time-charts in the fourth year, but it seems to me essential to have time-charts from the beginning of this scheme which takes in English history,

European history and world history. Although most teachers would agree that story and biography are natural approaches and some effort should be made to reach beyond 1600, yet the diet of political history in the fourth year is far too constipating for both teacher and class. Yet this suggestion was carried out in textbooks written by the same author for children to use and this method book went through at least five editions. It was obviously an accepted and popular approach as far as schools were concerned.

The second book, on similar lines, is R. J. Unstead's *Teaching History in the Junior School* which has tended to be more long-lived than Strong's. This book is made more useful by very practical photographs of models made by junior children as well as a detailed bibliography of useful reading books for teacher and taught. Unstead is in no doubt that a chronological treatment of English history across the four junior years is the basis of the scheme and that local history may be used as illustration rather than in its own right. His scheme is very practically modified by the author for one- or two- teacher schools to cut down teacher preparation, and a very full time chart from one million years BC to 1961 is given (for the teacher presumably) and divided into:

Approximate dates   Periods and people   Events   Background

This scheme may try to cover too much but it is definite (no alternatives) and very thoroughly worked out by a practising, enthusiastic, and knowledge-able teacher of history. Many primary schools today which do make some attempt to teach the past adhere to this through the many textbooks, reading books, and topic books which complement it. In a recent report on the results of a survey of fifty primary schools in Cheshire, the authors write 'A wide variety of textbooks were in use in the sample schools, yet Unstead's *Looking at History* was the most common general text.'[2]

The third publication of the 1950s was a Ministry of Education pamphlet (No. 27) published in 1952: *Teaching of History*. It is mainly concerned with the secondary school but has one chapter on the primary school. This pamphlet is mainly inspirational and does not set out to give a framework. Instead, it suggests historical methods of story-telling and the use of authentic evidence, such as the 'very words' of Mary Stuart and Thomas More just before their executions. The early years (7–9) should concentrate on myths and legends and the later (9–11) on stories of adventure and stories of British history grouped chronologically. Some reference is made to a study of the neighbourhood and interrelated work but the main emphasis is on a well-read teacher stimulating the imagination of her class by well-told and selected stories.

The 1950s books were didactic in most ways and therefore helpful to the majority of non-specialist teachers. The 1960s and 1970s were to bring a more optional and uncertain approach which may have led to the lack of confidence of teachers of history in the 7–11 age-range. The 1960s was a

Year
1   Family history
2   The school in its environment: links with other disciplines
3   Line of development on local history — use of evidence
4   Integrated patch of local history and geography

Fig. 2.1   Scheme for an integrated curriculum (from *History in the Primary School: A Scheme of Work*, Moray House College of Education, 1965)

period which saw the effects of the post-war population explosion in the schools, the expansion of teacher training and in-service work, and more opportunities for experiment and re-thinking of the place and purpose of history in the 7–11 curriculum. In both books considered here, the influence of the integrated curriculum is shown. In 1965 the lively History Department of Moray House College of Education, Edinburgh, published a pamphlet called *History in the Primary School: a Scheme of Work*. In keeping with 1960s thought the syllabus outline is as shown in Fig. 2.1.

There may seem to be a repetition in this scheme and too much emphasis on local history at the expense of a wider outlook of national or world history. Yet it bears out the viewpoint of Professor J.S. Bruner that a 'spiral curriculum' involving study of the same material successively in different ways provides the best learning sequence. Many primary schools, helped by active Teachers' Centres and record offices, have pursued this narrow but efficient approach and by now have built up valuable resources for children's activity. This could, even now when resources are scarce, be enlivened by, though not based on, stories from a broader background and found on BBC and/or ITV programmes so ably prepared in actual production and notes for children and teachers.

A second individualistic approach appeared in 1966 with John West's *History, Here and Now* (Teacher Publishing Company) – a startling title and a strong plea for younger children to use source material, written or otherwise, and imaginative stories in order to become 'aware' of the past. Therefore, to him, past history lives in the present – 'here and now' – and is not irrelevant to the modern child. Like Catherine Firth in the 1920s, John West is the only recent writer who dares to consider the past as a fit study for 'infants'. Catherine Firth recommends stories and pictures of the past grouped according to topic or period. John West suggests the study of artefacts and their relationship to their likely uses and their oldness. He does not actually work out a four-year scheme but implies that good stories of 'heroes brave and invisible' are vital for one of the years; he suggests that teachers should make a list of twenty heroes and heroines and think out why each one has been included. His own list ranges from Mohammed through Robin Hood and Guy Fawkes to Dave Crockett and Winston Churchill.

Somewhere also in the 7–11 years should come a local study and, like Strong and Unstead, he gives a detailed breakdown by weeks of different local studies. He starts with a term's work on environmental studies, then goes on to a term's work on seventeenth-century local history and finally gives a year's work to a study of a village in the thirteenth and nineteenth centuries. All schemes involve use of sources in the record office or library, and field work. It is therefore to be presumed that the local study is for 9- to 11-year-olds for at least part of their year. As in most books published since 1960 he does not suggest a framework for the four years or the order in which the work should be studied. Time charts are strongly advocated throughout.

The 1970s continued this uncommitted attitude of the 1960s with one or two exceptions in individuals writing of their own particular approach. In the *Handbook for History Teachers* (Methuen, 1972 edition) Kay Davies sums up the dilemma of the period in her chapter on 'The syllabus in the primary school' when she speaks of 'the present uncertainty in this area of the curriculum'. Current practice is given of the infant school in which 'incidental talk' through stories, pictures, and visits outside school will make young children aware of the past. She then outlines the practice with junior children of topics and patches in history as the teacher chooses. Yet she emphasizes the need for 'depth and progress in learning' so that children are not just collectors of facts without learning how to use them. Thus Miss Davies is more concerned with standard of work and quality of thinking than actual content of syllabus. This is in keeping with the period in which the Historical Association published Jeanette Coltham's *The Development of Thinking and the Learning of History* (1971) and Coltham and Fines' *Education Objectives and the Study of History: A Suggested Framework* (1971) as well as the initiation of the Schools Council 8–13 Project, *Place, Time and Society* in 1971. All these developments emphasize the need to teach skills and concepts rather than a particular content-based syllabus.

Two individualistic approaches are interesting and inspiring to the experienced historian but possibly a little too free for the non-historian who is looking for security. Alan and Roland Earl in *How Shall I Teach History?* (Blackwell, 1971) recommend variety: 'Variety of content and variety of treatment are the secret of success in teaching History'. They presume that the syllabus has been decided and proceed with considerable liveliness and humour to show how content can be taught to children between 7 and 13. Each chapter takes a different topic of history; medieval, Norman Conquest, the Age of Discovery, ancient civilization, world history, local history and Elizabethan England on a 'patch'. These are obviously selected as satisfying areas of content for the age group but no mention is made of sequence or order for these worthwhile patches. It is presumed that the headteacher will have some golden plan at the back of her mind and the class teacher will work from that. The second book, *History with Juniors* (Evans, 1973), is by Michael Pollard who has a definite view of what scheme of work there should be. He believes that history should be taught backwards for juniors, starting from the present and not going further back than about 1800. Most of his content is English history and much of it local sources and field work. His use of folk music as a method of teaching industrial history is most useful. This book limits the teachers' content during the four junior years but its very limitations give security, and much excellent detailed work may be done in the four years. In his book the *rapport* between primary experts is shown by his references to John Fines and John West. Therefore the 1970s have given teachers many excellent ideas and encouraged them not to isolate history in the curriculum, but have left wide open specific advice about a 'framework' for a scheme.

The 1980s have not helped to resolve the content issue, though the fact that most infant teachers want to use historical material has pushed the need for a framework down the age-range and therefore altered what is taught in the junior school. The DES Circulars 6/81 and 6/83 required LEAs to provide guidelines in all areas of the curriculum. Teachers' groups were formed to do this work in History/Humanities and many have published their guidelines.[3] My own research[4] and three books for teachers have consistently advocated some framework in the infant years.[5] The influence of John West's major research[6] began to be felt in the 1980s in that it encouraged other workers to use his methods and concentrate on small areas in more depth. For example, Hilary Cooper's[7] and Peter Knight's[8] work have shown that children can tackle more difficult work requiring thought, discussion and the need to introduce plenty of people of the past into the content of schemes. There have also been a number of smaller studies concerned with methods of teaching which have influenced content planning: Paul Noble (schemes of work),[9] Martin Forrest (artefacts),[10] Valerie Bone (sequence and time),[11] Susan Perrin (artefacts)[12] and Stephen Tofts (resources for infants)[13] are only some names to mention. Classroom experiments in oral and family history (spearheaded by Sallie Purkis)[14] and role-playing (Jayne Woodhouse and Viv Wilson)[15] have encouraged teachers to use areas of the past involving real people or documents as evidence. A research team in Australia have emphasized the difficulty of teaching the concept of time, the importance of connecting time and change and the great relevance of the time-line.[16] The most incisive and clear stimulus to action is the work of Paul Noble whose advice to a school as to how to set about constructing a scheme of work is shown in Fig. 2.6 (p. 26). These examples show that primary teachers are slowly and painfully reaching certain common conclusions relating to an outline national curriculum. More discussions are needed, at present led by the Historical Association, before a consensus can be reached, published and gradually accepted by the profession. Therefore, in 1987 the construction of a national curriculum in History for the primary school has become urgent.

Fig. 2.2 A 7-year-old's view of time

2.4 The beginnings of awareness of the past in the infant years

Junior teachers need to know what infants are capable of doing; in small schools they may teach in vertical groups and have to know. Yet many primary teachers, both infant and junior, take it for granted that no one tells or writes down how the past should come into the 'integrated infant day'. In this section of the chapter I am going to suggest a two-year framework which I believe is flexible enough to be easily assimilated into the normal infant day. More detailed consideration of schemes in this age-range is given in my recent book.[17]

In this scheme the first two terms are stories, at first each story complete in itself and in the second term grouped round one personality or event of the past to give a little more continuity. This would enable new children entering the school in September, at Christmas, and at Easter to start afresh. By the third term of the first year all children continuing into the second year are likely to have joined the class and therefore more purposeful work could be started on artefacts, at first selected by the teacher to illustrate a specific period or even widely different periods chronologically. Many museums are willing to lend certain treasures or replicas for a limited period (say a month). After that children know what you want and usually bring too much y in primary schools

	Term 1	Term 2	Term 3
	ɔries of the st	Stories of the past grouped in topics — role-playing	Study of artefacts brought first by teacher then by class
6—7	Family history	Local topics of own village, town, area	Local visits

Fig. 2.3 Framework for a two-year scheme for infants

material for comfort. By the second year children are more likely to be starting to read and write, which broadens the methods through which they are taught, though at present there is more suitable material for them to look at than read. Finding out about the teacher and her family and then their own lives and families, and building up their own books becomes an enquiry-based exercise, more obviously 'true' than stories told by the teacher and artefacts brought from the museum or their own homes. The second term of this second year could take them from themselves and their own little world to their local environment (linking with 'the place' of the curriculum) be it village, suburb or town. The local visits in the third term are closely linked to the work in the second term but carried out in the summer term for better health and weather conditions. Some liaison between the infant school and the teachers responsible for history in the junior school should be possible in the latter part of the summer term.

From myth to artefact in the 5–6 age-range

Kieran Egan has put forward the idea that between the ages of 4 and 9 or 5 and 10 children go through what he calls the 'mythic stage' of learning. Children's love of fairy stories involving the deep emotions of 'love, hate, joy, fear, good, bad' should be fostered, as this will engage their interest and attention most readily. Mythic stories involving stark opposites such as life/death, security/fear and courage/cowardice are clear as they have the black and white nature of the unreal rather than the grey haze of the real past. Egan believes that children must be fed by such mythic stories and will suffer if hurried on too quickly to such matters as artefacts and family history which are real and therefore more complex.[18]

Most public libraries have suitable collections of stories from the past and some infant schools possess copies in their own libraries or book corner. Obviously, beautifully illustrated, large books are the most suitable, and children look forward to seeing a particular book in the teacher's hands. Many children look at the illustrations in their free time even if they cannot read the words. Two or three books including the same stories, but having different illustrations, make for useful comparisons even if the teacher uses only one for the stories. Two most useful books for teachers to use for reference are Elizabeth Cook's *The Ordinary and the Fabulous* first published by Cambridge University Press in 1969 and Ralph Lavender's *Myths, Legends and Lore* published by Basil Blackwell in 1975. The former is concerned with myths, legends, and fairy tales of many European countries for children between 8 and 14. Elizabeth Cook names the myths, suggests how they may be presented to children and then takes seven 'crucial scenes' in books and analyses them critically. Ralph Lavender's book is more of a bibliography of myths but his preface is concerned with 'why' and 'how' stories should be told. He gives additional information about films, filmstrips, music, and discs to accompany the stories. Both books are written by enthusiastic specialists very much concerned with the practicalities of the classroom and both authors provide detailed lists of myths suitable for different ages.

Listening to stories from myth and legend and discussing people, actions, and consequences is excellent preparation for the second term when true stories of the past may be told and read more systematically. The teacher should decide which two periods of history are of greatest interest to her and tell five linked stories about each period. For example the conversion of England to Christianity could involve stories of St Augustine, St Columba, St Oswald and St Alban. Stories about King Alfred of Wessex and his heroic fight against the invading Danes could form another block. Each story may be used for simple role-playing with different groups of children used for different episodes. In these cases the story-time could come earlier in the day as children should not be tired when role-playing, otherwise they become silly and giggly.

In the third term, children are introduced to the fact that the past is not only learnt from stories told by the teacher, which have to be taken on trust, but from actual artefacts used in the past.[19] After the earlier imaginative representation, children are introduced to commonsense, down-to-earth life by this change. Artefact work needs longer than story-telling and in many cases could use a whole afternoon very effectively. Some period from about 1800 onwards should be selected first and about six well-preserved articles should be chosen to illustrate different sides of social history: for instance a lady's hatpin of Edwardian days, a parasol, an Edwardian toy, an Edwardian school-book, a bowler hat, and a gentleman's tie-pin. These should be representative of as many family members as possible (father, mother, children, servants, etc.) and should be easy to compare with similar articles today, if they exist. By this means the 'then and now' approach of comparison, an historical skill, can be used naturally. Children should thoroughly investigate these articles which therefore should not be too fragile. The children should have 'intuitions' as to their uses, in the words of Professor J.S. Bruner.[20]

Another collection by the teacher could be concerned with the Second World War period of 1939–45 supplemented by artefacts lent by the children's grandparents. For this to be really effective the teacher should invite parents and grandparents to an evening coffee party to discuss the reasons for doing this work; in this way she can gain their support and loans of suitable articles from their homes so that a temporary classroom museum may be built up, cared for by the 6-year-olds as they would care for a nature table or a guinea-pig. It is usually better to have a locked display case so that these precious exhibits can be labelled by the children but handled only with the teacher present.

A third stage in the artefact work is a collection of old objects brought by the children, and compared with the first two collections for 'oldness'. By constant discussion, feeling the objects, and observation, the children gradually become accustomed to comparisons of oldness. Some Museum Education Officers bring collections of objects to school to illustrate particular themes but this has to be for one afternoon only. This type of work is best limited to two different collections in one term, otherwise there is a lack of thorough investigation.

By the end of the first year in the infant school children will have started to be aware of people long ago and old objects belonging to a past they did not know. This naturally leads on to family history work in the second year.

From family history to local visits in the 6–7 age-range

Contact with parents and grandparents during the third term of the first year should be revived by the work on family history in the first term of the second year. This is essential not only to provide the children with first-hand information about themselves and their families but also to find relevant artefacts connected with the family to establish a link with the previous year's work. In one 6-year-old class I taught, one of the most shy little boys created a stir in the group when he brought to school a *Soldier's Bible* of the First World War which his grandfather had owned and which was inscribed with the grandfather's name and the date 1919. Perhaps a more important

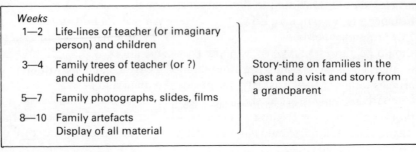

Fig. 2.4   Ten-week study of family history

reason for talking to parents is to forestall any difficulties which may arise from strained relationships at home and any knowledge purposely kept from children for their own benefit.

A study of family history may be undertaken for one afternoon a week for ten weeks, including 'story-time' at 3 pm. It can be divided into four distinct areas as shown in Fig. 2.4. This is obviously work on the contemporary family of the twentieth century, spanning not more than sixty to seventy years. If found successful, and with more input from the teacher, it could be taken backwards to the Edwardian and Victorian family, and the excellent material by Sue Wagstaff could be used (*People Around Us* published by A & C Black in 1978: Unit 1 – *Families, Koli's Family, Two Victorian Families*).

Local topics in the second term should be attempted as a line of development, using a simple time-line as in family history. Specific topics within the village or town should be studied, first as it is now, (links with 'place'), and then taking two other periods for comparison, dependent upon the age of the town and the information at the teacher's disposal. If interest is shown in one period and can be developed there would be no need to cover more than two periods altogether. The scheme shown in Fig. 2.5 for a term's work may be helpful. This unit will depend upon the information available and the motivation of the teacher. Most libraries now contain pamphlets and books giving outline histories of villages and towns chronologically. Teachers can select and adapt topics from these. Many include helpful maps and pictures which can be simplified. The term 'local topics' is very flexible and allows movement through two different periods (contemporary and one other).

The third term of the second year could be a continuation of the previous term with visits to places too far away for the winter months. Margaret West, one-time Infant Adviser for Wolverhampton, developed a field study centre for infants to visit for a few days with their teachers. More will be said about this later. An example of how to integrate terms two and three may be taken from the city of Southampton. In the second term of the second year Southampton could be studied in the seventeenth century from the very

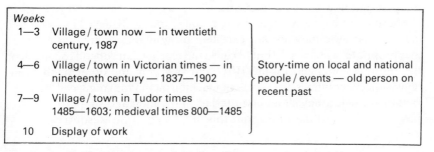

Fig. 2.5 Ten-week study of local topics for infants

clear 1611 Speed map of the city (Fig. 3.4, p. 74). The excellent Tudor House Museum could be visited in the third term and Southampton 'below bar' and 'within-the-walls', including old and modern buildings, could be an extension of this work. Thus about three visits might be made including Mayflower Park, so named to celebrate the sailing of the *Mayflower* from Southampton in 1620 – a topic which is, at least at the descriptive level, vivid and interesting to 6-year-olds.

This scheme for the infant years is intended to give the structure and sequence needed to see progression and variety of approach in relation to the past. It should not involve teachers in undue preparation; the only difficult part would be the second and third terms of the second year when local history has to be dug out from one or two local sources, the right book(s) found for preparation, and the information and pictures adapted to the needs of 6- to 7-year-olds. Otherwise material can be gathered from the children and their families or from easily obtainable reading books on conventional lines.

I am not suggesting any other schemes, as I shall for the 7–11 age-range. This is partly because teaching the past to very young children is an adventure and very few experiments have been made. As a result few materials have been offered to teachers for the specific age-range but the suggestions I have made can be taken up successfully by teachers with the minimum of preparation. They can also be spring-boards for work in language (oral or written), number, art work, R.E., literature, and drama. Therefore this particular scheme can easily be integrated into the normal infant routine and adapted as required, each term forming a unit on its own, joined only loosely to the rest of the scheme. The idea behind the scheme is to prepare very young children to have some interest in the past outside themselves, using as a starting point their natural interest in stories and objects, themselves and their families. In her book *Children's Minds* Margaret Donaldson shows the need for young children to 'decentre' in Piaget's sense by having vicarious experience beyond their own egocentric lives. This descentring helps to master all skills more quickly. Much of the scheme I have suggested may be considered as being part of this policy. In addition they come to their work in the junior school with some awareness of the past and how to think about it.

I hesitate to base any general scheme of work on BBC or ITV programmes, not because they are not excellent programmes in every way or are inappropriate in approach, but because the teacher can depend too much on the resources supplied by the BBC and ITV. On the other hand, some television programmes are excellent teaching media for young children who cannot yet read; they should be used as illustration and support wherever possible. More will be said about this in Chapter 4 on Resources.

2.5   History in the junior school

Since the 1978 Primary Survey many LEAs and schools have designed schemes of work appropriate to their own needs, some on interrelated (integrated) work, some still called Topic and often a mixture of all these. In many cases a Humanities consultant has been appointed to lead this work. Two HMI documents are being influential in this developing work – *The Curriculum 5 to 16* and *History in the Primary and Secondary Years*, both published in 1985 (by HMSO). These endeavours have been overtaken by the government's call for a national curriculum. Historians welcome the inclusion of History and most primary teachers accept the need for a national framework if it does not become a straitjacket or 'tramlines', in the words of Paul Noble. The Historical Association has put forward proposals in two documents and held regional conferences to formulate a response to the DES move.

Let us look at these four documents as pointers for the national curriculum in primary History which will become the basis for schemes of work in state primary schools. *The Curriculum 5 to 16* (Curriculum Matters 2) favours the unity of knowledge and areas of learning rather than lists of subjects to be studied; History comes into the area of 'human and social'. It advocates subject area consultants to initiate more specialized work in the 9–11 age-range though it supports Topic work (often integrated) in the 7–9 age-range. Environmental Studies, politics and economic understanding should have a definite place in the curriculum. It is encouraging to read that literature should illustrate and enrich many subject areas; this particularly applies to History. I believe that this should include good literature written for children. This publication takes up the basic ideas of the Schools Council *History, Geography and Social Science 8 to 13 Project* (1971–6) in that knowledge in itself is only one part of the curriculum; concepts (such as change), skills, attitudes and progression in learning are equally important and should control suitable content to a large extent.

History in the Primary and Secondary Years is a detailed document conceived with the years 5 to 16 in mind and is likely to become the 'blueprint' for many years to come. It is good to see a separate section of the pamphlet devoted to the 5–8 age-range, giving examples of outstanding work in local history. It emphasizes again the importance of a teacher responsible for the subject in each school. Admitting the impossibility of basing a scheme of work solely on either a concepts/skills approach or major themes in mainly British History, the pamphlet advises teachers to adapt their plan to the location of their school, and to develop their pupils' understanding of contemporary society, based on the concepts of cause, change and evidence and the development of specialized historical skills. Content will also be influenced by the need for each pupil to construct an historical time-line of work in the four years in the primary school. The

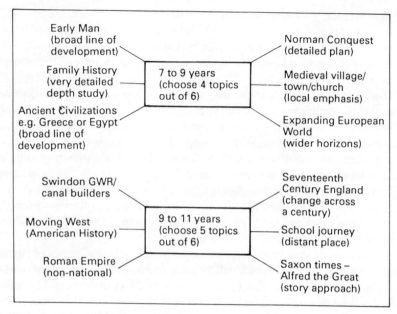

Fig. 2.6 A suggested framework for History in the junior school. (Adapted from *History in the Primary and Secondary Years*, DES, 1985, pp. 41–4.)

example of one school's scheme is given in some detail as in Fig. 2.6. Thus children will experience different teaching approaches, local history and areas of the world rather than Britain. The flexible organization allows for two half terms free from History as a separate subject in the first two years and one free in the last two years. Greater emphasis is put on History as a separate subject as envisaged in *The Curriculum 5 to 16*.

The two Historical Association documents are less clear and precise than the DES ones but are useful as a basis for discussion. *History for Life* (1986) only considers children aged 5 to 11 for one page in five paragraphs. It limits infants to stories and artefacts, omitting family and oral history which is placed in the 7 to 11 years. History is presumed to be submerged in topic work in one paragraph yet a 'very popular part of the junior school' in another paragraph. Which 'end' should one believe? A whole term on the microcomputer may alienate many primary teachers since junior schools seldom have enough machines to occupy a whole class, even in turn. It highlights the guidelines of Barnsley LEA in relation to historical skills but never tries to outline the scheme of work as is done in the DES booklet. It rightly emphasizes the need for better initial teacher training which the Historical Association is actively following up with the Advanced Diploma in the Teaching of History. *Proposals for a Core Curriculum in History* (7 to 14 years) (1987) has proved more controversial as being too prescriptive. The date 1890 as the dividing line at 14 years is considered unfair to children who drop History at that age and therefore never study twentieth century and contemporary history. That the sixty topics listed by the document should be compulsory in the seven years is a factual imposition to be compared with a final Honours Degree and not calculated to help most children to think historically or learn to enjoy finding out about the past. Yet the limitation of local history to some 10% of the time (instead of all the time in some primary schools at present), and 30% of the time being free for teachers to introduce their own topics, are good recommendations.

How far have the four documents helped us to plan our own school History scheme? From all of them it is evident that schemes of work must consider objectives, concepts, skills, attitudes and assessment; these must be stated clearly. It is also evident that a chronological scheme is unnecessary and indeed may be harmful in the attempt to teach chronology. But sequence and time lines and charts are essential, whether or not there is chronological teaching. They should be used throughout the years 5 to 11, taken up the school and those for different years related to each other as each new year starts. In other words, as John West has proved, *one need not teach chronologically to teach chronology*. Continuity and progression are closely linked to planning a scheme and assessing attainment. Most primary teachers are strongly opposed to 'benchmarks' at 7 and 11 but if they are imposed, work will have to be tested easily – which will have influence on content. A final outcome of these 1985/6 documents is the idea that a broad flexible scheme, offering plenty of choice to teachers – a 'framework' – is more acceptable to primary teachers than a prescriptive historical content for each term.

2.6   Integrated work in the junior school

The type of scheme in which history can, but might not, play a vital part is known by various names. It can be interrelated studies, topic, centre of interest or environmental studies. The essential argument for this approach is that the 'subject' divisions of the secondary, examination-orientated, school should not spoil the wholeness of approach which comes naturally to the 5 to 11 school. Since the Plowden Report of 1967, and indeed long before, much work has been done evolving schemes of this sort, and many able teachers have had the flair to implement them during the period of expanding resources. Mixed ability teaching, 'discovery learning', and individual assignments have all added to the need for this type of syllabus. So the ambitious individualized instruction and topic work, inspiring at its best and pointless at its worst, began. Various factors are now militating against this approach. By 1980 there were fewer junior children, and therefore classes tended to be smaller; there were fewer teachers and less time for preparation and above all resources were becoming more and more limited.

There is no doubt that the integrated scheme still has attractions and that many schools have carried out worthwhile work allowing the children to study the past in depth and relate it to other disciplines where natural in a 'patch' of history.[21] Schemes which forced all manner of disciplines into the framework found some rather unhappy, obtrusive alliances, such as the past trying to take a part in a topic on 'Water', a favourite but not necessarily suitable theme. Honest teachers boldly omitted certain areas of the curriculum, and this is where history suffered. In *The Times Educational Supplement* for 26 April 1968 Michael Wynne of the Schools Broadcasting Council wrote:

> In primary schools the integrated curriculum is the new orthodoxy and 'history' is out; yet the pendulum may swing back a little in response to the child's needs to arrange his accumulated information about the past into a recognizable framework, and this framework may conveniently be labelled history.

More will be said in Chapter 4 about how the BBC responded to this new difficulty in providing programmes for junior schools.

A general view appears to be arising now that younger juniors (7–9) enjoy integrated work and that the last two years (9–11) should allow separate disciplines to appear in the scheme in 'patches', or 'lines of development'. This has the incidental advantage of enabling the teacher to prepare more difficult work in the earlier years when children work more slowly and the amount of material for them to collect from diverse areas is not as great.

It is impossible to do justice to the many worthwhile integrated schemes worked out by colleges of education, advisers, Teachers Centres' wardens, and teachers but they seem to fall into certain well-defined categories. The most prolific are those concerned with geography, the locality, social studies, rural studies and environmental science, generally known as 'environmental studies', Historians differ as to whether history is more closely associated with geography or with literature and the arts but this usually depends upon the particular teacher's interests and training. Another type is concerned with music, dance and drama, using the past as a backcloth. Third is the link with science, particularly inspired by the *Schools Council Science 5–13 Project* though it has been more explicitly discussed by its predecessor, *Nuffield Junior Science* (Fig. 2.8, p. 37). Then there is the work mainly connected with art and those just called 'topic' or 'project' which involve many disciplines but are essentially based on an historical event, movement, or period of time. More recently heavier emphasis has been placed on multi-cultural considerations as an integrating factor in the curriculum and an example of one teacher's work, based on this assumption, is included. Finally, the Schools Council Project *Place, Time and Society* devised a strategy to be used either through separate subjects or through an integrated curriculum, and confined itself to examples and suggestions that schools were free to adopt or adapt as they chose; an example of History in an interrelated scheme completes this section. An attempt is made to maintain a clear historical thread as well as continuity and progression.

Environmental studies[22]

Most frequently, geography has dominated the environmental studies scheme in junior schools, possibly because of the greater interest of academic geographers in younger children and in field work, as well as their belief that 'place' could be taught effectively even to very young children. Michael Storm's *Playing with Plans* (Longmans, 1974) is an amusing and lively approach to the beginning of map work with infants. More recently Simon Catling has helped the infant teacher with *Your Mapbook* (Arnold/ Wheaton, 1981), *Outset Geography* (Oliver and Boyd, 1981/2) and *Ordnance Survey Mapstart* (Longmans, 1987). In the same way, two scientists and a geographer edited a text called *Teachers' Handbook for Environmental Studies* (Blandford, 1968) specifically for 9–13 pupils and the only contribution by an historian, D. F. Vodden, is on 'Environmental Studies in Surrey'. Linked thus to geography and social studies, the type of history taught is entirely small-scale history, usually local history. This has tended to lead to a scheme of history 'stories', often disjointed and at the whim of the teacher, during the first two years, and local history during the last two years of the integrated scheme. This has excluded world history of any sort, supposedly left for the secondary school. Yet it has enabled the past to be studied in much greater depth using local archival evidence and it also encouraged teachers to undertake field work in History locally, and sometimes residential field work in another area. The work has been approached in topics, centres of interest or themes lasting about half a term and usually culminating in a display. It has depended upon team teaching and cooperation between at least two members of staff. This could become difficult if one member of staff left and the replacement did not prove as co-operative or able. In describing his work on Surrey, Mr Vodden shows how lack of local material led him to supplement his chronological survey of the years 0 to 1500 by using standard class examples such as the Lascaux cave paintings, the Roman villa of Lullingstone and London medieval town life. The topic approach allows teachers wide choice from a number of disjointed titles, each able to last half a term, e.g. roads; doctors and health; houses and buildings; the Highway Code. This method could include an historical line of development, but that would depend upon how the topic was approached. For example, when studying the sea-shore the plan of a seaside town could be used showing buildings dating from the fifteenth century to the present day. This would be effective if the area was near enough for children to visit it and study the types of period houses.

Two other approaches to environmental studies should be mentioned.

One already discussed comes from Moray House College, Edinburgh; it is really a history scheme with a strong local bias and some integration with geography. The second is the *Schools Council Environmental Studies 5–13 Project* (1969–72). This was principally based on geography and the team members found difficulty in providing historical material for their trial schools. This was made clear in their Working Paper No. 48 *Environmental Studies 5–13: the use of historical resources* (1973). It was concluded that an expert historian or archivist (often a trained historian) was needed to compile and interpret material in order to ensure that it was significant enough for children to spend time on it.

History, music, dance, and drama

The journey of man through time, which is the story about which history is written, has been closely linked with man's efforts to express himself through different media. This expression of man's thoughts and feelings has often most truly reflected the image of the past and has been a constant delight to the child, the adolescent, the mature man, and the old. So much of the true past is with us in art, architecture, music, dance and drama which are such active subjects for children to pursue. Teachers concerned with history should emphasize that the past is the basic factor that these approaches have in common. From the scheme point of view it means a topic approach as it would be almost impossible to construct a chronological scheme based on the creative arts that was suitable for the 7–11 age-range.

Although music and movement have become the sphere of the specialist in junior schools many class teachers can play the piano and most schools have recorder groups; some even have orchestras or bands. All schools encourage children to sing, sometimes in elaborate presentations such as *Noyes' Fludde*, the opera by Benjamin Britten. Medieval history lends itself naturally to music, dance, and drama; this is the time when people make their own instruments and music in an unsophisticated and impromptu way. Longmans has had the courage to publish a unit of work called *Music from the Past* by Alison and Michael Bagenal (1988) which gives supportive advice on medieval dances, three plays with musical accompaniment, and instructions on how to make three medieval musical instruments. In addition, suggestions are given for further work on two of the plays and a most useful bibliography and list of recordings is included. This information figures in the teacher's book but there is also a colourful book for children with instructions and music for the three plays, amusingly and truthfully illustrated from medieval manuscripts and carvings from misericords. A cassette may also be bought with the music for the three plays on one side, and medieval music for listening and improvising dancing on the other side. The whole project could last from half a term to one term or could be used incidentally, one play at a time, the instruments being made in craft work as time allowed. If the teacher follows the thorough and scholarly instructions no child could go untouched or unable to appreciate the medieval sense of fun and joy in music and movement in the period 1250–1400.

Alison Bagenal has also linked history, music, dance, and art in collaboration with the National Portrait Gallery in London. More will be said in Chapter 5 about museums and galleries as a resource for the history teacher. Writing in *The Times Educational Supplement* for 15 August 1980 Mrs Bagenal describes an Elizabethan Masque held on three successive days at the National Portrait Gallery for different groups of 9- to 15-year-old children. The day was well staffed as a group of musicians and a costume expert were added to the Gallery's education staff. The day started by the group of children being shown detailed slides of the famous Elizabethan picture of Sir Henry Unton and his life in tableaux around him. The main concentration was on the area showing Sir Henry and his family about to be entertained to a masque after a banquet (National Gallery). Then the children chose to be musicians, dancers, or craftsmen and dispersed into three groups to be taught their different functions. 'Craftsmen' used the children's studio in the gallery to prepare properties and costumes (masks, head-dresses, and decorations); 'musicians' and 'dancers' practised in the other galleries. Towards the end of the afternoon the masque took place helped by adult musicians. This was a memorable day for the participants who will not easily forget the Elizabethan picture, an original source, and particularly the detailed scene in it which they 'lived through'. From the point of view of the junior school, this highly integrated day using outstanding resources could not form a regular part of the syllabus and depended upon knowledge of the Elizabethan period having been taught in school beforehand. The 9- to 11-year-olds would obviously be helped by the 11- to 15-year-olds but the work could probably be tailored to 9- to 11-year-olds on their own.

If teachers find the expertise and organization of these projects rather awe-inspiring, they might find it easier to link history with drama. By drama I mean 'role-playing' and informal class miming of short scenes or incidents. It does not involve large full-scale productions on the school stage at the end of term for parents. Drama as a learning medium only helps history if the individual class teacher provides an informal structure with plenty of discussion with the class, to stimulate disciplined imagination of the past through systematic use of questioning and empathy. The work of Dorothy Heathcote lately of the University of Newcastle upon Tyne stands out as the right historical approach. In her work, children are made to feel and understand by discussion the people of the past even though their historical knowledge may not be great and their 'stage properties' simple.[23]

An example of this remarkable teachers' work may be worth quoting. Mrs Heathcote ran a three-day in-service course in 1973 at the Gilmour Development Centre, Liverpool, called *Making History – An Approach through*

Drama. She used a large class of 10-year-old children from a neighbouring school. The general theme was transport from the nineteenth century and then stretching back to the sixteenth century. The stimulus for the first day was a large coloured paper cut-out of a train on the Liverpool to Manchester Railway. This in itself was of local interest to Liverpool children, many of whom had studied the first, second and third class coaches of this railway in the Transport gallery of the Merseyside County Museum. From this small knowledge the children eventually imagined that they were sitting in the train and several of them told the audience what roles they were playing. This made them think carefully about which people would be likely to travel on this train and in which coach they would sit. The nineteenth-century cotton magnate from Manchester coming to a meeting in Liverpool? The Manchester family of six children visiting their grandmother in Liverpool? Endless possibilities were discussed before the children had parts, big and small, to play.

The second morning their disciplined imaginations (*not* fantasy) were taxed a little more, starting from the picture of an eighteenth-century coach. In this case they imagined that they were a household of servants moving their landowner/employer from one residence to another. Mrs Heathcote used the blackboard to jot down all the articles they would have to remember to pack. This required detailed discussion as some children suggested modern articles, such as a television and film projector which had to be abandoned as anachronistic. Children's previous study of the past became very useful here as the majority opinion discarded obvious anachronisms and some even suggested obvious period pieces such as pendulum clocks and silver dishes. Eventually, after much bustle, they climbed into their coaches and wagons in an order of precedence, laden with articles, and reached the new house with great excitement.

The third morning posed the even more exciting problem of sailing to the New World in the *Mayflower*, starting from the picture of a seventeenth-century ship. This time some of the watching audience was used as crew while the children played the role of pilgrims. The difficult concept of 'pilgrim' as a certain sort of traveller, very different from travellers today, was discussed. Why were they leaving England? Where from? If they felt so strongly in 1620 about having freedom to worship how they liked, would they mind leaving their homes and many of their possessions? Did they take only essentials? What were the ships like to cross the stormy Atlantic? Do you think they were very brave? Would some be frightened, especially children, and need support and comfort? As the class boarded their ship and hoisted the flag there were mixed feelings and they faced many perils on the way. This led to much fervent and unabashed praying and the children were so relaxed by now that they broke into united singing of a hymn as part of their Sunday service. It will be noticed that the particular interest of this teaching was that Mrs Heathcote posed problems for the children to solve by thought and discussion rather than by seeking information from books. She was also 'teaching history backwards' in the chronological sense. Thus she gradually accustomed the class to 'difference' between 1973 and 1873, and more difference to 1783 and even more to 1620. In this way she used the 'similarity/difference' concept given prominence by the *Place, Time and Society Project* in a way that runs contrary to the chronological syllabus and leaves its merits less self-evident than an author such as Unstead suggests. She also used the uniting element of 'travel' and yet the different vehicles of train, coach, and ship; this could have led to more discussion with more time. The class will probably never forget their individual feelings as they represented passengers on the train, servants in the coach, and pilgrims on the ship. It seems to me that this 'historical awareness' of 'difference' and 'change' is the most important part of 7- to 11-year-old children's study.

The work of Dorothy Heathcote has inspired History teachers amongst others during the last twenty years. Most directly she influenced Ray Verrier and John Fines in their teacher training,[24] but indirectly such teachers as Jayne Woodhouse and Viv Wilson in their co-operative work with Roger Day, Drama Adviser for Wiltshire.[25] They planned and executed work with two classes of 8- to 9-year-olds in a Southampton school on the Court Leet held on Southampton Common in 1566. This involved preparation in class, co-operation of parents on costume, a rehearsal out of doors and the final great day which was videotaped.[26] They write here of their similar work with 9- to 10-year-olds on the Iron Age.[27] Vivienne Little has also experimented with role-playing.[28]

Danebury solstice — an Iron Age history through drama project

The year is 400 BC. Iron Age tribes from the surrounding area have gathered together at Danebury hillfort to mark the occasion of the summer solstice. As part of the celebrations there have been tests of strength and skill amongst the warriors; some of the young people have marked their ritual entry into manhood or womanhood with a secret ceremony. Soon, there will be music, feasting and dancing, and the bards from each tribe will compete for the honour of telling the best story. Finally everyone will come together in the Great Dance, to salute the sun and ask for the gifts of peace and prosperity on the land and its people.

The date is June 23, 1987, and this is a 'History through Drama' day. The Iron Age tribes are nearly 270 children aged between 7 and 12 from three Hampshire schools with their teachers, and lecturers and students from La Sainte Union College of Higher Education. For the staff and pupils of Mount Pleasant Middle School, St Mark's Middle School and Swithun Wells Primary School, this is the culmination of a long-term project on the Iron Age which involved extensive classroom preparation and research into the period. The children examined the archaeological evidence of the Middle

Fig. 2.7   The Iron Age solstice: Segovax tells a story during the feasting (by permission of Tom Holder)

Iron Age and considered its uses and limitations in telling us how people lived. They visited local sites and museums to look at examples of pottery, metalwork and other crafts and to examine modern reconstructions of buildings and farming methods. At the same time, extensive use of drama role-play in the schools helped to deepen the children's insight into the period by emphasizing the individual and corporate concerns of real people living in an Iron Age community.

This summary of the Danebury project illustrates our particular approach to the teaching of History through Drama. The three key elements of this method are background research into the period, the establishment of a 'personal identity' through drama role-play and finally, as the culmination of the work, an entire day spent in role at an authentic historic site. By placing a major emphasis on utilizing the local environment — in this case a nearby Iron Age hillfort — we feel that it can be adapted by teachers anywhere in the country.

The central feature of the project was the preparatory work leading to the final day at Danebury. We were fortunate to have the support of the Archaeology and Education Unit at Southampton University who introduced the children to the evidence for the period and the means employed by archaeologists to interpret it. It was emphasized that any statements about Iron Age society could be at best only inference, or as the children were encouraged to say, 'a good guess'. At the same time as examining primary source material, drama role-play was deepening the children's sense of involvement with the period.

In order to establish a 'personal identity' each child was given an authentic Iron Age name, drawn from the later literature, and each school nominated as a separate tribe. Iron Age communities were developed through class discussion, map making, mime and group work. All these methods were directed towards enabling the children to answer certain specific questions about their backgrounds. They were asked to decide where their village was situated and what it was like, who they were related to and what their function was within the settlement. This combination of background research and role play allowed the children to explore aspects of everyday life in the Iron Age through the eyes of an individual character.

An important aspect of developing the children's personal identities was the wearing of clothing appropriate to the period. The evidence for what people wore during the Iron Age is sparse, but here financial considerations were more important than accuracy. We confined ourselves to the wearing of cloaks and simple tunics embellished by jewellery made in the classroom. The children were given ample opportunity to wear these various items during the school day so that they would feel familiar. It was important that by the time the children reached Danebury they had lost all sense of 'dressing up'.

On the day of the Solstice the children approached Danebury via a walk which would lead them well away from modern day intrusions. However, unknown to teachers and children alike, there was danger on the path! A band of ruthless marauders (a group of reputedly type-cast lecturers and students) were lying in wait, ready to seize trade goods and supplies. Under terms of truce, their motives for the attack were revealed; as outcasts they were dependent on robbery for food. Peace was established when one tribe offered to adopt them into their community. The tribespeople then proceeded to more peaceful business. Goods were exchanged, inter-tribal allegiances were reinforced by gift giving, and coming-of-age ceremonies were enacted for the young men and women. The highlight of the day then proved to be the oral story-telling contest, when bards from each tribe shared their best tales.

As the day drew to a close, the tribes joined hands and moved together in the Great Dance. The dance spiralled before the ramparts until the circle was complete. At the exact moment when all those gathered raised their hands together in praise of the sun, the first rays of sunshine we had seen all day broke through the clouds. It seemed a fitting — and moving — end to a term's hard, but worthwhile, work.

It remains to stress one vital point concerning the authenticity of the experience which History through Drama provides. We are not attempting to reconstruct the past but rather to offer one of many possible interpretations of an historical event. For example, we do not know whether the solstice was ever a cause of celebration at Danebury, and if it were, we cannot say with any certainty how the day was conducted or what ceremonies occurred. There is simply not enough evidence for us to approach the spiritual world of our Iron Age predecessors in such detail. However, within these limitations we believe it was possible to offer a single view of an event which was consistent with the available evidence. The archaeological record combined

with ethnographic parallels suggests that all the activities in which we participated *may* have taken place. A vital part of the preparatory work was to stress
to the children that the viewpoint we had chosen to adopt was in no way
definitive, and to encourage them to suggest alternative interpretations. The
children did not 'become' Iron Age people; they brought their own experience to bear upon an imaginary situation. While we firmly believe that the
drama role play took them closer to an historical understanding of the period,
the children at all times remained themselves, looking at the past through the
eyes of the present. In this way we believe that the day at Danebury brought
the past alive to the children by its immediacy and through their direct involvement.

Jayne Woodhouse and Viv Wilson
La Sainte Union College of Higher Education, Southampton

Chapter 4 considers the National Trust and English Heritage as purveyors of
role-playing and drama in a professional form with productions given at
appropriate buildings, usually involving large numbers of children in role-
playing. A recent example was at Corfe Castle, Dorset, where the YNTT
(Young National Trust Theatre), supported financially by Lloyds Bank,
re-enacted scenes from the Civil War period.[29] After a considerable period
of gestation and trials in London schools, ILEA has produced a pack on
Celts and Romans: Learning Through Drama (1986). This seems to be
intended for 9- to 11-year-olds though I was involved in using the pack with
7- to 8-year-olds in one of the trial schools. The pack emphasizes that this is
drama for learning, not performance as self-expression. It is divided into
'Raising some issues', 'Exploring the issues' and 'Developing the children's
own lines of thought'. The whole theme of the pack is the problem the Celts
encountered when faced with the Roman invasion. I can thoroughly recommend this pack as it is very detailed and instructive. The work of 'Archaeology Alive' at the University of Manchester also takes role-play into the
classrooms (Chapter 4).

Most role-playing is undertaken to live out a particular day or crucial
event in the past. Thus Hereward the Wake's resistance to William the
Conqueror, Wat Tyler's 1381 revolt, Ket's rebellion of 1549, the Jacobite
rebellions of 1715 and 1745, the Peterloo Massacre of 1819, the Tolpuddle
Martyrs of 1834 and the 1926 General Strike are suggestions for role-
playing. These themes of revolts against authority and the power structure,
show how individuals were involved and how they felt. They also show how
conflict influences the course of History and is captured in drama. Which-
ever approach is adopted, Heathcote or otherwise, drama adds to the
dimensions of thought and feeling for the individual in the past.

History and science

Emphasis on integration and science in the junior school in the 1960s led to attempts to involve History with Science. Two attempts will be described here, both being projects sponsored by large grants of money.

The Nuffield Junior Science Project published its findings in a pamphlet called *Science and History* (Collins, 1967). From this pamphlet the able teacher can be helped to link the disciplines of science and history through 'discovery learning'. Two approaches are suggested. One is a series of stories, told by the teacher, of famous scientists who made discoveries, such as Pasteur, Ron and Grassi (malaria), David Bruce (sleeping sickness), Ronx and Behring (diphtheria), Walter Reed (yellow fever), and Humphrey Davy (safety lamp). These would be simple stories with no experiments. The second approach would involve the children in more activity and

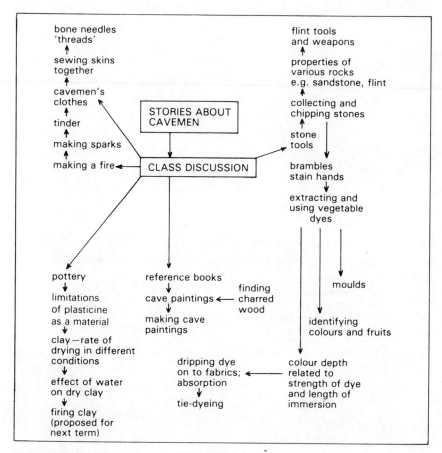

Fig. 2.8 Stories about cavemen (from *Science and History*, Teacher's Background Booklet, Nuffield Junior Science, Collins, 1967)

actual experimentation. The period most easily used is early man and his need for food, shelter, clothing, illustration in his cave (paintings), and weapons. The diagram named 'Stories about Cavemen' (Fig. 2.8) may help to amplify this for a class of 7- to 8-year-old children. Other topics to be tackled in this way are the voyages of discovery, involving ships, chronometer, and new foods; and transport, starting from moving stones to Stonehenge and at Stonehenge, in order to build the temple to the Sun God.

The second project is *Science 5–13*, sponsored by the Schools Council, the Nuffield Foundation and the Scottish Education Department. In 1969 it published two pamphlets on *Time* through Macdonald publishers. One is subtitled a 'background book' and the other 'a unit for teachers'. Children would work on units of time (day, week, year, etc.), time measurement (clocks), standard time, places and time (Greenwich and ships), biological clocks, and people and time (e.g. Galileo). An interesting topic developed from a display of old clocks which involved the making of a candle clock as

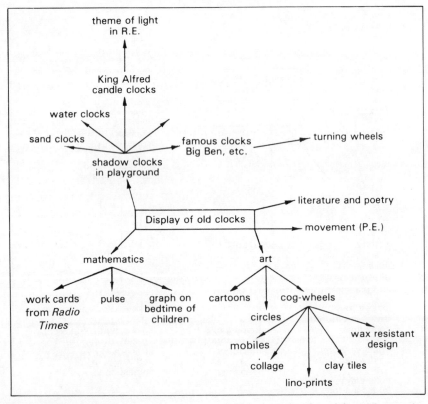

Fig. 2.9   A variety of activities connected with time developed from the starting point of a display of old clocks (from *Science 5–13*, Schools Council Project pamphlet on *Time*, Macdonald, 1969)

King Alfred did in order to plan the many activities of his day (Fig. 2.9 for flowchart). Older children interested in the measurement of time by famous men of the past could study Isaac Newton, Galileo, Christian Huygens, Robert Hooke, Thomas Tompion, and John Harrison. This would also involve practical work connected with time. Since history teachers find difficulty in teaching children an understanding of historical time and therefore feel insecure in their teaching of the past, this approach of time as used every day might be another way of looking at the problem. Once the concept of 'time' has been grasped, sequence, change, dates, centuries, 'periods' of history, and time charts will fall into place in the child's mind.

The Nuffield Junior Science Project and *Science 5–13* view the syllabus as a series of topics, complete in themselves and unrelated to each other except through science. However, the integration of science and history appears to be rather a strained relationship and could only be worked by an able, experienced and highly-motivated teacher. It may be more practicable to link History and Mathematics.[30]

History and art

Sybil Marshall, an experienced primary teacher who became an English specialist, believes in the integrated approach to the curriculum, with history very often as the basic component. She thinks that: 'Historical events are like pearls on a string of time', and that 'History comes into its own in the integrated thematic approach'. As the headmistress of a small village school at Kingston, Cambridgeshire, her main interest was in art and this combination of interest in the past and creativity produced some outstanding work described in *An Experiment in Education* (Cambridge University Press, 1970). A model brought to life an early lake village, and a term's work on Roman Britain led to a co-operative painted frieze showing a Roman procession. Old objects lent by villagers were examined, sketched, painted, and modelled. The church and the churchyard were used in the same way, stone rubbings of gravestones being made and the old writing deciphered. At one stage all the children in this all-age village school made a *Book of Kingston* telling the story of their village, using illustration freely. They also made a history of their village green culminating in a frieze of a procession of villagers. Since drawing, painting, and creative work are the natural medium of primary children and the past presents objects, buildings, and scenes needing representation, history and art are more natural bed-fellows than history and science. Art thus becomes a necessary form of record for the past.

Integrated topics based on history

In the four integrated frameworks so far suggested, history is the handmaiden

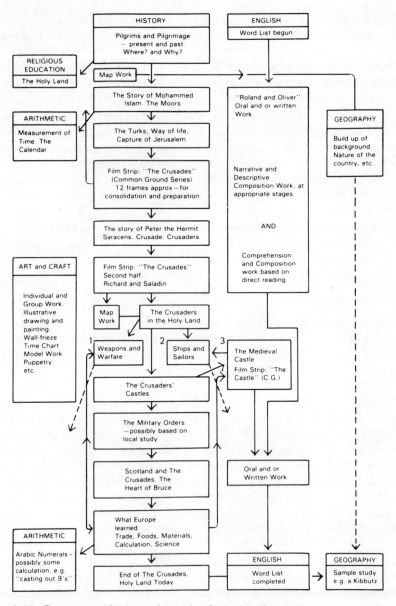

Fig. 2.10   Programme for a patch on the Crusades (from *History in the Primary School: A Scheme of Work*, Moray House College of Education, 1965)

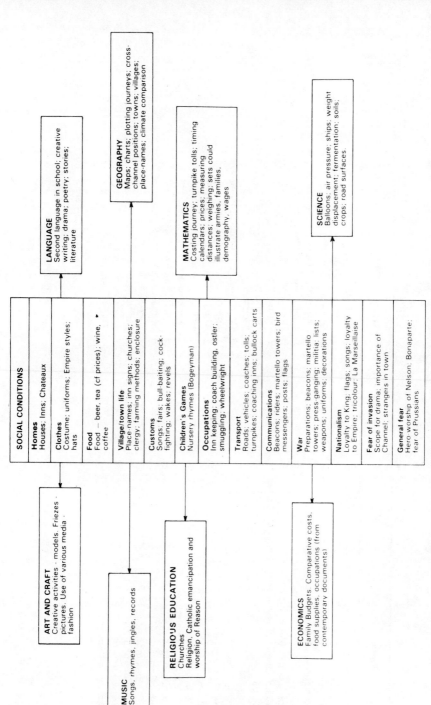

ART AND CRAFT
Creative activities - models. Friezes - pictures. Use of various media - fashion

MUSIC
Songs, rhymes, jingles, records

RELIGIOUS EDUCATION
Churches
Religion. Catholic emancipation and worship of Reason

ECONOMICS
Family Budgets. Comparative costs, food supplies, occupations (from contemporary documents)

SOCIAL CONDITIONS

Homes
Houses, Inns, Chateaux

Clothes
Costume; uniforms; Empire styles; hats

Food
Food — beer, tea (cf prices); wine, coffee

Village/town life
Place-names; inn signs; churches; clergy; farming methods; enclosure

Customs
Songs; fairs; bull-baiting; cock-fighting; wakes; revels

Children's Games
Nursery rhymes (Bogeyman)

Occupations
Inn keeping, coach building, ostler; smuggling; wheelwright

Transport
Roads, vehicles, coaches; tolls; turnpikes; coaching inns; bullock carts

Communications
Beacons; riders; martello towers; bird messengers; posts; flags

War
Preparations; beacons; martello towers; press ganging; militia; lists; weapons; uniforms; decorations

Nationalism
Loyalty to King; flags; songs; loyalty to Empire; tricolour; La Marseillaise

Fear of invasion
Scope for drama; importance of Channel; strangers in town

General fear
Hero worship of Nelson; Bonaparte; fear of Prussians

LANGUAGE
Second language in school; creative writing; drama; poetry; stories; literature

GEOGRAPHY
Maps; charts; plotting journeys; cross channel positions; towns; villages; place-names; climate comparison

MATHEMATICS
Costing journey; turnpike tolls; timing calendars; prices; measuring distances; weighing; sets could illustrate armies, families, demography, wages

SCIENCE
Balloons; air pressure; ships; weight displacement; fermentation; soils; crops; road surfaces

Fig. 2.11 Life at the time of Napoleon 1806: a comparison

Sources of information	Materials suitable for classroom presentation
1. Visits	1. Booklets
2. TV, Films, Radio	2. Friezes, collage
3. Filmstrips	3. Diorama
4. Archives and study kits, transcripts required	4. Tape-recordings
5. Maps	5. Slides with commentaries
6. Cartoon pictures (Art prints)	6. Drama
7. Books (e.g. Quennell)–Reference / Historical Stories	7. Films
8. Post cards	8. Artistic presentations–paintings / pictures
9. Newspapers	9. Models
10. Recordings (Music Readings)	10. Costumes, uniforms, dolls, puppets
11. Museums / Churches	11. Poems, creative writing
12. Firms	12. Musical activities, songs, jingles
13. Stories, rhymes e.g. Opie *Language and Life of Schoolchildren*	13. Ballads, records linked to slides
14. Personal Contacts–Relatives	14. Newspapers
15. French materials	15. Children's news sheets
16. Historical Societies	16. Maps–routes–France / England–Channel
17. UNESCO Bias in History	17. Registers
18. Diaries–contemporary	18. Militia lists
19. Calendars	19. Posters
20. Memorials and Statues	20. Flags / Heraldry
	21. Coins
	22. Displays–Interest Tables e.g. French / English food

Fig. 2.12   Life at the time of Napoleon: sources and resources

of other disciplines. In some topics, however, history uses other disciplines as supportive material. Two good examples of this approach are: 'The Crusades' suggested by Moray House College of Education, and 'Life at the time of Napoleon 1806' evolved at an in-service course held in Liverpool in 1969.

In 'The Crusades' (Fig. 2.10) such units as 'Weapons and warfare', 'Ships and sailors' and 'The medieval castle' could be treated in more detail. This particular topic is more relevant to history and English; geography, art and craft and R.E. would not be extensively involved. 'Life at the time of Napoleon 1806', also based on history, is suitable for a 9- to 10-year-old class. It should be integrated with mathematics, geography, science, language, music, R.E., art and craft, and economics. The theme running throughout is a comparison between the life of an English girl or boy in 1806 and a French girl or boy at the peak of Napoleon's power and therefore a period of great danger to England. A similar comparison between young people of both countries in 1940 would lead to interesting discussions, as 1940 was the year of the fall of France to Hitler, the isolation of Britain and the Battle of Britain. The aim of the work is to study a patch of history dependent upon a particular year (1806), and to invoke other disciplines where appropriate. The patch would last for one term, one afternoon a week. The work could be introduced by an active stimulus, such as a novel, film, poem, song, story, or picture. Teacher and class should discuss this introduction and see where it leads, using the diagram (Fig. 2.11). Half the class could take on the French role and half the English, and each group could imagine they were journeying from a town in England or France to the coast to watch the soldiers massing for the wars. *En route* they see how people lived and report back their findings at various stages of the journey. Comparisons could be made between the groups at each stopping point. Alternatively, the 13 topics under the heading 'Social conditions' could be divided into four groups, some studying the French children and some the English children in each group. Visual presentation should be an on-going activity and other classes should be invited to view the progress and the culmination of the project. Other disciplines (as suggested on the diagram) could integrate with this work to a greater or lesser extent. Help is given in Fig. 2.12 with sources and resources.

In a recent article entitled 'The drawbacks of projects', John Eggleston says 'A feature of many projects is not so much their spontaneity, but their open organization. Often the detailed structuring of the activity is left to the child or group of children.'[31] The two projects outlined in this section, on the other hand, are exceptions to this rule as they are highly structured and demand detailed preparation from teachers before they start. Yet when any interrelated work is undertaken, either the balance between subjects is maintained in a rather contrived fashion, with history claiming its proportionate share in the four-year (or two-year) programme as a whole, or history taking its chance of being the central subject, depending on who decides on the syllabus. Thus a syllabus based on topic work of some kinds could have little historical continuity or purpose, or even historical content, while elsewhere it might be history undisguised and perhaps unjustifiably overstressed.

The place of multicultural education in the primary school

Multicultural education should be an integral part of any primary school curriculum; it should not be confined to various subject areas such as History or Geography. It is an approach to learning, a way of thinking and feeling, rather than a set of rules to follow, or specific information. It is a fact that Britain has become a multicultural society. Many pupils in our schools today are the descendants of those who came to Britain not only in the 1960s but long before. These pupils rarely think of themselves as 'immigrants' but rather as British citizens with their own distinct cultural roots. This fact has major implications for all schools regardless of location and ethnic composition. As is now widely realized, all pupils should experience some form of multicultural education.

There are many multicultural resources available for teachers today. These can be found in local museums, art galleries, libraries and organizations such as the Commonwealth Institute in London. There is also a great deal of written and visual information in the form of books, pamphlets, posters, photographs and educational magazines (for example, *Religious Education Today*).[32] Often the main source of information is the children themselves. Even for those schools with very few or no ethnic minority children there is a lot of material available today in daily newspapers and on television and radio. When I was working on a topic called 'Ceremonies' with a class of second year juniors, one child brought a newspaper article into school about a certain pop star who had recently got married. From then on our topic work centred on wedding ceremonies in particular.

After discussing the pop star's wedding, which took place in a registry office, the children went on to find out more about the different types and places of wedding ceremonies in Britain today. One child had recently been to a friend's Greek wedding and brought photographs into school to show the other children. We also watched television programmes which highlighted different types of weddings.[33] I managed to borrow some artefacts used in various wedding ceremonies from the local church, a Hindu temple, a teachers' resource centre and from some of the parents of children in my class. The photographs, the television programme and the assortment of artefacts helped to stimulate the children's interest further. Three main areas of interest became immediately obvious; the clothes worn, the food served and the traditional music played at different weddings.

I divided the class into four groups and asked each group to find out as much as possible about a certain type of wedding ceremony — a Western Christian church wedding, a Greek Orthodox wedding, a Hindu wedding and

WEDDINGS

People at Weddings

1. Looking at photographs of weddings (past and present)

2. Looking at family wedding photos of children in class (perhaps even a video recording)

3. Important relationships e.g. Best Man, father figure who gives away the bride . . .

4. The part played by different people during different types of weddings e.g. traditional role of bridesmaids, maid of honour, page boy . . .

Symbolism and Imagery at Weddings

Looking at the different symbolism and imagery used at weddings and where it originated from e.g. chimney sweep and horseshoe from Christian wedding, e.g. symbolic fire, coconut and mendi patterns at Indian wedding comparing wedding cards from different types of weddings

Changing Fashions at Weddings

1. Looking at the clothes worn at weddings then and now (concentrating on past 25 years i.e. within experiences of children's family)

2. Clothes worn at different types of weddings — Hindu, Greek, Chinese . . .

3. Traditional significance of some clothes

4. Making life size models and peg dolls to represent different wedding clothes

Wedding Traditions

1. How traditions have changed and why

2. How traditions originated

3. Traditions from different cultures

4. Music played at weddings

Weddings in Britain Today

1. Difference between registry office wedding and that in a place of worship

2. Wedding ceremonies — traditional ceremonies of main ethnic minority groups

3. Places of worship where weddings take place e.g. church, temple, synagogue

Transport for Wedding Parties

1. Types of transport used today compared with that over the past 25 years

2. What the different modes of transport mean to different ethnic groups in Britain today

3. Decoration of wedding transport — origin and significance of certain imagery e.g. flowers, coconut shells

Food at Weddings

1. Comparing food now and in the past

2. Comparing different types of food served at different types of weddings

Fig. 2.13 Weddings (by permission of Anne Joyce)

a Chinese wedding. By doing this I tried to include the four major ethnic minority groups represented in the local environment. Each group of children completed their research and then presented their findings to the rest of the class in a role-play situation with the help of appropriate music, artefacts, clothing and food. We then moved on to look at how weddings had changed over the years and the historic traditions involved in wedding ceremonies. The historical element of the work we covered tended to fall into seven main areas although there was scope for many more (Fig. 2.13).

Teachers who do not feel confident in their own knowledge of multiculture may approach this area of learning with many doubts and fears. The first step is to think about the multicultural element when planning work. The second step is to ensure the support of your headteacher since she should be able to give moral support and help with resources. The third step is to find out what resources and facilities are available locally. Often this type of information is available from teachers' centres, LEA Advisers, libraries and local information bureaux.[34] Some of the larger secondary schools in the area may have a selection of multicultural resources which they would be willing to lend to primary school teachers. I have always found parents, religious leaders and other members of the community most helpful. Personal contact is by far the most successful way to get parents involved in the school. For example, it can be very helpful to have a number of parents to accompany the class during a visit to a place of worship, particularly if one or more attend the place of worship themselves and can pass on their own knowledge and experience to the children on return to the classroom.

Anne Joyce
Primary Advisory Teacher, Leicestershire LEA

(The school referred to in this account is fortunate in having four cultures substantially represented. It is often more difficult when there is a bewildering plurality of belief, and perhaps even more so when there is only one.)

The Schools Council and integrated frameworks

During its two decades of existence, the Schools Council supported several projects with cross-curricular implications for primary history. Some of these have already been mentioned: *Science 5–13; Environmental Studies 5–13* and *Place, Time and Society 8–13*. The last of these has had considerable influence, especially recently, through its ideas rather than its materials, and in the following section an integrated scheme of work according to its principles is discussed. However, in its later years, the Schools Council also supported some other projects which have had implications for primary history.

One of these, which built partly on *Place, Time and Society*[35] was based in the London Borough of Merton and considered continuity and development in children's learning in social studies across the whole age-range 5–16, thus anticipating current emphases. Another important initiative was *Developing Pupils' Thinking Through Topic Work*,[36] based at the University of Nottingham. Although the scope of the topic work considered in this project was quite wide, history was included, and a useful guide to teachers' self-improvement in planning topic work is now available. In *World Studies 8–13*,[37] jointly funded by the Rowntree Trust and now based at St. Martin's College, Lancaster, the main emphasis is on contemporary issues and on the importance of developing world perspectives and understanding, but the project has evolved lively suggestions for considering the claims of other cultures in place and time. Some historical content also figured in the *Curriculum Enrichment for Gifted Children*[38] project for children aged 8–11, based at Nene College, Northampton. Humanities is one of the four curriculum areas which were explored, and the project's 17 packs of pupil material included one, intended for eight-year-olds, on the Normans, with emphasis on the Bayeux Tapestry. Here, the question: How do we learn? is constantly reiterated, and children are given a tape of source material, a slide pack, and a workbook with which to undertake self-directed work. The Bayeux Tapestry materials are excellent and might well be used, under teacher supervision, with a wider range of children. Another project with a more explicitly psychological emphasis was *Listen, Think and Speak*,[39] based in the Metropolitan Borough of Sefton. Here too the Bayeux Tapestry figured in the production of materials and it is encouraging to see such good use made of a valuable resource, though unfortunate that the same degree of expertise could not be extended to other topics, especially since the resource materials produced in the course of these projects are neither cheap nor easy to obtain.

The Schools Council also supported a number of local small-scale initiatives, some of which are still bearing fruit in different parts of the country, and this form of support for grass-roots initiatives has been continued by the School Curriculum Development Committee, itself now to be superseded by a National Curriculum Council. The fostering of local initiatives ran, in a sense, counter to the centralizing trend more generally evident in curriculum development.

Finally, mention should be made of SCIP, originally the Schools Council Industry Project but now the School Curriculum Industry Partnership, involving a number of agencies concerned to promote the interests and image of industry. Mainly since the end of the Schools Council, SCIP has extended its activities into the primary years, and now represents a growing component in the primary curriculum, relatively well funded, and responsible for several useful guides to practice. It has added to the primary repertoire at least one new feature, the 'mini-enterprise', but has also led to a considerable interest in the history of local and other industries and to resources for this kind of study.

It remains to be seen how far the National Curriculum Council will be prepared, or permitted, to give to primary history even the measure of support that the Schools Council and SCDC have shown. The underwriting of history as a foundation subject in the national curriculum should help to allay the fears of those who feared the consequences of 'merger' in integrated frameworks. The actual treatment of history in the new structure is another matter. In order to extend the range of thinking derived from the Schools Council projects into the age of the national curriculum, and to suggest one way of promoting historical (and other kinds of) understanding within an interrelated framework, an example is given of a scheme of work based on the ideas of *Place, Time and Society 8–13*.

2.7 Place, Time and Society 7—11: history in an interrelated framework

The Schools Council Project *Place, Time and Society 8–13* was established in 1971 to develop ideas and materials for the middle years of schooling. These ideas were to be applicable whether in a subject-based or in an integrated curriculum, in what were then the new Middle Schools but also, where appropriate, in primary and secondary schools. They were also intended to promote structure and progression in learning, at a time when project and topic work was often lacking in both. Now, after nearly two decades, the tide no longer flows towards middle schools or towards a free choice of integrated curricula, but towards nationally-defined subjects in primary and secondary schools. The one aspect of the original strategy that does still remain embodied in current thinking is the emphasis on structure and progression and on the consequent continuity from one phase to the next. Meanwhile, many local initiatives in curriculum-making continue to make use of the thinking developed by this project in the 1970s, and are now seeking to adapt it to changing circumstances. To assist this process, the following example of a scheme of work for junior Humanities has been designed to combine the requirement of a national curriculum with the principles of *Place, Time and Society 8–13*, modified in the light of fifteen years' experience.

Although the *Place, Time and Society* project did not pretend to cater for infant or first schools, it represented a long-profile approach to the curriculum as a whole that has implications for the infant years as well as for the upper secondary school. It assumed that the youngest children in school would encounter some 'pre-disciplinary' experiences of a kind that are recognizably concerned with the past, with the physical, natural and human environment, and with social and economic relationships. This may sound pretentious, but it is quite compatible with the pursuit of themes such as Family, Shops, and Where we Live, and also with imaginative and expressive work based on stories some of which are from the past. It is also compatible with finding and looking at 'old things' and learning to think about them, as well as about animals and plants and physical objects as seen through the eyes of artists and scientists. So the scheme of work for *juniors* that follows is based on the assumption that the children, in their infant years, will have enjoyed some experiences of that kind, and will in fact have begun to meet Place and Time and Society, in school and outside, though probably not in as defined a way as when they start in junior school with something termed Topic or Humanities.

Since the scheme itself is an attempt to embody the principles of *Place, Time and Society*, with some adaptations, those principles should first be summarized:

1 The emphasis should be on curriculum process, that is, on the development of a range of skills (intellectual, social and physical) and relevant concepts, and personal qualities (interests and attitudes) and only then on knowledge-content suitable for these purposes, selected in accordance with the characteristics of children, individually and collectively, at different age-levels.

2 The separate 'Social Subjects' (i.e. History, Geography, the Social Sciences) should be regarded as resources on which to draw, and as ways of thinking and problem-solving, rather than as bodies of knowledge certain parts of which should be prescribed as essential, or as ways of determining what is good or evil.

3 These social subjects should be considered in interrelation with each other and with other aspects of the curriculum, rather than in isolation, but their distinctiveness and coherence as ways of understanding should be brought out progressively between 5 and 11, and given recognition as separate fields of study in secondary education, probably from the age of 11 and certainly from 13. (That does not imply that only one of them should continue in isolation after the age of 14.) The use of the major concepts treated within the separate social subjects – period and government, region and location, employment and markets, community and society, and so on – should enter progressively into the study of Humanities during the primary phase.

4 The selection and organization of actual subject-matter in primary Humanities should be made by teachers in the light of their potential for the development of these major concepts and in particular of four substantive key concepts integral to all the social subjects (Communication, Power, Values and Beliefs, Conflict/Consensus) and of three methodological key concepts involved in the thinking that they all require (Similarity/Difference, Continuity/Change, and Causes and Consequences).

5 The actual choice of themes or topics for study in a particular class should also take account of the development, interests and experience of the teacher and children concerned, though there should be, over the four

years of junior-school life, an overall balance between historical, geographical, economic and social emphases, and a planned continuity and
progression in the development of skills, concepts and knowledge proper
to each of the social subjects.

6 The sequence of themes or topics should also allow ideas to be developed
  outwards in space, forwards and backwards in time, and with increasing
  complexity in economic and social understanding.

7 The methods of study adopted should encourage investigation, mature
  social interaction, empathy, and a sensitive acceptance of differences of
  opinion. They should all promote the understanding of real people:
  individuals and groups, past and present.

A scheme designed to comply ideally with all of these principles would be
a contradiction in terms, since each teacher and each class would need a
separate scheme. But in a national curriculum, that contradiction in terms
must to some extent be enforced. So this scheme constitutes avowedly an
attempt at compromise, a shared framework that could serve the claims of a
national curriculum to ensure progression and continuity, to cater for
multicultural considerations and economic awareness, and to enable
children to move from place to place without losing their foothold in time
and society, while preserving as much flexibility as possible in its actual
implementation. In any case, it allows for a small and decreasing part of the
time allocated to Humanities (whether separately or in an integrated
structure) to be spent on current issues that call for attention but cannot be
anticipated in advance. For the structured part of the Humanities curriculum, two themes are suggested for each year in the junior course, except that
the final year has three. All of them are open to negotiation and adaptation,
but they are intended to constitute a coherent whole (Fig. 2.14).

First year 7–8

Characteristics of children: (here, and subsequently, no attempt is made to
indicate the range of characteristics, including those of children with special
needs; a composite 'average' is given.) Transition from infant-school practice; partial mastery of language skills; growing response to stories of
general appeal; growing capacity to understand broad distinctions in place
(here/there), in time (now/then) and in society (we/they).

Themes:

1 FOLKTALES   Tales now established as part of the 'repertoire' of
  human heritage chosen (partly according to availability, including contributions from children's families) from contrasted cultures e.g. Homeric
  Greece, ancient India, the Caribbean, the American frontier, modern
  Nigeria; told, illustrated in art, poetry, song and drama; finally 'analysed'
  through questions such as: How old? Where from? (and then located on

world map, globe, and a new medium, the time-line). What sort of people started it? How do we know? What is there about it that has made it such a favourite? Perhaps the class, or some members, could then compose a ballad about some recent local or national or wider event.

2 REPORTERS   By contrast, this is intended to extend competence in noting distinction among events near at hand in place and time. The aim is to prepare a class newspaper emphasizing accuracy, sequence, design, imagination and interpretation. 'Reporter groups' could be set up, each to do some investigation and to write a brief contribution on the care-taker, the canteen supervisor, the traffic warden and other school cele-brities, including representative children of different kinds, and also on school amenities, events, and burning issues such as sports fixtures. Examination of the local press would suggest other features such as Letters to the Editor, a local-knowledge crossword, and perhaps a 'museum corner' to which family historical relics might be lent for reporting. (The local newspaper itself might be drawn directly in, as an example of local history.) In the actual make-up of the class newspaper, special attention would be paid to accuracy of sequence, location, deci-sions about what is important, and ways of communicating information and opinion, including maps, diagrams and time-charts.

AGE	'OPEN' TIME	THEME
7–8	OTHER TOPICS INVOLVING HUMANITIES	1. FOLKTALES
		2. REPORTERS
8–9		3. ROOTS
		4. EXPLORING
9–10		5. GRAN'S WORLD
		6. WORKPLACES
10–11		7. KNOWING OUR PLACE
		8. HERE AND THERE
		9. OTHER PEOPLE'S LANDS

SUMMARY OF A SCHEME FOR PLACE, TIME AND SOCIETY 7–11

This summary now requires expansion in a little more detail.

Fig. 2.14

Second year 8–9

Characteristics of children: extension of skills of language and perception; greater ability to take independent initiative and to develop social sensitivity, as individuals and groups, both inside and outside school.

Themes:

3 ROOTS   Starting with the class's own Roots, in place, time and society; development of social skills and empathy through respect for the class's variety of Roots; imaginative accounts of how two different fictitious families might find their Roots; extension to the idea that all people have Roots, some stronger than others; further extension from Roots to Origins; the origins of human settlement in and near this place, with use as evidence of nearby museum and archaeological material, resulting in imaginative but disciplined construction of model of an early settlement (prehistoric or later); brief consideration of other kinds of local and other Roots important to the class (school, public services, places of worship of different faith communities, the last carefully related to the R.E. scheme); bringing together of the later parts of this theme in a frieze of Origins and a long time line. Underlying the whole theme is an emphasis on continuity/change and on power and beliefs.

   Note No handling of Roots will satisfy everybody; that in itself illustrates the nature of conflict in society. But it should be undertaken with as wide an awareness, sensitivity and warmth of understanding as possible.

4 EXPLORING   Looking first at children's own explorations in their shared environment, perhaps along the lines suggested by Robin Moore,[40] and also elsewhere; making maps and explorers' logs; the idea of 'joining up the world'; a list of the eminent explorers who extended knowledge of the geographical world for their own peoples; plotting these explorations in place (globe, atlas) and time (time-line); stories of two of these explorations, one from past centuries and one from the twentieth (polar or space exploration), chosen according to interest and availability of material, and developed with emphasis on evidence, accuracy of knowledge, imaginative reconstruction from the point of view of the culture from which the explorers came, the explorers and their companions, the cultures which they 'discovered', and a discussion of the social and political consequences.

Third year 9–10

Characteristics of children: further development of the potential shown at 8–9; considerable increase in manipulative skills and in, mainly, 'concrete' reasoning; beginnings of understanding of concepts such as 'period' and 'region'; growing capacity for more sustained and complex co-operative study if suitably guided.

Themes:

5 GRAN'S WORLD   An attempt to build up an impression of life locally and nationally after the Second World War, starting like Roots from family experience, but extending it more systematically; group and individual work on aspects of Gran's World chosen initially by the children themselves and including those whose Grans were in different worlds; extended to include the local, national and international context emphasizing the choice and limits of choice that different people experienced; critical examination of the evidence adduced, including oral evidence; introduction of tabular then/now comparisons involving continuity/change; presentation of outcome in an exhibition or mock TV programme; introduction of the idea of Our Children's World and use of disciplined imagination to draw up a now/future table; selection of material that a future class could find useful if they were to repeat the exercise in the 2030s.

6 WORKPLACES A deliberate introduction of the concept of Work: What is work? Why do people work? Why do some people not work? Compilation of list of local workplaces (selective, not exhaustive); choice of one, not necessarily a factory, according to opportunity; liaison with that workplace to find out about its history and present functions; perhaps, development of a mini-enterprise in the class, thus emphasizing economic concepts such as supply and demand, division of labour, cost and price, added value, marketing, risk, control, etc; decision-making considered in relation to elementary computer-assisted simulations, leading to the emphasis on choice among possible explanations, and actions rather than assumption that there must be a right answer; culminating in a presentation involving advertising and its ethics and limitations, the role of management and unions, and the concept of legal control of workplaces and their related functions; a brief comment on workplaces elsewhere.[41]

Fourth year 10–11

Characteristics of children: continuation of the preceding, with increased mastery of written expression (by most) and with greater feel for distinctions and change within past time; increased capacity to develop hypotheses and generalizations and to consider alternative explanations, related to mastery of greater complexity in language structure and especially in adverbial clauses; increasing capacity for empathy and for understanding of conflict in human affairs.

Themes:

7 KNOWING OUR PLACE   A more systematic local study than Reporters or Gran's World, based on a variety of data: maps, documents, observations, collated statistics; selection of topics for group study, by

groups, but under guidance to encourage balance between historical, physical, economic and social topics; representation of outcomes in (a) maps, including a date-map with surviving man- (and woman-) made features coloured according to their period: the choice of period would itself be a valuable exercise, as would the modification of symbols needed to denote alteration and restoration; (b) time-charts, diagrams, graphs, photos, descriptions, and perhaps the insertion of data on suitable software; (c) oral and dramatic presentation; analysis of outcomes by statistical and other methods; consideration of local issues of communication, power and conflict, together with possible solutions; a concluding look into the future and how planning might help or hinder desirable change, from different points of view.

8 HERE AND THERE   Choice of another accessible environment contrasted in geographical, historical, economic and social features but preferably linked through school twinning, so that each 'twin' could draw on the other's resources and experience; preferably a week's residential exchange to promote direct interaction and to develop social skills; presentation by each school of a 'report' on the other place, pursued under the headings already in use of Knowing Our Place: if those headings require modification, that would teach a further lesson about the two environments.

In addition to the direct contribution to Humanities, HERE AND THERE could contribute powerfully to informal education.

9 OTHER PEOPLE'S LANDS   Title deliberately chosen on multicultural grounds but also to emphasize 'land' rather than 'country' or any political designation; a start would be made from the sharing of experience of other lands, through residence or holiday, by members of the class; extension to expectations of future visits; choice partly from this collective experience of two lands, both of manageable size and with available data, and one of them near to the United Kingdom, but otherwise contrasted characteristics: examples of such pairs might be Spain and Pakistan; France and Hungary; Norway and Tanzania; planning of journeys to each of the pair chosen by use of timetables and tourist literature – giving some introduction to historical and contemporary culture and a taste of the country's own language; preparation of a report on the two imaginary visits, including maps, and illustrated travelogues incorporating hilarious as well as serious experiences but bringing out the significance of the historical and cultural context, and of current problems; preparation of a tabular comparison between the two. This final theme would draw together a fair proportion of the skills, concepts and task procedures developed during the four junior years, and would provide a foretaste of the study of larger units including the superpowers at the secondary stage.

In addition to its development of skills and concepts important in the social subjects, this scheme has cross-curricular implications that scarcely need to be spelled out. These, too, present an overall balance across the four years, though they are not equally represented in each individual theme. At the same time, it must be emphasized that this scheme is about Humanities, and is not a piece of pedagogic imperialism attempting to annex the rest of the curriculum. For its effectiveness, indeed, it depends on the concurrent development of language and mathematics, science and technology, the creative arts, P.E. and moral and religious education, all of which represent distinctive and essential ways of understanding and endeavour, as Humanities does.

Yet Humanities may be considered to represent more than one of those ways of understanding and endeavour. History and the social sciences have their own distinctive characteristics, and both resist any attempt to include them within the other, while geography tries, not unsuccessfully, to establish a distinctive approach independent of both the others. Since the present purpose is to indicate how the historical way of understanding figures in the scheme, a brief comment will first be made about how geographical and social-science skills and concepts can be built up, before the historical component is considered more fully.

The development of mapwork skills and other representational skills in geography, the use of the globe and atlas, the development of notions of location, nodality and distribution, and of physical/human interaction, all figure in the various themes. Meanwhile the spatial structure of the locality, the idea of a region and of a political unit, and a feel for the 'otherness' of Other People's Lands, is built up along with a growing grasp of the major distribution of continents and oceans and an ability to know one's way round the world. Similarly, the economic ideas deliberately introduced in Workplaces are extended in Knowing Our Place and Here and There, and touched upon in Other People's Lands, while the social concepts of family, community, organization, interdependence, innovation and conflict can be traced through the entire sequence, so that children reach secondary education with some awareness and experience on which subsequent studies can be built.[42]

Turning now to the specifically historical elements in the scheme, mention should first be made of the principal tool skill, the capacity to sequence or seriate events and people and periods, and then its elaboration into mastery of the conventional time-scale, as distinct from mere date-labelling. Attention is paid to this kind of skill acquisition in every one of the nine themes, and requires constant practice and reinforcement. Some form of time-line, on the wall or suspended like a clothes-line with pegs for dates, should be part of the regular equipment. At first there would be a long line, representing as much as 10,000 years, with the Folktales located on it; this would be an opportunity to explain and emphasize the BC/AD division. The very vagueness of the timing of some folktales presents a learning situation in itself. Reporters is at the other extreme: it is the accurate sequencing of events over a very short time that matters here. For Roots and Exploring, the longer line is in use again, but this time with events bunched into the AD part. Gran's World introduces the notion of 'period' and also brings out the need to use more than one line, thus introducing the idea of different scales into time measurement at the stage at which it is also being met in the mapping of place measurement. The last four themes, especially Knowing Our Place, take this familiarity with the conventional time scale further and project it into the future. The one extension not specifically mentioned is the large-scale charts required to take in all of prehistoric, and geological, time. This may be touched on in Knowing Our Place, but in spite of the dinosaurmania frequently met, and perhaps beneficially developed through primary science, the full significance of immense spans of time and space is left for secondary education to explore.

The use of reference and study skills and the evaluation of evidence are promoted over the four years through the use of an increasing range of sources. By the final year, independent searching for historical evidence and evaluation of the relative significance of conflicting or unrelated material becomes possible, especially when focused on the local area of its 'twin' in Here and There. The appraisal and interpretation of original sources, including material actually collected by children, begins with Reporters and Roots, continues through explorers' journals etc. in Exploring, extends to oral evidence in Gran's World and official publicity material in Workplaces, and takes in a further range of archaeological, architectural, documentary and even palaeographical material in the final-year local studies. By then, too, it begins to be clear that evidence looks different to different people.

One of the key concepts in *Place, time and society*, Continuity/Change, is central to historical thinking. It is found in Reporters and Roots, and on a wider canvas in Exploring, considered more systematically in Gran's World, and absorbed into the methods of study necessary in Workplaces and in the fourth-year themes, in which there is a clear indication of how the historian's perspective interrelates with the others in Humanities.

A sense of period is a characteristic feature of the historian's craft, and historians sometimes criticize interdisciplinary studies on the grounds that this sense of period is sacrificed to somewhat problematic and inhuman 'lines of development'. In this scheme, it is not sacrificed, but gradually built up, first through Exploring and then through Gran's World, after which it is included in the approach to study required particularly in Knowing Our Place and Here and There, and ventured in Other People's Lands.

It is possible that historians, hearing of a scheme of work of this kind, will still regret the lack of a basic chronological structure and of content that has acquired the sanction of tradition. There is no sequence from Cave Men to the Victorians, it is true. On the other hand, historical content that promotes genuine historical understanding is regularly introduced and systematically related to the time sequence in such a way that the major divisions of History (that is, of British and Western history) such as the Iron Age, Middle Ages, Seventeenth Century, Victorian times become known, and the importance recognized of the way in which one follows and is influenced by another. A more systematic, sequential, study would follow in secondary education, with some emphasis on British history because for all young people that has the significance of proximity, but with samples of periods and cultures elsewhere in place and time in order to avoid ethnocentric parochialism, and with a more consistent chronological continuity over, say, the last two centuries.

There is, however, one piece of content that does claim specific inclusion in its own right in a junior-school scheme, and that is the locality. It figures, though never exclusively, throughout all the themes from Reporters onwards, and incorporates some systematic local history in Knowing Our Place and reciprocally in Here and There. It is of course possible to stray into much too much detail even for 11-year-olds, for the potential content of local study in its wider context extends through secondary into further and higher education; but enough can be done to give children some sense of coherent understanding of, and feeling for, and identification with, their own place, rather than dismissing it as humdrum or hostile. In a national curriculum, it must still be that unique local knowledge that children need in order to locate themselves, even if they do not all see it the same way. Moreover, it is something that they can bring into secondary education, as they will have already brought it into Here and There, alongside others bringing similar understanding of adjacent and more distant places that are their own. It is a positive way of starting the process of cohesion within a first-year secondary class in History, Geography, or Humanities.

A teacher considering this scheme and its implications may be pardoned for wondering whether some sort of Mastermind (paid on the basic scale) is required in order to attempt to implement it. Some understanding on a teacher's part is certainly necessary. It should not be approached simply on the basis of sketchy knowledge dredged up from the personal past and enlivened by snippets of current interest. The necessary amplification of knowledge and understanding is, however, less formidable than it looks. The sources recommended in Chapter 4 can provide for much of the historical content needed for the nine themes, especially Folktales, Exploring, Gran's World, part of Roots, and the fourth-year studies. Local libraries and museums are usually able to provide substantial supports for Reporters, Roots, and Knowing Our Place, and for some aspects of Workplaces and Gran's World. An additional source for Workplaces is the School Curriculum Industry Partnership's publications (see also Chapter 4). Among the many sources for Gran's World, mention should be made of the familiar Granada Television series *How we used to live* (see Chapter 4). For

Other People's Lands, as already indicated, much can be derived from standard travel literature, enlivened by phrase-books; the established series of guide-books provide substantial historical data for anyone unfamiliar with the general historical context, though it has to be remembered that tourism has its own principles of selection that shanty towns might not endorse.

These references to source material are to be set alongside the major source of information, the adults in the locality and the children themselves, all of them, enquiring and sharing experiences. The analytic use of such information is a central purpose of the scheme itself, and figures in every one of the themes; consequently, the teacher is never left with the whole burden of providing information, so that she is left free to concentrate on the organization of the work and on what material is required in order to maintain balance and extension of understanding.

As time passes, an archive of material can be built up in a school and shared with others nearby as well as interchanged in Here and There. This database would require updating, thus affording further evidence of continuity/ change, and further opportunity for children to exercise critical judgment about the material they use. The establishment and maintenance of such an archive should not be left to individual teachers but should be part of the responsibility of Humanities consultants within schools and of Humanities advisers in an area, supported where possible by HMI. The same archives could be expanded for secondary-school use, too; their value for GCSE projects is evident. The resourcing of a national curriculum should include specific provision for this purpose; it would pay splendid dividends.

So the problem of resources is not daunting; only substantial. Even so, a teacher facing any one of the year-programmes in this scheme could still wish she were a Mastermind. Yet everyone can make a start, perhaps on a reduced version of one such theme, and build up towards a more fully-implemented scheme, one term or one year at a time. This scheme of work is not intended to be a national curriculum in itself, sprung full-grown from the head of *Place, time and society*. Rather, it is meant to be a reasonably thought out guideline to be adapted by those who want to steer between the 'random, repetitive, risk-free' array of topics that the Schools Council project originally aimed to supersede, and the traditional, factual, history and geography that could now all too readily re-appear.

Alan Blyth
Formerly Director of Place, Time and Society 8–13

2.8   Conclusion

No scheme for the 7–11 age-range is appropriate without due recognition of the development of children and their interests and abilities at different stages. Kieran Egan views the 8–14 years as those influenced by romance. Following, but reinterpreting, Whitehead, and even Hegel, he calls it the Romantic Stage. Any syllabus, therefore, should emphasize 'the most exotic and bizarre societies', very different from their own – 'the more alien the world with which students (i.e. children) can be connected, the more relevant is knowledge about it to their educational development'.[43] This use of the very different is not only interesting but *necessary* to the 8- to 11-year-olds for them to advance to the next stage of learning. It should also allow, I believe, for studies in depth, since 8- to 11-year-old children have the ability to master and memorize considerable detail if adequately structured. This would not mean that all patches should be studied in equal depth. Although children of the 7–8 age-range also enjoy stories of 'the exotic and bizarre' and children of 8–11 are more competent to undertake and enjoy local field work, this reminder is salutary in making sure that we do not lose sight of dramatic personalities and events in the 8–11 syllabus. I believe that Kieran Egan's view of history at the romantic stage is true of all study of the past in the junior school. 'History is best understood at this stage as a kind of mosaic of bright elements – anecdotes, facts, dramatic events – which are composed into a small story, which in turn is a segment of a larger story'.[44] It is to be hoped that this chapter will enable teachers to help 5- to 11-year-old children to experience a small story, which is a segment of world history, a larger story.

Notes

1. P. Sudworth, 'An Analysis of Teaching History in the Primary School since 1960' in *Teaching History*, No. 33, June 1982.
2. R. Swift and M. Jackson, 'History in the Primary School: a Regional Survey' in *Teaching History*, No. 49, October 1987.
3. P. Noble, 'Seeking a Sense of Direction' in *Times Educational Supplement*, History Extra, 12 April, 1985.
   Examples of recent LEA initiatives are:-
   H. Cooper, 'Patterns of Development' in *Times Educational Supplement*, History Extra, 20 November, 1984 (Greenvale Primary School, Croydon).
   Primary History Guidelines, Metropolitan Borough of Solihull, 1986.
   Cumbria Education Committee, *Humanities in the Primary School*, Cumbria County Council, 1987.
   Manchester Education Committee, *Humanities Curriculum Guide*, Manchester Education Committee, 1987.
   East Sussex Curriculum Working Papers: *Humanities in the Infant Classroom; Primary History 7–13; Learning Skills*; East Sussex County Council, 1984–7.
4. (a) J.E. Blyth, *Understanding the Past: Children 5 to 9*, Research report, Froebel College, Roehampton, 1985.
   (b) J.E. Blyth, 'Sequence and Time Sense with Children 5 to 9', in *Times Educational Supplement*, 25 November, 1985.

5. (a) J.E. Blyth, *History in Primary Schools*, McGraw-Hill, 1982 (revised edition Open University Press, 1988).
   (b) J.E. Blyth, *Place and Time with Children 5 to 9*, Teaching 5–13 Series, Croom Helm, 1984.
   (c) J.E. Blyth, *History 5 to 9*, Primary Bookshelf series, Hodder and Stoughton, 1988.
6. J. West, *Children's Awareness of the Past*, Ph.D., University of Keele, 1981.
7. H. Cooper, *Questions Arising in an Attempt to Interpret the Historical Thinking of Primary School Children Accordng to Theories of Cognitive Development*, Diploma in Child Development, University of London, 1982 (A summary of results may be found in 5(c) above).
8. P. Knight, *Children's Understanding of People in the Past*, Ph.D., University of Lancaster, 1988.
9. P. Noble, *Curriculum Planning in Primary History*, T. H. 57, Historical Association, 1985.
10. M. Forrest, *The Teacher as Researcher: the Use of Historical Artefacts in the Primary School*, M.Ed. Dissertation, University of Bath, 1983.
11. V. Bone, *An Investigation into Children's Understanding of Historical Sequence*, Diploma, Froebel College, Roehampton, 1984.
12. S. Perrin, *Using Historical Objects to Stimulate Talk with Infants*, Diploma in Advanced Studies in Education, University of Bristol, 1986.
13. S.G.C. Tofts, *History in the Infant School: an Empirical Study of the Way in which Historical Material is Used with Infants in the Integrated Curriculum*, Diploma in Advanced Studies in Education, University of Bristol, 1984.
14. S. Purkis, *Thanks for the Memory*, How do we Know Series, Collins, 1987.
15. J. Woodhouse and V. Wilson, 'History through Drama: An Enactive Approach to Learning' in *Education 3–13*, Vol. 15, No. 3, October, 1987.
16. Y. Larsson and G. Johnston (eds.), *Issues in History Teaching: Understanding the Time Concept in History, A Unit of Work on Teaching About Time in History, Years 7–10*, Faculty of Education, University of Sydney, New South Wales.
17. See 5 (c) as above.
18. K. Egan, 'Children's Path to Reality from Fantasy: Contrary Thoughts about Curriculum Foundations' in *Journal of Curriculum Studies*, Vol. 15, No. 4. 1983.
19. K. Hodgkinson, 'How Artefacts can Stimulate Historical Thinking in Young Children' in *Education 3–13*, Vol. 14, No. 2, Autumn 1986.
20. J.S. Bruner, *The Process of Education*, Vintage, 1963, p. 60.
21. A good example of integrated topic work, based on a book with a local historical flavour, was carried out by Mrs Sheila White of Kilkhampton County Primary School. She was one of a group of teachers working with Olga Collier of the Cornwall County Inspectorate. Mrs White used David Wiseman's *The Fate of Jeremy Visick* (Kestrel Viking 1982, Puffin 1984), a tale of Cornish tin mining a century ago, as a stimulus for a whole range of understanding and feeling.
22. M.B. Gauld, *Seeking Progression in the Historical Strand of Environmental Studies*, Occasional Paper No. 2, Aberdeen College of Education, 1986.
23. L. Johnson and C. O'Neill, *Dorothy Heathcote: Selected Writings on Education and Drama*, Hutchinson, 1984.
   B.J. Wagner *Dorothy Heathcote: Drama as a Learning Medium*, Hutchinson, 1979.

24. J. Fines and R. Verrier, *The Drama of History*, New University Education, 1974.
25. See 15.
26. *The Court Leet of 1566*, Wessex Educational Television Consortium, King Alfred's College, Winchester SO22 4NR, 1986.
27. J. Woodhouse and V. Wilson, 'Celebrating the Solstice: A History through Drama teaching project on the Iron Age' in *Teaching History*, No. 51, April, 1988.
28. V. Little, 'History Through Drama with Top Juniors' in *Education 3–13*, Vol. 11. No. 2, Autumn 1983.
29. A. Tinniswood, 'Play-back to History' in *The National Trust Magazine*, Spring, 1987, also *Country House Visiting*, National Trust, 1987.
30. *History in the Primary and Secondary Years*, op. cit., Appendix 3, History and Mathematics.
31. J. Eggleston, 'The Drawbacks of Projects' in *Times Educational Supplement*, 12 September, 1980; also G. Rogers, 'Project Work and the History Curriculum' in *Education 3–13*, Vol. 14, No. 2, Autumn 1986.
32. *Religious Education Today*, Christian Education Movement, Middlesex.
33. *Watch*, BBC, 1984–5 (An Indian Wedding).
    Tomorrow's People, ITV programme 7, 1985.
34. M.M. Ahsan, *Muslim Festivals*, Wayland, 1985.
    S. Barrett, *The Tinder Box Assembly Book*, A. & C. Black, 1984.
    O. Bennett, *The Sikh Wedding*, Hamish Hamilton, 1985.
    J. Mayled, *Marriage Customs*, Wayland, 1986.
    S. Mitter, *Hindu Festivals*, Wayland, 1985.
    J. Snelling, *Buddhist Festivals*, Wayland, 1985.
    A. Souza, *The Sikhs in Britain*, Batsford, 1986.
    R. Turner, *Jewish Festivals*, Wayland, 1985.
    People Then and Now, Macdonald, 1986 (contemporary families all over the world).
    T.V. Programmes on multicultural ways of life:- ITV *Believe it or Not, All Year Round, Seeing and Doing* (Greek/Cypriot), *Going Places* (life styles in India).
35. A. Blyth et al., *Place, Time and Society 8–13: Curriculum Planning in History, Geography and Social Science*, Collins /ESL Bristol, 1976, obtainable from School Curriculum Development Committee.
36. H. Bradley, J. Eggleston, T. Kerry and D. Cooper, *Developing Pupils' Thinking Through Topic Work: A Starter Course*, Longmans for School Curriculum Development Committee, 1984.
37. S. Fisher and D. Hicks, *World Studies 8–13: A Teachers' Handbook*, Oliver and Boyd, 1985.
38. Schools Council Curriculum Enrichment Packs: *Discovering History*, Globe Educational for Schools Council, 1980.
39. R. Norris, G. Hennessy and D. Harmes with Sefton Local Education Authority, *Listen, Think and Speak*, Yellow Section, Holt, Rinehart and Winston, 1984.
40. R. C. Moore, *Childhood's Domain: Play and Place in Child Development*, Croom Helm, 1986.
41. D. Smith (ed), *Industry in the Primary School*, Falmer Press, 1988.
42. For geographical, economic and social aspects of Place, Time and Society see J.

Bale, *Geography and the Primary School*, Routledge and Kegan Paul, 1987; A. Ross, *Social Studies in the Primary School*, Falmer Press (forthcoming) and S. Wagstaff, *People Around Us*, A. & C. Black, 1978.
43. K. Egan, op. cit. p. 47.
44. ibid. p. 45.

3 The classroom operation

3.1 Introduction

At the beginning of the last chapter I emphasized why I regard methods of teaching and the resources of the classroom as more important than the content of the scheme of work. Each discipline has its established methods and in following these, the teacher will find teaching easier and more effective. 'Methods' of teaching have been equated with the 'tips for teachers' of older training days, yet *how* teachers structure and plan their work and provide activities for children must always be crucially important. How teachers conduct 'the classroom operation' is closely linked to what resources they have at their disposal. In writing this chapter I shall assume that teachers have very few resources at their disposal and shall suggest ways of overcoming this.

The natural methods of the historian as outlined in Chapter 1 should always be borne in mind. Story-telling at any level of teaching history is one of these methods. More story-telling is done at certain ages, but explanation of events and people is always needed by the good teacher. As a story is usually told from beginning to end there is a strong time and sequence element and a teacher must tell the story in the right order to make sense. Second, the historian is closely concerned with people and events, especially in the 5–11 age-range; historical movements and ideas are not suitable at this stage. A third intrinsic method is to ask questions about evidence; how do we know that this or that happened? Teachers should always be asking children questions even if they have not taught them the facts, and showing them books about history as the way to find out. Fourth, teachers should also bear in mind that change and difference are fundamental to the subject and, therefore, comparisons between the 'then' and 'now' and different people and periods should constantly enter teaching methods.

These four essentials seem to be mainly concerned with oral work, discussion, question and answer. Teachers should beware of being 'the

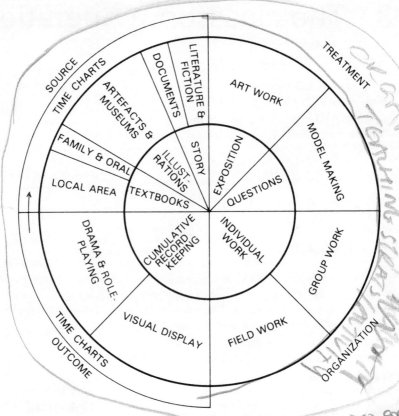

Fig. 3.1   The classroom operation

fountain of knowledge' and dominating the learning situation, which can easily be done in history. They must purposely think out activities for their children, particularly in this age range, remembering that 5- to 8-year-olds find reading and writing a slow method. Most preparation time for this age range will go into preparing suitable activities rather than collecting and remembering information. Although I shall provide suitable bibliographies at the end of the book (to read the most appropriate book is half the battle in preparation), teachers can make a good lesson out of a less good book if their methods are well thought out. It is natural for some methods to appeal to some teachers and it is tempting to keep to a method 'which works', but variety of approach is the secret of success and teachers should be daring enough to experiment with new approaches gradually as confidence builds up.

In this chapter, different methods will be discussed and at the same time experience from past teachers and different approaches for varying ages will be considered. The approach advocated in this chapter is summarized by Fig. 3.1 in which the centre circle is concerned with basic methods indispensable to teaching the past and the outer circle shows more ambitious and experimental ways of teaching. Both circles are grouped into four inter-dependent concepts of how the work is treated by the teacher, how children are organized, what the outcome of the work is, and what sources may be used. Time charts finally link 'outcome' and 'sources' since they form the result of work and also the basis or source of other work (in another year of the school). Drama and role-playing have already been discussed in Chapter 2. Story, illustrations, and time charts form part of this chapter. In this way Chapters 2, 3, and 4 are closely linked and are the heart of the book.

3.2 The story lesson

Two well-known methods of teaching the past are telling a story, and a lesson starting with a story and leading to related children's activity. Both are now considered 'old-fashioned', mainly because they give sole initiative to the teacher and involve her in a considerable amount of oral work. In actual fact, both methods are more difficult than they appear at first sight, but they still remain the essence of history teaching. They are difficult because they require detailed preparation and reading, they necessitate good discipline and above all a high standard of presentation in order to hold the attention of children of any age. But there are certain pieces of advice that are very helpful to teachers. It is better to start learning story-telling by reading a short, suitable story and then progressing to telling it, first with your book open and finally without it, but always helped by as large an illustration as possible.

Story-telling is not only a successful method but has been discovered more recently by one historian and teacher to correspond to an essential stage in a child's development which, if missed, will jeopardize his future educational development. For example, Kieran Egan writes of 'the power of stories in the mental life of young children'. In his amplification of this theme, 'the necessity of the story form', his main contention is that the real past is too indecisive and grey for young children, but that the story form is satisfying because a story, according to Aristotle, 'has a beginning which sets up expectations, a middle that complicates them, and an end that satisfies them'.[1] In other words, the historian's problem to be solved by seeking out relevant sources and reading different viewpoints, becomes to the young child the description of a person relating to an event (the problem), made more interesting by crises and complications (added problems), and re-solved by a usually satisfactory end (problem solved). Therefore 'an end' is essential in a story and what happens afterwards does not matter.

This idea, developed for the 'mythic' stage of education, was practised by an outstanding story-teller, Freda Saxey, for many years. To her the principles of story-telling were clear. The teacher starts by reading and re-reading her story from its original sources (many such sources are translated if originally written in other languages), trying to visualize the people and actions as vividly as possible. The second stage is to plan it into four to six parts 'like the acts of a play and find a title for each part'. The teacher should jot down at the foot of her working page phrases and ideas from the sources which will appeal to children of the age group concerned. Third, the teacher should go over each titled part and put specific words (if possible exact ones) into the words of the characters. R. J. Unstead suggests Becket's reply to the knights looking for him in Canterbury Cathedral – 'Lo, I am here, no traitor but a priest of God' – if a story was being told of Archbishop Becket's murder.[2] Last, Freda Saxey advises teachers to try to *see* the action of the story happening, as this will help memory and add to the vitality of the telling. Obviously, a visual illustration is very helpful. More will be said about pictures later in this chapter. Freda Saxey does not think of story-telling as 'talk without chalk' but as a shared experience of teacher and class. If the advice is to be followed, stories of people, actions, and crises are the best. At whatever age stories are told, and they are basic throughout the primary age range, discussion should be planned and leading questions asked in the second part of the story session. In this way 'good and bad' and 'right and wrong', 'selfish and unselfish' may naturally form part of the curriculum. Shirley Makin, a pupil of Freda Saxey, writes about telling a story to blind and partially-sighted children in this chapter.

Another teacher with a flair for story-telling is John Fines. His advice on how to teach about castles to 6-year-olds over a period of six weeks hinges on the 'half story'.[3] This means telling a story up to an exciting point from which the story could go in several directions. This stimulates children to use their thinking and imagination to complete the story, and leads to much discussion as to how the story should end. In one example, John Fines imagined that he was Sir Ralph, a medieval baron owning a castle. Sir Ralph was short of money, was expecting a visit from the king and had many other problems; he went to bed one night with these problems unsolved and the children were left to solve them. Although Dr Fines had the help of six student teachers and was teaching a class of bright 6-year-olds, his methods could be adapted to the normal class situation. It would only be possible for the class to work in groups, tackling Sir Ralph's problems, if the work was attempted with 7- to 9-year-olds. The half-story could lead to model-making of a castle(s), a coach trip to Porchester Castle (ruined) and preparations to furnish the castle for the royal visit. The teacher, taking on the role of Sir Ralph, could still act as the promoter of discussion to solve the problems and the final episode could be a role-playing of the royal visit. Thus the six sessions start with story and lead to drama in Dorothy Heathcote's style of living the parts. For this type of work to be effective the teacher should know a good deal of detail about castles and life in castles and the children should be able to refer to reading books on castles, of which there are plenty. The advantage of this half-story technique over the previous method is that the children have to solve the complications of Egan's 'middle' of the story in order to reach 'the end'. This necessitates thought, discussion, and knowledge. At the end, they will remember the difficulties a Norman baron had in entertaining the King.

Although the two teachers mentioned so far happen to be particularly skilled as story-tellers, most primary teachers would agree that every teacher should be able to tell a story reasonably well. In *Why Teach History?* (University of London Press, 1974) Pamela Mays recognizes that not all teachers are gifted as story-tellers and wisely suggests that stories can be *read* by the teacher if suitable books are used. She names a very simplified series called *Awake to History* (Pergamon, 1964), Ladybird books (Wills and Hepworth) and Eileen and Rhoda Power's *Boys and Girls of History* and *More Boys and Girls of History* (P. 1927–1953). Her good reason for this is that children will gain a more varied vocabulary if the teacher reads from different books rather than always putting stories into her own language. Therefore teachers fearful of embarking on the task of learning how to tell stories should gain confidence legitimately by reading them. This will also depend upon the nature of a particular class and their place in the 5–11 age-range, younger children preferring 'telling' and older ones 'reading'. Suggestions of stories from modern historical fiction are given in Chapter 4.

The Historical Association published a very valuable small pamphlet entitled *Story-Telling: Notes for Teachers of History in the Junior School* (T.H. No. 13) but unfortunately this is now out of print. Five different specialists considered areas of the past in detail, giving sources and assessing the value of their particular area. The five areas were:

1 Stories of Alfred the Great.
2 Stories of the Norman Conquest.
3 The Canterbury Pilgrims and Thomas à Becket.
4 Discovery of the Mississippi valley.
5 Roman Britain: an archaeological approach.

The five authors consider their topic in relation to the whole age range of 7–11 and suggest ways in which their particular stories may be used. For example, D.M. Dannett makes it quite clear that her stories of Roman Britain are best treated as introductory material for a museum visit and possibly an archaeological dig and therefore are more suitable for the last year of the junior school. The second part of the pamphlet is a list of suitable stories with books in which they may be found and illustrative material to be used with them. However, the bibliography is out of date and needs revision as many more suitable books are now on the market and teachers will find them readily in public libraries.

Thus story plays a fundamental part in any teaching of the past particularly in the 5–8 age-range when reading and writing is so much slower for children. In the first two terms of the 5–7 scheme of work (Chapter 2), it is the basic teaching method, and stories should be grouped round important figures or events. It is a good introduction to any work done even from 8 to 11 but need not be used as frequently in the last two years of the junior school. One way of getting older juniors to read history in their own reading time is to set aside one part of a term, with preparation, for groups of children, after discussion, to read or tell their favourite story of the past. This would involve the class in reading, group discussion of stories, decision as to which one to use, and selection of a pupil capable and willing to read to the class. If the class had six groups it could lead to a competition, in the presence of the headteacher, as to which was the best story and why. Story can also be a base for role-playing and dramatization. Children should be reminded that every story must have a beginning, a middle, and an end. If they have been told stories well by the teacher from 5 years upwards they would be in no doubt how to judge a story of the past.[4]

How I tell the story of 'The Assassin' to a visually handicapped class of 8- to 11-year-olds

The children range in age from 8 years 11 months to 11 years 6 months and form a very receptive class in a school for the visually handicapped. Three of the children have some residual vision, the other five are almost or totally blind. Some of the children have additional problems: one has difficulty in walking, one can eat only liquidized foods and one is emotionally disturbed. Two of the children are above and two or three are below average intelligence. Two are girls, six are boys.

The Assassin is a story about the attempted murder of Prince Edward (later King Edward I, 1272—1307) by a Moslem messenger in the Holy Land during one of the crusades. At the time Edward, accompanied by his wife, Eleanor, was resting after a battle. The meanings of a few of the words to be used in the story were discussed, e.g., assassin, Crusade, Moslem, Christian, knight.

I had made myself very familiar with the text of the story so that when I needed to adapt to the feel of the class and be more forceful I was able to tell parts of the story rather than read them. However, I did read most of the story because I did not want to lose any of Dr Mowl's* choice adjectives, fine phrases, or patterns of repetition. She wrote this story in such an excellent manner, always using direct speech, that even when the story was being read, it sounded as if it was being told. The children were asked not just to listen to the story but to imagine that they were living in those times and conditions, and were the people in the story. They were asked to think about what they would hear, smell, feel, or see, if they were able to. They listened to the story very receptively and obviously enjoyed it and found it interesting. They asked many questions, e.g., Was it a true story? Which King Edward did

---

* Dr Mowl was the same person as Freda Saxey, mentioned earlier.

he become? Which King Henry was his father? When was the crusade? How could Eleanor be Queen; Prince Philip is not King?

The children were asked what they could imagine most vividly. The two girls both chose to describe gentle parts of the story. One described the chess pieces beautifully and the other the scenes where Edward told Eleanor the reason for his placing a cross on the shoulder of his cloak and the people attempting to persuade her not to go on the crusade. The boy with emotional difficulties said 'Eleanor saving his life'; when asked how, he resorted to his favourite answer, 'I don't know'. After discussion he said, 'nursing and looking after him'. One boy whose speech is a little incoherent, when helped by the other children, settled for 'When he was given the paper by the little brown man'. He was referring to the letter. The brightest of the boys said confidently, 'The keystone falling down and smashing the chair'. Another boy referred to Edward killing the Assassin and the guard picking up the stool to strike the dead man. This was immediately corrected to 'the minstrel' by the other children. The oldest boy said, 'Riding a horse getting hotter, paler, and dying'. The most boisterous of the boys said, 'When the assassin took the dagger out of his belt and stuck it in Edward's arm'.

I asked them a few general questions, e.g., What do the words 'fair', 'brave', 'loyal', and 'sweet' mean? What are the differences between a soldier, a knight, and a general? Do you think that Edward was right to say that it wasn't knightly to strike a dead man? Should people hurt each other because they are not members of the same religion? Did Eleanor do the right thing to accompany her husband? Did Edward do the right thing to go on the Crusade and free the Christian knights? How was the climate different from England? What was different in those days from today?

Another day the children were asked which parts of the story they remembered and if they remembered any of the words or phrases used in the story. I found that they had remembered most of the actions that had taken place in the story but found it difficult to recall phrases apart from 'the little brown man' and 'three hundred English knights'. Unfortunately there had been over a week's interval between the two lessons. I decided to re-tell the story quickly as I felt they needed to be reminded about some of the detailed descriptions and phrases before they could dramatize it, write about it, or illustrate it. Each child was then asked to tell me about their favourite part of the story. Most of the children re-told a section of the story; the assassination scene was the most popular. Two children re-told the conversation between Edward and Eleanor after the keystone had fallen. One child wrote about the climate in the country of the Crusade. Two of the children managed to repeat several of the phrases and adjectives used in the story and others an odd one.

The three children who have some residual vision did illustrations. They chose scenes rather than isolated figures. One was the bed scene done by a child who is obsessed by time so he insisted on putting a clock in the picture. This led to a discussion on how people told the time in those days. Another child chose the scene where Edward and Eleanor returned to Windsor Castle as King and Queen with crowns on their heads. The third child chose the scene where the keystone fell. These illustrations were all done in wax crayons.

The class made two models, one of Edward and one of Eleanor. The cardboard centres from toilet rolls were used for the foundations. They chose red velvet for Edward's cloak and the selvedge of the material for the cross which was pinned on with a safety pin. Blue taffeta and white lace were used for Eleanor's dress. The materials were attached by rubber bands and staples and parts were just tucked inside the rolls. The faces were drawn with felt pens on white adhesive labels by the children who could see. Their crowns were made from tinfoil and attached with staples. One child made models out of plasticine.

The story provided stimulus for lively discussion and imaginative experience. It gave impetus to the children's creative individual and group work. They listened purposefully and their vocabulary was enriched as a result of hearing words and phrases skilfully used. They remembered in detail incidents, words, and phrases. They thought about and discussed emotions, feelings, and ethical values. An interest was aroused in what life was like 700 years ago. They enjoyed the story and asked if they could hear more historical stories.

Shirley Makin
The Royal School for the Blind, Liverpool

3.3   Interpreting illustrations[5]

A second basic method used by most primary teachers is the use of illustrations in the classroom. It may seem a truism to emphasize the value of visual evidence, especially to younger children, but in recent years teachers of all ages of pupils have found that 'seeing is believing' and that many pupils can understand and remember better from a visual approach. Therefore this method is not to be considered childish or unimportant. Although books on teaching history to primary children seldom make a specific effort to show teachers how to do this, they all presume that illustrations are vital. Sir Fred Clarke said, 'Pictures will always have a very high value to imaginative reconstruction', though he did not favour model-making in history, seeing that as really handwork or art and craft. Catherine Firth had a whole chapter on 'Pictures and their uses', decrying *Little Arthur's History of England* for including only six pictures. She called the use of pictures, 'A precious means for the learning of history'.[6] She had to rely on postcards from London museums and the Quennells' *History of Everyday Things in England* series (Batsford), but today teachers have much more help than this. Gillian Evans concentrates on what to look for in medieval pictures.[7] In this part of the chapter I am concerned with how the teacher uses illustrations rather than how children make them. The latter will be considered later when expressive work is discussed in more detail.

'Illustration' covers a wide field and it is impossible to give much detail here where we are concerned with uses. The most useful are those made by the teacher either before the session or during it on blackboard or paper. The building up of a picture, in the style of Rolf Harris or Tony Hart, has obvious advantages. But this is a gift, and most of us have to rely on commercially published pictures. Macmillans' large 'class pictures' of English history, though highly coloured and therefore not always accurate for real life, are at least a starting point. So are the illustrations from the long-running *Junior Education*. These old faithfuls are often still to be found in school where newer illustrative material is hard to come by. A second type of illustration is a black-and-white line drawing copied from a contemporary picture and simplified. In many respects these are more correct historically though the lack of colour makes them lose some appeal to infants and younger juniors. A third category is contemporary pictures, either medieval manuscript illustrations, actual contemporary sketches or maps. The teacher has to be very careful to select clear and fairly large examples, and earlier maps, such as John Speed's seventeenth-century ones, which are really simple plans. A delightful, but somewhat dated, book for 7- to 11-year-olds is *The Map that Came to Life* by H. J. Deverson (Oxford University Press, 1967) which is a story about a walk taken by two children using part of an Ordnance Survey map shown in the book. On each page a full-colour picture illustrates a detail (amplified) of the OS map which is very well explained. A fourth type of illustration is a genuine painting done by an old master such as the Sir Henry Unton picture in the National Portrait Gallery already mentioned, *Portrait of the Artist's Daughter* (Fig. 3.2), *Portrait of Arabella Stuart* (cover), the famous *Thomas More Family Group*, the *Coronation Portrait of Queen Elizabeth I* or the well-known picture of *The Field of the Cloth of Gold* when Henry VIII met Francis I of France. An embroidery such as the *Bayeux Tapestry*, depicting the Norman Conquest, falls into the same category. Lastly, there are illustrations in most textbooks and reading books, some of which require careful selection. The publication of resource packs, archive teaching units, and 'Jackdaws' over the last fifteen years may be used with careful selection of the fairly large pictures used as support to the archival material. All these types of illustrations provide starting points for discussion with the teacher or by the children in groups. The visual approach is more likely to elicit response, comment, and questions from most children than the spoken word.

Using two specific pictures and one map I hope to show how a lesson may be taught mainly from illustrative material, probably more effectively than using the spoken word. My first picture is a contemporary early Tudor one of *Lord Cobham and his family at table*, used as a Frontispiece to this book. This could be taught to 6- to 7-year-olds either as part of a patch on the Tudors or as part of a line of development on 'children'. The picture could be a 'starter' for a session on meals in a noble household at the time. There are

Fig. 3.2   Portrait of the Artist's Daughter by Cornelius de Vos from Devonshire
Collection, Chatsworth (Reproduced by permission of the Chatsworth Settlement
Trustees. Photograph supplied by Courtauld Institute of Art)

comparisons with today crying out to be made: a family of six children, a
nurse, grown-up clothes for the children, their ages (written above five of
the children), the great amount of fresh fruit eaten, animals including a
monkey and birds actually on the table, pewter plates, and parents in the
background showing the growing importance of children in the family. This

Fig. 3.3   Fighting fire in the seventeenth century (by permission of Liverpool Education Committee)

picture is so rich in contemporary detail that only a poor teacher or a very unresponsive class would not learn from it; in fact the picture actually teaches the lesson.

My second picture for 6- to 7-year-olds is a sketch made from a contemporary line drawing in *A Town Under Siege: Liverpool in the Civil War 1642–4* (Fig. 3.3). It shows townsmen fighting a fire with leather buckets; the scene could easily be drawn and coloured by children in their own inimitable way. On the other hand the teacher could sketch in the main outline of the sloping street and house roofs and duplicate copies for children to complete. Children will quickly see the simplistic ways that people of the seventeenth century had for fighting fires in their wooden houses; water in leather buckets, long hooks to pull off the flaming wood to stop it causing more fire, taking goods out of the house, and praying to God both inside and outside the house. A child can also be seen being let down on a rope from a window. Certain references from *Liverpool Town Books* enforcing law and order may easily be understood by very young children as relating to the illustration:

1619   We present Richard Lune's wife for carrying fire in the open streets uncovered.

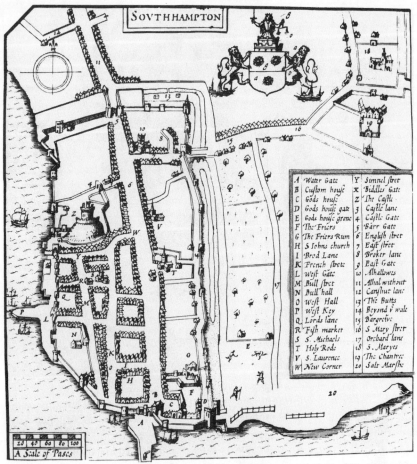

Fig. 3.4 John Speed's 1611 map of Southampton (by permission of Southampton City Council)

1636   We do order that the now Bailiffe of this Town shall provide and have in readiness for the Town's use a dozen leather buckets for such use as the Town shall have occasion or need of.

1641   Item. We do order that there shall be no fire carried through the streets either in the night or day.

A story could be started from these extracts and the picture, based on Richard Lune's wife unwisely carrying fire in the street to warm an ill neighbour and a fire starting. The children could suggest how the story might be developed (the middle) and completed (the end) and pictures could be drawn and coloured for notebooks. Thus again, one contemporary illustration and a few extracts provide the lesson, and could lead to other stories of town life in the seventeenth century.

My third illustration, also for 6- to 7-year-olds, is *John Speed's 1611 map of Southampton* (Fig. 3.4). This has the great advantage of delightful little models of the castle, bargate, All Hallows Church, Holy Rood Church, the Customs House, as well as ships on the sea, the medieval wall, the 'Butts' for archery and small figures playing ball in the fields. The area within the medieval wall is still clear today and can be walked round and many of the streets today have the same names. This map gives endless scope for discussion, drawing, mapping routes, and even field work for very young children. Most of the maps drawn by John Speed contain the main town in one corner in more detail. Local Record Offices usually sell them. They are wonderful illustrations for intensive work in detail and for display. It is possible to 'read' modern pictures in reading books, if they are big enough, but the contemporary illustrations yield much more detail for discussion and children between 5 and 11 are very observant of detail which they find intriguing.

3.4   Exposition and questions

Constant use of story-telling in the early years of the 5–9 age-range gives the teacher of junior classes the confidence to start a session by a short stimulus talk involving question and answer as well as description and illustration from blackboard, chart, or pictorial illustration. The teacher can also start from a poem, source reading, or short tape recording. Although the teacher takes the initiative in this type of lesson she should be training her class to participate in oral discussion. Most history is not taught by specialists in the primary school, and one teacher, as suggested in the 1978 Primary School Report, should be encouraged to become a history specialist in order to at any rate advise her colleagues. Thus the class teacher already *in* authority in her own classroom, may become *an* authority to some extent in the scheme taught. The oral lesson is one sure way of indicating that the teacher is *an* authority. This does not mean that she must know all about the work or have read all the books which the children have read collectively, but she must be thought to know more than any one child and should not be prepared to start her class on any period of the past regardless of her own knowledge. The oral approach also transfers the enthusiasm of the teacher to the class more quickly than any other method.

It is obvious that many questions are asked and answered informally in group work but these are not planned by the teacher and they often seem to be questions of fact or finding out about source material. Well-known work in the primary school on language, conducted by Dr John Tough in Schools Council projects (*Listening to Children Talking*, Ward Lock, 1976), has shown the importance to very young children of the teacher 'talking' and 'listening' to children (*Talking and Learning*, Ward Lock, 1977). This develops towards the top of the junior school into planned discussions with purposive questions of different sorts. The Schools Council Project *Place, Time and Society 8–13* has experimented to some extent on two types of questioning, 'closed' and 'open', as a means of encouraging critical thinking skills. 'Closed' questions are those expecting a factual, right or wrong answer. These are the questions usually associated with history teaching, too many of which lead to rote-learning. They are a good way to start a session as they are easy for all to answer, revise what has been done earlier, and help a class to settle down and concentrate. They may also be used effectively in ten-point oral tests checking on names, dates, and main events, as well as words difficult to spell.

'Open' questions usually expect longer, less cut-and-dried answers, requiring thought rather than memory. They do not expect the right answer (as there may not be one) but to anticipate other questions from the teacher as follow up, to clarify the question further. Thus they play an essential place in the cumulative, planned piece of teaching. They also are a teaching method which helps children to use historical material relevantly since a face-to-face questioner usually obtains a relevant answer to a question. 'Open' questions have three objectives: to encourage children to use evidence to draw conclusions; to encourage them to be aware that all evidence is not trustworthy; and to encourage them to use thought and common sense in their reasoning. Thus 'open' questions follow the base of fact and knowledge laid by 'closed' questions and .... n result. 'Open' questions may be used regularly fr.... *Open / closed* ....ld up an attitude that history is not all fact. To un.... *questions* ....teacher should know her class well and so have er.......................hildren to listen to the questions and answers of ..... *Not discovered* .... t make sure that as many children as possible are ..... *without teaching* ...d that other children *listen* to each other's answe..........................n with their peers through the teacher. The chart s...........................ecific example of Henry VIII to show how 'closed...... *open depend on* .....ad to critical thinking. It is obvious from this ....these questions cannot be 'discovered' without ...... *open depend on* ....pen' questions depend upon the answers to the '..... *closed being* ....rect. As soon as questioning becomes at all c..... *correct.* ....well advised to prepare three or four leading 'ope.........................ring the oral lesson. This means that she must ....her 'open' question related to the answer to he..........................the thinking of the class further. She must a..........................the discussion back to the oral lesson in order t..........................he story approach, i.e., the beginning and t....... Questioning is an essential part of the oral lesson and has to be learnt by the teacher.

The obvious request from the non-specialist teacher is for good, concise, and easily obtainable reading material to help to prepare even a short

Closed questions		Open questions		Critical thinking
Asking for memorizing of names, dates, events	Encouraging children to sequence and break down the past into understandable parts	Encouraging children to use evidence to draw conclusions	Encouraging children to be aware that all evidence is not trustworthy	Encouraging children to use thought and common sense in their reasoning
Examples	*Examples*	*Examples*	*Examples*	*Examples*
What were the names of the six wives of Henry VIII? On what occasion did he meet the King of France to show off his wealth and power? In what year was Thomas More executed?	Put the wives of Henry VIII in their order of marriage to Henry. Can you think of one reason why each wife was discarded?	Did Henry VIII want a son badly? How do you know? What makes you think he was very sad even when a son was born to him?	Did the evidence of Thomas Cromwell's visits to monasteries show them to be inefficient and therefore necessary to 'dissolve'? Did Cromwell visit the monasteries intending to close them before compiling his evidence?	Can you think of any reasons why Thomas Cromwell agreed with Henry VIII about the monasteries? Why did Henry VIII execute Cromwell in the end?

[handwritten annotations:] LOOK AT ROSETTA STONE. WHAT WAS ROSETTA STONE? WHERE FOUND IT? WHY WHEN FOUND? carl Champollion WHO? Understood it

Fig. 3.5   Encouraging critical thinking through questions in later junior years (topic: Henry VIII)

introductory oral lesson. Rather than search out the many excellent reading books now on the market I suggest two particularly succinct books specially written for this purpose. One is *Teachers' Handbook: History*, edited by John Fines (Blond, 1969). After a general introduction this book is divided into five sections, written by different specialists, all of which are concerned with historical material, different approaches, illustrations, and references to source materials, films, filmstrips, and BBC programmes. The five topics are comprehensive in range: prehistory, the Roman period, the Middle Ages, early modern times and contemporary history. There is enough in each section to construct a series of good lessons without any further reading. (Year by year advice on further reading and source material may be built up.) The section on the Middle Ages is conveniently divided into subsections such as heraldry, children and childhood, town-building and urban life. The book is not written to provide material for a specific age range but most of the material is suitable, with some selection, for the 8–11 age-range.

My second book is one already mentioned in the previous chapter – Alan and Roland Earl's *How Shall I Teach History?* (Blackwell, 1971). This less detailed book may be useful to the teachers of 5–8 children as well as 8–11 children. It covers most of the ground of the other – medieval history to the Norman Conquest (a patch), the Age of Discovery, ancient civilizations, world history and local history and Elizabethan England (a patch) – but is more humorous and less academic in style, as well as being much cheaper in price. It includes some references to further study and gives the excellent advice which all teachers of history should heed – 'Be ruthless in selection'. The two books complement each other and together form an excellent basis for oral teaching.

3.5 The essential product: cumulative record making

So far we have looked at three 'musts' in the classroom operation for the teachers of history in the primary school: the story, interpreting illustrations, and oral work. Before more varied methods are discussed a fourth essential is written work of some sort. People sometimes ask what there is to show for the history that children have studied, what 'the product' should be. Much of what they write is necessarily transient, part of a particular display. What really matters in the long run is what they retain and make part of themselves. This is 'the essential product'. For this purpose a special kind of written work is particularly useful: cumulative record making. Since most people, including children, find talking easier than writing and young children have to *learn* how to write, there has been a tendency to overlook the need for young children to write about the past. Informal methods of teaching have encouraged this, as well as the drudgery of marking or even looking at work repeated thirty times. Yet if over the six years of primary education we are hoping to provide some framework related to time, children must have some record to aid memory, to relate to their time charts, and to see for themselves where this or that year's work 'comes' in chronology. Thus, work is built upon as the pupil goes through the school. Therefore, I am naming this part of the chapter 'cumulative record making' which is also related to assessment (Chapter 5).

Very little attention has been paid to this side of history teaching on the assumption that a child who can write English can also write history. Although this is true from the point of view of language (spelling, punctuation, handwriting), a start should be made in the primary school on the unique features of writing about the past. The particular pitfalls when writing about the past are the temptation to copy whole sentences and paragraphs from books (often regardless of their meaning), to write at far too great length in the belief that knowledge is what the teacher wants, and finally the habit of writing on scraps of paper. It is only too usual for these scraps of paper to be read once, fastened to a display and then discarded because there is nowhere to keep them. More will be said later about the last pitfall, which is most easily overcome by making history workbooks. The other two difficulties can be avoided to a large extent before children reach the secondary school by careful training as to how to write about the past. As in other methods of teaching, variety in record keeping is the key to success.

The only primary teacher who has written about record keeping in History is R.J. Unstead in a section of his book called 'Written work'.[8] He rightly emphasizes the importance of display of work, particularly by 5- to 8-year-old children, and believes that this is one way of avoiding copying from books, as the children check on each other with warning from the teacher. The teacher also must read the books that her children read and look at work to check on copying. It is usually easy to find this out, as children do not usually write as adults however able they are. In Appendix 1 to Unstead's book he gives a very useful list of suggestions for written work in history (pp. 81–85).

How to get primary children to write easily and well, except by luck, does not seem to have been tackled. I believe that there can and should be a building up and progression of techniques from the infant stage to top juniors. Starting from story-telling in the first two terms of the first infant years, children may build up Books of the Past; these are large books of different coloured paper stapled together to avoid disintegration and decorated on the front by the child concerned. Each story should be illustrated by a drawing or crayonning, a title put by the teacher at first, until the child has learnt to write, and the papers pasted into the book in order of the telling of the stories. The same could apply to the artefacts studied, though representation of real objects is more difficult. The family history studied might include a child's life-line and brief family tree, both of which could form part of the book. Local history could be represented by simple plans, perhaps completed from the teacher's outline, and the visits might be recorded by a brief account (at age 7) completed from the teacher's account with key words (on the blackboard) omitted. When teaching 6-year-olds I was surprised to find how keen they were to complete an account of a visit we had made to the museum. To them this was the favourite piece of recording though it possibly smacked of old-fashioned junior practice. Looking through their Books of the Past, taking pride in them, and showing them to parents proves an enjoyable way of putting the term's or year's work together. I have found 6-year-olds anxious to 'remember' what has been studied and pleased to have some record to jog their memories. These books would show in retrospect not only what history had been 'done' but also how the child had developed it's powers.

Many infants reach the stage of writing one sentence about their pictures and this may be built on in the 7–9 age-range. Children of 7–8 years should be encouraged to write at least one sentence under their pictures (models) and

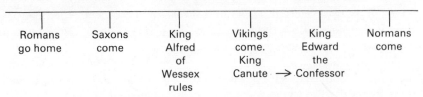

Fig. 3.6   Horizontal sequence line

then to develop from one to two and more so that by the end of the second year in the junior school most can rise to a short paragraph about one person, event, or building studied. By 8–9 it might be possible to build up a simple horizontal sequence line of about six events in sequence as in Fig. 3.6. This purposely takes no notice of *length* of time between events and is only concerned with order or *sequence of events* (i.e., what comes before what, in time). The book may also contain an answered worksheet and a cartoon strip with 'balloons' depicting the voices of historical characters. If a topic or patch approach has been adopted for a period of half a term a scrapbook of photographs, postcards, and newspaper cuttings might be made with sentences about them. This would replace the book for one part of the year.

The years 9 to 11 should again build upon the record making of the younger juniors. The one-paragraph accounts should be developed into three- or four-paragraph accounts and later imaginative accounts of the same length. The final stage of top juniors should be to get beyond the *account* of fact to a beginning in writing relevant work on a more specific, less open-ended title. Examples of such titles are:

How a Victorian school was different from ours.
How did the Romans improve Britain?
Make a list of some reasons why Francis Drake deserves his fame.
Write a letter from one of the Pilgrim Fathers to a brother who stayed at
   home.[9]

For children to undertake any of these last tasks, the teacher should build up on the blackboard the main topic of each paragraph and advise children to write only about that topic in one of the three to four paragraphs. Thus, in the Victorian school answer, comparison paragraphs might be:

BLACKBOARD

How a Victorian school was different from ours
Paragraph 1. The school buildings ('then' and 'now')
Paragraph 2. Teachers and punishment ('then' and 'now')
Paragraph 3. Lessons ('then' and 'now')
Paragraph 4. Games ('then' and 'now')

For the work on the Romans, paragraph headings might be:

BLACKBOARD
How did the Romans improve Britain? Paragraph 1. Roads Paragraph 2. Fortresses and Hadrian's Wall Paragraph 3. Villas

More complicated maps and diagrams can be expected in the fourth year and it is a good time for children to keep a list of important dates from their year's work on a vertical time-line at the end of their book. The use of both horizontal and vertical time-lines can be understood by the fourth year. As in the third year, contributions are made to group work in one form or another, either written, artwork or modelling. This planned method of slowly developing a page of paragraphed writing will also help all other written work and ease the transition to secondary History.

So far I have been concerned with the content of children's books. In his most useful booklet, *Activity Methods in History* (Nelson, 1967), John Fairley gives two types of workbooks which children can make for themselves. One is a loose-leaf book with decorated cover and the other a zigzag concertina type which folds up and is tied by tape fastened at one end. He gives instructions on how to make both types of books. The advantage of the loose-leaf workbook is that pages may be added and taken out. It is much more suitable for older than younger juniors.

Children should be encouraged to take pride in the neatness and appearance of their history workbooks and to keep them from year to year for reference by teachers, and to develop in their next class. From the point of view of marking this could replace written work in English or other subjects at certain times.

3.6   The organization of individual and group work

Referring back to the classroom operation chart (Fig. 3.1, p. 64) we now advance from the inner circle of basic essentials for teaching the past to more specific methods, probably used less frequently but needing in some cases more preparation. Although these methods are teacher-controlled in organization they do not depend so much on the teacher for classroom functioning. The methods to be considered in this and following sections of the chapter are: individual and group work, field work, art work and model-making, and the regular use of time-lines and charts.

It is unwise to give the impression that individual and group work are distinct methods. Group work often includes children working on their own chosen piece of work contributing to the group, and if a group is as big as eight children, smaller sub-groups will be formed according to friendship patterns. Most writers take it for granted that group work is done only with older juniors, presuming that children below 9 will be unable to co-operate enough to accomplish a task. With training in this more open-ended form of learning along the lines I shall suggest from John Fairley's experience (*Patch History and Creativity*, Longmans, 1970), I believe that it is possible to start this type of work, developed from individual work, at the age of 8. An absolute necessity is plenty of resources in the classroom: books, pictures, paper, coloured pencils, documents, artefacts, photographs, art and handwork materials. More help will be given with this in Chapter 4 on 'Resources'. John Fairley says in his excellent book:

> It is an assumption that the individual will occupy different work situations at different times. Thus, according to the nature of the task, so will he find himself involved as a member of a class, or of a group, or simply as an individual employed in some unique pursuit.[10]

Let us first consider generalizations about individual and group work but looking in detail at more specific examples that have been tried and found satisfactory. Infants spend so much of their time doing individual work at their own speed that it is unnecessary to emphasize its importance in the 5–7 age-range. It would seem wise to try some group work (four children in the group at the most) with the rising sevens as preparation for future co-operation with their peers. Therefore individual work is the staple diet of all 5–11 children though it should be intermixed with group work and other forms of organization from the 8-year-old stage onwards. After the exposition of the oral lesson most of the session is spent in children's individual activity. During this time they are preparing their records based on the stimulus of the oral lesson. So they will be reading books, looking at pictures and time charts, touching artefacts, and reading source material, drawing or preparing for a short test at the end of the session. This individual work provides an opportunity for the teacher to help individual children either by going round the classroom or having them at her desk or table. If many children are having difficulty with word meanings or a document the whole class may be stopped and more oral work undertaken, possibly using the blackboard, before individual work is resumed. Children who have completed their work can have it checked and then return to another area of the curriculum. This is the period for writing sentences underneath drawings, and paragraphs, building up a piece of work as suggested in the previous section. Benefit is gained by all if a quiet atmosphere is maintained as far as possible to allow concentration and the use of initiative by individual children.

Group work is usually more suitable for 8- to 11-year-olds. The size of group varies according to natural divisions of the topic, resources available, and the friendships and interests of different children. Obviously, trouble-makers will have to be separated and groups rearranged if necessary. Groups usually choose their own leader who helps the teacher to organize the group and to find suitable material for the work. I have found that one afternoon a week for six weeks is usually about the right length of time for one topic. The culmination of the group work is often a big display with or without some dramatic or expressive presentation, each group having a section of the classroom. This leads to considerable healthy competition. From the historical point of view this provides ideal opportunity for a 'patch' study in depth.

In addition to these general views about individual and group work it is helpful to refer to two writers who are particularly concerned with this method. Alan Jamieson in *Practical History Teaching* (Evans, 1971) has a chapter called 'Projects in the classroom'. By project he means a period of history, often interrelated with other disciplines, studied in depth and for longer than a normal lesson would allow. It is sometimes called a topic or centre of interest and may be tackled through individual or group work, the latter being most usual in the 9–11 age range. He praises this method as allowing children of different abilities to work at their own speed. The most useful part of this chapter is the section on 'Materials for use in projects' in which Alan Jamieson subdivides material into visual material, picture books, postcards, wallcharts, and printed books. More will be said about this in the next chapter.

John Fairley, in *Patch History and Creativity*, puts forward a three-staged approach to accustom children gradually to greater freedom in organizing their own learning. He writes about this for the 9–11 age-range but on consideration I believe that it is suitable for 8- to 11-year-olds, given suitable resources. Figure 3.7 is a summary of Fairley's three-stage approach with his suggested content. In this way children are gradually weaned from too much dependence on the teacher and are allowed more choice as they reach their final year. Helpful detailed information is given in Fairley's book, including making models and pictures.

Three other uses of group work have figured in my experiments with older juniors. The first is on the lines of Fairley's patches, as it expects teacher and class to find suitable material. The other two are based on *Liverpool History Packs* (archive teaching units) made for top juniors and lower secondary children. The advantage of ready-made packs supported by a handbook for teachers is that the basic material is already prepared and, although more reading books are needed, much work can be done just from the packs. For a class of about thirty children six packs are needed and one for the teacher for preparation.

Stage 1 8—9	Ancient Rome	Life at home School and work Leisure	Teacher controls with an oral lesson before each topic and then individual work on assignment cards by class after each introduction
Stage 2 9—10	The Norman Conquest	Bayeux tapestry and Battle of Hastings. Buildings Dress and pastimes Village life	Teacher controls Bayeux tapestry and Battle of (1) Hastings as core study; all do (2) individual work on this (3) Three groups choose *one* topic for group work
Stage 3 10—11	The Voyages of Captain Cook	The Anglo-French struggle for Canada. Voyages of Captain Cook My town in 1780 Transport changes 1700—1800	No teacher exposition (1) Groups choose *one* of four topics and start work at once (2) (3) (4)

Fig. 3.7   Summary of patch study examples by John Fairley (from *Patch History and Creativity*, J. Fairley, Longman, Education Today Series, 1970)

The work on 'Voyages of discovery' was undertaken in a city primary school with a top class of very mixed ability (about forty children). The headmaster was interested in history and had stocked up suitable books on the subject in spite of limited accommodation. The organization was simple and rather loose-knit but gained the desired results. It lasted half a term for one afternoon a week. I introduced the topic at some length in the first session both from the content point of view and from the point of view of how we were going to organize it. Friendship groups were formed and each group concentrated on one of the following topics: Drake, Hawkins, Raleigh, Gilbert, Frobisher, Columbus and Magellan, Diaz, and Prince Henry the Navigator. As the class was very mixed in ability, resources were not prolific, and space was at a premium with few level surfaces on which to work, I kept the numbers of groups small enough for me to be able to help each group every session in order to suggest 'ways forward' when the group came up against problems of books, materials, etc. The concentration on well-known (obvious) personalities also had its purpose as more material could be found in public libraries on them and some children had encyclo- paedias at home. Towards the end of the afternoon each group prepared a short account of the work done that afternoon and the group leader read or 'said' it to the class. I found this an efficacious way of checking up that all children had been trying to do something! Towards the end of the half term I made plans with group leaders for a display of the work. The children became very enthusiastic about this as the headmaster allowed us to use the school hall and keep the display up for three days to enable parents, most of whom lived in the area, to visit in the evenings. Each group contributed to the large relief model of the world showing the routes of our adventures; this became the central feature of the display as all viewers had to look at the model first before reading other parts of the display concerned with the different explorers. Each group made one model (in addition to their contribution to the relief map) and also a group booklet to which each member contributed. The enthusiasm of the parents living around the school was our reward.

The second experiment was undertaken with the help of a published archive teaching unit in a stiff envelope. This was more highly planned as the unit gave the structure and much of the material. The result was work of a higher standard in the same time. The teacher can concentrate on finding resources in addition to the unit as the work proceeds, instead of having to assemble them in the first place. I used *A Tudor House: Speke Hall and the Norris Family 1500–1700* (ed. M. Cook and J. E. Blyth for Liverpool Education Committee 1971) with third and fourth years at different times in a suburban school in good buildings and with a tradition of solid history teaching. A pamphlet *How to Use the Teaching Unit* discusses how illustrations, documents and booklets may be used by children both individually and in groups. The content of the unit falls naturally into six groups; the Norris family, the building of Speke Hall, secret hiding places, Royalists in the Civil War, fashion, and furniture. In order to give children a broader view of the work I gave a short oral lesson with aids and board-work (e.g., the wall picture of a simplified bird's eye view of Speke Hall) at the beginning of *every* session. All children had to record the main points of this in their own words (from a skeleton plan on the blackboard) before they proceeded with their specialized work in groups. All groups had display space on wall and table near them for temporary display to assess progress. This silent recording replaced the reporting back in the previous experiment. Therefore, each pupil had a folder of the main history of Speke Hall at the beginning and more detailed work on their own topic in the second half of the folder. The work was further improved by a visit to Speke Hall about half way through the period of time and the use of documentary material for many pupils. More will be said about the use of source material in the next chapter. A classroom display completed the work.

Before the publication of history packs for sale, John West, then a General Adviser with Liverpool Education Authority, was the power behind the Liverpool Teachers' Archives Study Group which compiled a large box of documentary and other material on the *Liverpool–Prescot–Warrington Turnpike Road 1725–1871*. This was the basis of my third experiment with top juniors. The box is kept in the Teachers' Centre and lent to Liverpool schools for half a term. This box contained enough material for thirty pupils to have their own copy of most items to use in individual or group work. It also contained several copies of reading books, slides of the road today, a filmstrip, and maps of the road. The documents were divided into five categories: maps; how the road was administered; tolls; travellers and traffic; and finally road-making and repair. I organized the work in a similar way to the Tudor House project but a coach trip from Liverpool to Warrington replaced the visit to Speke Hall. On the trip we stopped at important points on the road related to our work, such as a coaching inn and a toll house, the original buildings still standing. In the same way I gave five lessons on the five topics at the beginning of most sessions, and folders were kept in the same way, covering general and particular information. On this occasion our display in the classroom was enlivened by the showing of a short film made during the seven weeks, as well as art work of quality relating to the topic. The film was also shown to parents at a Parents' Evening and is an encouraging record of work and a display long since destroyed.[11]

All the types of work detailed in this section involve children in activity of their own, demand much more reading to be done by children and allow individual initiative to be shown, while also exposing those who might be tempted to slack. The variety of tasks set is so great that most children want to participate fully and group work ensures the checking of work by peers in this age range when 'fair play' and 'justice' are of paramount importance. Thus individual and group work are a form of 'discovery learning', yet emphasizing the teacher's vital role. There is no doubt that if the teacher is going to carry out group work effectively as a learning experience much preparation is needed and it is indeed a 'classroom operation' of the highest order.

3.7   The organization of field work

History teachers realized rather late the critical importance of field work to the learning of their discipline and therefore even now few schools, either primary or secondary, insist upon this way of teaching as essential. Geographers and scientists have long made practical experiment a built-in obligation in the curriculum of all young people. Yet this way of teaching and learning is a natural way of looking at, and finding out about, sources of the past, and is as important as written records. One has only to read Herodotus, Thucydides, Gibbon, Macaulay, and Trevelyan as well as contemporary writers such as A. L. Rowse, Asa Briggs, W. G. Hoskins and E. P. Thompson to know that 'seeing is believing' and that no professional historian can afford to overlook the 'history around us'. Nor can teachers, particularly of younger children, ignore this dimension of their work. Here is the built-in 'activity' we make such an effort to create in the classroom. In addition, field-work is the natural 'visual aid' of any local history content in the syllabus – the evidence of what is learnt in the classroom. It broadens the outlook socially for children normally kept within the walls of the classroom and school to go on a visit, and it is also a gift to those who want to integrate disciplines, particularly history, geography, and sociology. It is essential for those favouring a skills/concepts basis for their work, since no other way of teaching enables many important skills of the historian to be taught and used. Observing, discussing, recording in a variety of ways, using indexes and parts of reference books, team work with others, and finally synthesizing work by display as a final record, are all skills which are used to the full in field work. Incidentally, it is also valuable in that it demonstrates, directly, that the record of the past is imperfect. Some parts have survived intact; some have been partly destroyed; some have vanished completely. So we can never be quite sure how things were, still less how people were.

When considering the most helpful literature on this topic three types of books may be found. The first category is of books specifically written on field work (as distinct from local history). One particularly for primary schools, *Look Around – Outside* by Henry Pluckrose (Heinemann, 1984), has eight chapters starting with one on the types of materials used for building 'outside'. The other seven chapters offer constructive advice on houses, churches, places of defence, the road, village, town and a general theme on industrial sites, mills, docks etc. The book is fully illustrated by photographs, mainly taken by the author, the chapters are subdivided under useful headings; information and practical advice are interwoven into the text. The book is intended for teachers but is so clearly written in bold type that top juniors could use it themselves as a mine of information (Fig. 3.8). A second book is particularly addressed to teachers in urban schools – *Using the School's Surroundings, a Guide to Local Studies in Urban Schools* by Stephen Scoffham (Ward Lock, 1980). All the photographs are relevant to the inner city and the author shows how seemingly most unpromising material can be used effectively. Children's work is shown, and also their comments on the topic being studied. In addition there are full bibliographies for teachers and children, appendices on resources and more information for teachers and an index. This book could be used for work in History, Geography or Environmental Studies.

The second category of books is those with single chapters on field work or those concerned basically with local history or with secondary as well as primary children. Alan Jamieson has one chapter in his *Practical History Teaching* (Evans, 1971, pp. 67–79); he advises teachers to look at a building both inside and outside and to talk to a whole group of children from a vantage point of a building and then divide them into groups to complete different tasks on the building from prepared worksheets. Tom Corfe has edited *History Field Work* (Blond, 1970); in the section on 'Preparing for field work' John Fines advises teachers to visit the site and seek out information from record offices and museums before preparing sketch-maps, plans, and worksheets for the children. He goes on to warn teachers to

Chart no. _7_
Date of visit _10/5/72_

Church of St _Eban_ at _Spitwick_

EXTERNAL SURVEY

Tower } _Tower with broach steeple 119 feet high_
Steeple } _Weathervane – ploughman and horses_
Porch _✓ has 18C thatch remover – fire fighting – but no thatch now_
Sundial _None_
Gargoyles _Interesting dragons round tower and above porch_
Other interesting features _Old tomb near porch – Captain Spew_
sea captain 1792, man-o-war on his slab!

Gargoyle over porch

Materials used for walls/tower _Dressed limestone_
for roof _Slate and tile_
External length (E–W) _130 feet_

INTERIOR SURVEY

	Architectural Style	Roof	Tombs & monuments	Interesting features
Nave	Norman	Wood – not very interesting or old (or clean!)	Brass under tower 1450 John Platt	Wooden pews 15C Norman font (plain)
Chancel	Early English		Sedilia (2 seat) Piscina Jacobean pulpit	Misericords Squint from N. aisle
Transepts	Early English		N. Transept – Stuart tomb to Sir John Pole gentleman in waiting to Charles I	Stone Saxon coffins 
Aisles	Early English		Tablets and hatchments to Pole family, N. aisle.	Modern inscription to 9 miners who died in a pit accident 1956. 3 "vicars" died 1349 – plague?
Other chapels	None			

The Font

Church dates from _1162_
Church furniture of interest _Norman font, modern shaft._
Notable people _C. Dickens said to have worshipped here._

Jacobean pulpit

Fig. 3.8 A chart for field work on churches (from *On Location! Churches*, H. Pluckrose, published by Mills and Boon Ltd, reprinted by permission of Unwin Hyman Ltd)

tell children enough but not too much. For example, he took very young children to visit Silchester Roman museum as Roman soldiers having to leave Britain in a hurry and being asked by their commander to assess what to take with them; thus the children divided into groups and selected valuable or essential items from different parts of the museum. A valuable idea in 'follow-up' with young children is given by John Salt and R. R. Cumming in their outline map of an area to which symbols cut from coloured paper could be fixed.[12]

The last type of literature is that specifically about local history. I would recommend a full and scholarly reference book by W. B. Stephens, *Teaching Local History* (Manchester University Press, 1977) written from great knowledge and experience with exhaustive references and bibliography. One chapter is concerned with field work and presumes that serious attention has been given to the teaching of local history. From one point of view of the 5–11 age-range W. B. Stephens distinguishes between 'immediate' and 'intermediate' follow-up; the first is essential with younger children while the memory is fresh and the experience immediate and will probably take the form of discussion and immediate completion of quick records. The second will result from more reading and writing and will probably take the form of an end-of-term display or exhibition. It is certainly true from my experience that a field visit with 6-year-olds in the morning must be followed up by immediate recall through discussion in the afternoon of the same day; it also allows children to let off steam. W. B. Stephens believes that field work in history is important even if field work is also done in geography because, although both disciplines may be concerned with the same 'now', the 'then' of history involves 'at what point in the past'. The 'now' of history is compared with very many 'thens'.

Taking into consideration the experience of these writers and the needs of the three age ranges already discussed, teachers should work out three methods needed to accomplish successful field work. These are: preparation, field work visits, and follow-up activities. Preparation is very important because weak organization could lead to serious practical consequences with children of primary school age. These preparations include adequate staffing, insurance, informing parents of the visit, safe transport, and safety while walking round buildings and even walking on the streets. Knowledge of the facilities and pitfalls of an area is essential and teachers should work out in detail time schedules, places for rest and refreshment, and toilet facilities. Other preparation obviously means reading the appropriate sources, preparing information and a follow-up programme. All authors reiterate the need for thorough preparation. 'It cannot be emphasized too much that the value to be derived from field-work visits is in proportion to the amount of preparation done beforehand by both teacher and student.[13]

On the actual field day it is a good thing to divide the time into information given by the teacher (usually more tailored to the class than can be done by the curator), use of prepared maps and hand-outs for the children to follow, work in pairs or small groups on specific topics, and final putting together of findings before returning. If children are under 9 years old the visit should be well enough staffed for groups to work with individual teachers. It is impossible for children to work on more than one topic in detail (e.g., chairs or beds in one country house, or one room of a house) even though they learn more about the whole topic on their return to school. Too much information or finding out can spoil a visit and lead to superficial, unsatisfying work. The teacher should hold the visit together by referring to each group's work. Some teachers believe in structured worksheets and definite tasks to be performed on site, others prefer discussion and imaginative drawings and sketches. All work necessitates clip boards, waterproof covers, pencils, crayons, and large sheets of 'detail' paper if rubbings in brass or stone are to be done. It is usually wise to provide a sketch-map of the route and its interesting buildings. Recording on the site is different from more detailed recording back at school but all field work should be followed up in some way. Infants are usually satisfied by discussion and simple recording in their notebook or for a display. Top juniors are capable of using the visit of half a day or a week's school journey as a big stimulus for work on source material, visits to the record office, compilation of individual and group books, and the making of models and reading of reference material. The different work expected of 6- and 10-year-olds is a good example of progression in learning. Junior schools still involved with the 11+ examination can use the whole of the summer term after the examination for a week's school journey and detailed follow-up. Time allowed for such work as a whole naturally varies in the three age ranges. Infants find more than two weeks too much, whereas top juniors could easily spend half a term in useful activity. These weeks should fit naturally into the syllabus and therefore be planned as an exercise to be repeated by teachers. The work involved in preparation is too great for teachers to change the venue of the visit more frequently than every three years, unless they are already familiar with the locality of school and very well read in the history of the area.

Although it is impossible to suggest precise field work experiences for 5- to 11-year-olds in all areas of the country, certain themes are suitable at certain stages of development in order to show that a progression can be built up. General help may be given on many well-known themes and teachers should branch out from these outlines to illustrate the themes from their own localities. Obviously top juniors could undertake all the field work done by the 5- to 9-year-olds but if the work is properly planned they should already have done it and it is important not to repeat visits already made earlier in their school career.

During the infant years field work is usually restricted to half-days or days in the more immediate neighbourhood, though a visit to a small parish church or a walk round part of a medieval wall of a town is not precluded.

Three types of visits are appropriate to this age range: the environment of the school, a local museum, and a study of statues of famous people in the home town. A school founded in the nineteenth century is a gift for this work as children can get used to looking at the school building as a whole on known territory, then branch out to the local environment of the school and compare the 'then' of the school and the 'now' of the more recent buildings surrounding it. When taking such young children to a museum it is best to concentrate on rooms whose contents are well arranged and will appeal to them. Children should be given about four to six items to find in their particular room and be able to describe them from careful observation. Statues of famous people should be viewed from both near and far and photographs of them studied in school. Vantage points in tall buildings near the statues should be found for viewing. This work can lead to many queries as to why the statues are erected in their town. It takes considerable skill to take infants on field work lasting more than a day but Wolverhampton Local Education Authority has had the courage to set up a field centre for short courses for infants lasting from one day to several days. Margaret West initiated this work and describes 'Kingswood', the field centre, later in this chapter.

If possible, younger juniors should continue from this work in the infant school by studying the parish church as a complete building and then progress where possible to a walk round a town wall, from which much may be seen of the buildings in a town. Understanding ruined buildings is a more difficult concept than complete ones and children will need help with plans to study a Roman villa or a castle. Most books on field work devote much space to showing how castles may be used. Study of a castle from motte and bailey to Norman keep castles, and finally to Edwardian Welsh castles, is a progression in itself, and younger juniors are better concentrating on the first two and leaving the more complicated buildings to the later junior years. Alan Jamieson gives a detailed scheme for studying a castle in his *Practical History Teaching* (Evans, 1971, pp. 71–3). An interesting experiment was conducted by P. J. Rogers and R. H. Adams with a mixed-ability class of third year juniors to get them to make a scale model of a castle using two visits and considerable preparation and follow-up. This use of field work to make an accurate model of a castle required expertise in teaching and the use of sophisticated skills. Rogers and Adams concluded that 'discovery learning' was not appropriate in this work as the children needed a great deal of direct teaching and direct practice with skills.

> The worrying thing here, and the first danger of the 'Discovery' concept, is the implication that the techniques of enquiry are easily (if not automatically) acquired by the children themselves if only we provide them with plenty of books and pictures. But the use of these and other sources has, of course, to be learned; and they have not only to be used but criticised.[14]

Their use of a castle in field work was a very different way of approaching it from the 'guided tour' type of exercise which could be used with younger juniors.

The village is another favourite study for the 7–9 age-range and this may form a 'patch' study of a village at a certain historical period, or a 'line of development' approach showing how the village developed from prehistoric times to the present day. Edward Osmond's delightful book *A Valley Grows Up* (Oxford University Press, 1953) is an outstanding example of this type of work. Henry Pluckrose gives constructive help on how to prepare for a village study in *Look Around – Outside*.

Older juniors will find three topics a useful culmination to their field work. Starting with the monastery, they may use imaginative reconstruction to live the life of a monk in the twelfth century (Fig. 3.10, p. 104), to make a model of the building, and to learn about the medieval church. It is usually preferable to choose a 'substantial ruin' such as Rievaulx Abbey in North Yorkshire rather than a building with only low walls left. From the monastery, the town, if it is reasonably small, could be studied either as a 'patch' or a 'line of development'. For example, Ludlow in Shropshire is a small town replete with different types of historical buildings; a magnificent castle (the original venue for acting Milton's *Comus*); an impressive almost cathedral-like church; several streets of half-timbered buildings (including the famous Feathers Hotel) and Stokesay Castle (a fortified manor-house) within easy coach distance. In fact, Ludlow could well occupy top juniors with a week's field work, which would bring it into the purview of children from elsewhere, perhaps from Birmingham. The final topic may well be a country house, which can be very confusing and tiring unless a limited amount of work is done and the class is strictly divided into groups, each group finding out about one room. It is better to return a second time to a country house rather than undertake too much of it on the first occasion. On the second visit the children could make a quick tour of the whole house, after the unifying work in the classroom between the two visits.

Although I have suggested some of the very usual topics in order of difficulty from age 6 to 11, all topics can be handled by good teachers in some way for all age groups. As it is essential to fit the field work into the scheme it may be necessary to adapt these suggestions. It is usually better to undertake field work in good weather, during the summer term. But in all cases topics should form an integral part of the scheme, be prepared thoroughly, and used for several years.

Kingswood   An imaginative approach to history

Important as it is to predetermine the main functions of an education authority's resources, it is often even more necessary for opportunities to be built into the curriculum which enable children to explore and develop their own skills and interests. Our experience in Wolverhampton is a vivid illustration of this. In 1977 we opened what we envisaged to be a field study centre for infant and nursery children. An adaptation of a disused camp building with the addition of a nursery unit, it provides residential accommodation for 20 children and day visit facilities for 40. Some 14000 children aged between 3 and 7 have used the centre with excellent results during the past three years. Much credit must reflect upon the planned approach to each visit, a responsibility shared by the staff of the school and the permanent centre staff who combine respect for, and recognition of, the learning opportunities which the centre and its surrounding countryside provide. Additional facilities such as a mini-bus make it possible to follow through the children's discoveries and experiences without a dulling time lag.

Recently a small group of children visiting the centre entered into discussion with each other as to the King to whom the place-name referred. At the time they were crossing the common, and Amanda, one of the older children in the group, volunteered the information that she had at home a book about Staffordshire in which there was a story of a King named Charles who had hidden in an oak tree. Could this be the place, they wondered. The teacher was drawn into the conversation at this point and the children's interest further aroused by the new knowledge that the King had certainly been very near this place after his escape from the Battle of Worcester and that the position of the oak tree was known to be at Boscobel where he had eventually found shelter. Could they go to Boscobel and see, they asked excitedly. The teacher agreed, recognizing the need to catch the opportunity at interest peak and exploit it to the full. In a short time the children were actually at Boscobel looking at the oak tree and reliving history together, through story and imagination.

Although the name of the centre has been left in its most general form we recognize that 'language centre' would be an appropriate subtitle. We have always emphasized the need for all new experiences to be described accurately with the use of the correct words. For example, 'farrier' has become part of many Wolverhampton children's vocabulary as a result of a visit to Kingswood and a demonstration of his skill. A most appropriate follow-up to this experience was the discovery in a nearby field of an old long-forgotten horseshoe which consolidated the learning situation and gave rise to much interesting creative work. The country skill of alert observation which is fostered and encouraged at Kingswood has led to a collection of objects found on the site and the nucleus of a museum being formed.

Imagination has been seen to play a large part in laying the foundations for an interest in the past, and handling objects from that time of 'long ago' brings forth discussion and leads to conclusions which often show that we underestimate the young child's ability, and fail to offer sufficient opportunities for extension. This has been found to be true across the full range of ability. Objects as diverse as a large key, a squirrel trap, nails, and an old spade, have each in their turn given rise to excitement and speculation as to identity and use. Perhaps equally revealing are the occasions when the teacher has been reminded of the generation gap as, for example, when a

ging back to the centre his newly-discovered 'treasure', an old buck-
med on its usage because it was made of metal and not, as the child
, plastic.

ery nature of the countryside surrounding the centre leads to the
imaginative play and we are only now beginning to develop the use of drama
and the acting out of ideas stimulated by a setting unfamiliar to urban children. The uneven nature of the common gave rise to one such opportunity. A
group of boys thought that it would be a good place for a battle because the
trees would afford fine hiding places and they wondered if a battle had in fact
ever taken place. The noise overhead of an RAF jet flying low startled the
children at this point and, reminded them of hearing of air battles in the more
recent past, and of the need of protection from such attack. It was interesting
that immediately the mounds in the ground became a subject for conjecture,
some knowledge of trench warfare and of air raid shelters became apparent
as the children dug deeply into each other's minds for possible explanations.

We are continually finding that the opportunities of learning alongside
children at Kingswood are legion, and we recognize the value to teachers as
well as to pupils. Away from the more formal school environment we are
finding a richness in young children's minds of which we have been all too
often unaware and not least among our discoveries is the certainty that an
interest in the past should not only not be ignored but should be positively
fostered.

Margaret West
Formerly Infant Adviser for Wolverhampton LEA

3.8   Art work, model-making and visual displays

We have already seen that one of the basic ways of teaching history is
explanation and questioning. More ambitious and experimental ways of
teaching may be developed from this: art work and model-making is one of
these. It is especially applicable to primary teachers who usually have been
well-trained at college in these practical and interesting techniques. Children who find book learning difficult and oral work embarrassing can often
learn through drawing and model-making which necessitates record keeping
and assessment in this sphere as well as in the more traditional ways. The
primary teacher is in a much stronger position than the secondary teacher
since she has her ready-made 'history room' in the classroom. Yet this type
of work is only relevant to the past if the drawing, models, etc., are a ready
illustration of the history scheme and are also as authentic as possible.
Therefore, all practical work should be prepared with reference to historical
sources, and plenty of discussion should surround children's preparation of
materials, execution and follow-up. Evidence of children's real understanding of their practical work in relation to their history scheme is shown by the

captions, accounts, and setting out of their display. Therefore visual display is an essential method of the good teacher.

Many books known to art and craft specialists will be useful for teachers. Most local education authorities have at least one specialist art and craft adviser who will be very willing to help teachers. Also most LEAs run at least one short course a year on art and craft for primary teachers; unfortunately this is not yet regularly done for those interested in teaching history. Some of these books may be needlessly complicated and strike fear into the non-specialist. Therefore I am recommending two particularly useful short books entirely devoted to history and practical work. With either of these as one's 'bible', history will be very well taught through practical work. One is by John Fairley – *Activity Methods in History* (Nelson, 1967 – Teaching Aids Series No. 15) and the other is by Tony Hart – *Fun with Historical Projects* (Kaye and Ward, 1971). John Fairley, a historian rather than an artist, gives a comprehensive review of most methods involving practical work, ranging from visits to museums to dramatization. Every double-page spread has relevant sketches showing how the model should be made. Tony Hart, of television fame, concentrates more on houses and how people lived and gives detailed advice about four particular topics: early British settlement, a Roman villa, a feudal village, and a Norman castle. As an artist he has provided his own large drawings and sketches which are delightful artistic exercises as well as being practically helpful. The second book is less comprehensive than the first and possibly of most use to the teacher of 5–8 children rather than older juniors. Three more books have sections concerned with practical work. The most comprehensive is *A History of Everyday Things in England* by M. and C. H. B. Quennell (Batsford). Alan Jamieson in *Practical History Teaching* (Evans, 1971) runs over many types of 'active history' such as mosaics, friezes, stained glass windows, collages as well as models. He suggests reference to the monthly magazine *Junior Education* which often has one item on historical models and how to construct them from the paper of the actual magazine. Pamela Mays pays particular attention to the making of dolls representing people of the past. These are made from bottles, wire, pipe-cleaners, papier mâché, and rolled paper. She also describes how to make different masks which the children can wear to represent different historical characters. All these experts have their special interests and teachers must decide which suits them, their children and circumstances best. They all help children, especially the less academic, to feel for people in the past.

It is obvious that the enthusiasts who write about art work and model-making have been able to work in adequate surroundings physically. As already mentioned, primary teachers have the in-built advantage of their own classroom, occasionally with a store-room attached, and they can plan how to use their room's table and display facilities to suit their way of teaching. Thus it is essential to have more actual space than the space allotted for desks/tables and chairs, blackboard, etc. Certain parts of the classroom should be reserved for history, probably one table and part of the display boarding as well as a good share of reference books in the class library. In the store-room (if any) there should be different colours and types of paper, from plain white drawing paper to coloured sugar paper. Also card, cardboard and corrugated cardboard, shoeboxes, balsa wood, polystyrene, end-toilet rolls, and matchboxes should be stored. A large box could be kept for children bringing 'throw-out' materials ready for practical work. As well as these items, pencils, crayons, felt pens, paint brushes, glue, and paint are essential preparation for modelling. The ingenuity and resourcefulness of juniors, particularly older juniors, should not be underestimated and one should never be pessimistic about the reality of the final project if careful use is made of pictures in reference books. Shirley Makin shows how even visually handicapped children can make figures to represent 'Edward' and 'Eleanor' in her account of telling a story (Chapter 2).

Pictures, models, and friezes are three usual types of practical work in history. The first two are suitable for all age ranges between 5 and 11 but particularly for the 5- to 8-year-olds. From the reception class, children draw and crayon readily. In spite of their inclination to draw very small flowers/ figures/articles/animals on a large page, children should be encouraged to use wax crayons to draw bold pictures filling the page. Pictures should always be given a title by the teacher and as soon as possible by the child in a word or a sentence. From the point of view of the past children must know what they are trying to represent, even if their effort is not at all representative! Later on painting, collage work (glueing material to a background), cloth pictures, and embroidery are appropriate. Younger children usually prefer to make their own individual matchbox model, but as experience grows and they become more capable of co-operative work, collective models can be made (e.g., a medieval walled town). For example a 'line of development' built up in a topic such as 'the village through the ages' or 'the development of housing' may be undertaken by different groups of children providing the different stages of development. An all-age primary school in Liverpool built most of its history/handwork on models of buildings, landscape, figures, and animals described in local sources for the town. The additional advantage in this small school was vertical grouping so that the older juniors worked with infants to create sea front scenes of Liverpool in the seventeenth century and Everton Lane in 1790.[15]

Besides the free-standing model, made either individually or collectively, other types of model easily made are the relief model, the diorama, and the tableau. They are explained by John Fairley in *Patch History and Creativity*. The relief model usually depicts an outdoor scene or a map needing two-dimensional treatment. A strong wooden or cardboard base is needed and a paper scene up the wall at the back depicting the distant landscape. John Fairley's example is the Norman invasion fleet approaching the

English coast. He also suggests using shoe boxes for small dioramas depicting a single event such as William I's coronation in Westminster Abbey. This is usually the work of one or two children and can be easily moved about, suffering little damage in the classroom. Such dioramas at their best may be seen at the Geffrye Museum, Shoreditch, and the Science Museum, South Kensington. Tableaux are a cross between the free-standing model (large or small) and the enclosed diorama. They are easy to use if there is display boarding on the wall and tables pushed up to them. As they can be extensive, a group of children can be involved, some drawing and painting the back-cloth and others making the models of buildings and people for the table. R. J. Unstead provides a sketch of a tableau depicting a Tudor town scene with the cathedral on the back-cloth, street, part of the town wall, and a 'Globe' type theatre. He suggests attaching the background picture to stiff card or wood so that the whole tableau can be moved.

A form of craft work almost always undertaken by a large group of children, but more often by the whole class, is a picture sequence frieze. This requires adequate length of display board round the room or at least at the back of the classroom. This type of work is a great help to the building up of a time sense since the pictures must be arranged in the correct historical sequence. The obvious frieze sequence is the Bayeux Tapestry, an eleventh-century embroidery showing William of Normandy's preparations for invading England, his crossing the Channel, the Battle of Hastings, and William's final coronation as King of England. Although the whole tapestry cannot be depicted, key scenes may be selected; on pages 113-14 of his book John Fairley suggests eight scenes from Harold's oath of allegiance to William in Normandy to William's victory at Hastings and the death of Harold.

It is impossible to mention all ways of using art and model-making in the teaching of history, but more individualistic approaches than the one discussed are: the making of mosaics from potato, wood, or lino cut (Tony Hart, *Fun with Historical Projects*, p. 35), making stained-glass windows from polythene bags (John Fairley, p. 18), making medieval musical instruments (Alison and Michael Bagenal, *Music From the Past*, Longmans, 1988) and the whole industry of brass-rubbing and stone-rubbing. More is said about brass-rubbing in Chapter 5. Stone-rubbing in graveyards is less expensive though it requires permission; Liverpool juniors are 'developing skills of research and recording' while rubbing the grave of a member of the Norris family who died in 1726 (Fig. 3.9, p. 98). Kenneth Lindley's book *Graves and Graveyards* (Local Search Series, Routledge and Kegan Paul, 1972) is invaluable for teachers.

If children do not keep notebooks or files, display of work is the best form of recording and allows children to learn from each other. It would be nice to think of a history display for each term in which the past is taught and children should be encouraged to help with its mounting from as early an age as possible. So much depends upon the temperament and training of

Fig. 3.9   Developing skills of research and recording (by permission of Liverpool Corporation)

individual teachers, but one would hope for an artistic presentation, each item relating to the others and not too complicated, with clear captions telling the story of the past. The whole display should be at the correct level for the smallest children to look at and read. At least one session should be spent discussing it and getting individual children to talk about their contribution. If possible other classes should be introduced to the work so that all may benefit. Some teachers prefer to have an 'on-going' history table in the same way as the nature table, but this is more difficult to maintain intact without a display case. No display should be kept up for more than two weeks at the most. A most helpful booklet, written by an art specialist, Ruth

Phelps, *Display in the Classroom* (Blackwell, 1969), gives more detailed help which applies as much to history displays as to many others.

This section of Chapter 3 has been concerned with how children can learn about the past from art work and model-making. Earlier parts of the book have discussed how this type of material can be used for teaching purposes. Work of this kind should be done in the primary years both as an individual task, a group effort, and as a class project. The past has natural display potential which is a normal culmination for any topic in the primary school. Two considerations should always be borne in mind. One is that variety in the use of these different practical methods of work should always be retained. Yet one teacher should not take on too many different approaches, or he or she will never become reasonably successful in even one or two. The other is that practical work should always be an illustration, as in the case of field work, of some part of the normal scheme of work.

Claire Parker's description of an Elizabethan project illustrates a variety of teaching methods: model-making, field work, oral work as well as role-playing.

How I teach an Elizabethan project — Hinchingbrooke House to 9- to 11-year-olds

This work, based on the 'box of delights' provided by Mr Bagenal, our adviser, was done towards the end of the school year and the children were ready and able to approach a project in a mature and lively manner. I introduced them to the topic at the end of the previous term and sent home a brief plan of the proposed work for the benefit of the parents. I have found that in this way the parents often help their child to look forward to the term in a practical way by pointing out related TV films, books, and postcards etc.

During the holidays I prepared work cards in conjunction with those sheets provided by Mr Bagenal. These were mainly to be used as a formal hand-out type of card for those times when a child needs extra written work to enjoy or needs the security of a set framework within which to work. Also during the holidays I ordered the books most suitable from the school's library service and supplemented them with the best selection of pictures and postcard presentations available. These I arranged or mounted in readiness for the class's arrival on the first day of the term. My own personal preparation of the subject involved as much reading as possible of the more palatable biographies of Elizabethan personalities, novels based on the period, research into the history of the period, and the buildings of the time to be found in my own school district. This early work was by far the most valuable preparation and 'keyed' me up to the subject in such a way as to enable me to be brimming over with infectious enthusiasm for the project.

Our first afternoon spent on the project began with a dramatic description by me of the return home of Sir Henry Cromwell to Hinchingbrooke near Huntingdon. With the aid of some taped Elizabethan 'mood' music and the showing of pictures related to the theme, I endowed Sir Henry with the type of character I thought would most appeal to a large proportion of the boys in the class. This was the beginning of the role-choosing that I was so anxious to initiate. Within a very short time a large part of the class was keen to claim a role that suited their personality. Even within this one afternoon we covered most of the possible role-playing that could be used during the term, although I was very aware that I was rushing rather quickly into quite a few fields at once.

The net result of that first afternoon was a basic grasp of the following points:

1 Houses, transport, clothing, food etc. were very different and life was much narrower in all directions.
2 People could be put into four main groups:
   (a) the courtly set including famous personalities in the fields of government, the arts and explorers, as well as the queen herself;
   (b) the landowners of the countryside and their families who had power and money;
   (c) the domestic servant classes;
   (d) the outdoor and agricultural servants and those who lived a vagabond and roving existence.
3 The Cromwell family really existed and lived in our own district.
4 That research could fall into two categories: the particular, i.e. factual stories, and the general, i.e. ways of life, music, cooking, and gardening, etc.

The next lesson was taken up with making files to put their work in and drawing up a flowchart to their own specifications. This latter they had already had experience of and it helped them to see an overall picture of the work to come.

From this point on the work veered between the effort to experiment with the activities that would have been normal at that time, e.g., clothes making and cooking, writing and learning by heart of poems, music making, pretend falconry, and much enacting of daily life scenes at court, in the home, on the road, in the countryside, etc. — and the careful recording and research that would make up the basis of a written presentation. A large-scale model of Hinchingbrooke House and its grounds was made, many self-portraits of the children in their roles were painted or collaged, costumes were made ready for presentation acting, music prepared, and dances learned ready for a performance. Our final production, involving a visit by the parents, was much enjoyed by the children who had by this time become so involved in their role-play that they even spoke in their own style during such lessons as mathematics and P.E. In the production they enacted the visit of Queen Elizabeth to Hinchingbrooke House, her welcome there, the entertainment for her as provided by the locals, family, and members of the court itself, speech-making, dancing, music, and the proffering of real food made by the children from recipes of the period.

I think that the role-playing afforded the children the best chance to become totally absorbed in the project and while drawing many children out of themselves in the play-acting they were able to take refuge from the very beginning in choosing very much *their* type of personality. For instance the one or two retiring little girls who would have blanched at the thought of acting, quite happily set about being mouse-like maidservants who scuttled with real authority about the room doing their menial jobs with great confidence. At the other end of the scale the two children — boy and girl — who had the greatest confidence and greater imaginations were able to extend themselves enormously within the roles of Queen and courtier, going to the lengths of using rather period style speech and grandiose gestures while conversing about facts of the time in a fairly erudite fashion.

Other events within the scheme were a visit to the Fitzwilliam Museum, Cambridge, which was greatly enjoyed, an inclusion of the music studied into a concert of other music, and a parents' afternoon when the children entertained those parents who could not come previously. This time we made a link up with a Yorkshire school who had studied the same project.

Claire Parker
Milton Road Junior School, Cambridge

3.9   Time charts

In this chapter the classroom operation has been looked upon from the point of view of the basic elements and the more ambitious and experimental ways of teaching history. So we reach the most important and most difficult part of teaching history – a sense of time – which practically may be linked to time charts. Sequence charts of pictures for younger children are ideal as a starting-point. Time charts are a source of learning for children, since the time chart used in the 7- to 8-year-old class may be further developed in the other three junior years, and also an outcome of their work in a particular year and eventually in the four years.

Time charts not only relate closely to the classroom operation but also to the syllabus, since most of the schemes suggested in Chapter 2 necessitate constant reference to time in order to be understood. Thus it is possible to think of time charts as providing a unifying factor in teaching the past in the junior school and the framework suggested by the 1978 primary school report. The problem of whether time should control the syllabus or vice versa will be discussed later in connection with Michael Pollard's views.

Time is of the essence of the past and many teachers and psychologists have viewed this difficult concept as a sufficient reason for not attempting to teach history, except as story, until at least the later junior years. It would be burdensome to describe the mountain of research done on this topic, yet three names stand out as sufficient to summarize the pessimism prevalent until quite recently. Jean Piaget, the famous Swiss psychologist, though not directly concerned with teaching about the past, has strongly influenced all teachers of younger children by his belief that children go through stages in mental development roughly at certain ages. The stage needed to understand time is well into the secondary school! E. C. Oakden and Mary Sturt as long ago as 1922 found that the naming of a given year (at the time) was difficult up to the age of 7 or 8 and that only half a sample of 9-year-olds knew their own year of birth. Yet they were not entirely pessimistic since the concept of time apparently begins to develop at the age of 4 and teaching can improve this concept from that age. They concluded by praising the use of time charts in teaching:

> Time-charts could be much more extensively used than they are at present. The concrete and pictorial representation of a conventional and abstract thing is thus given to the child. In no school where the tests (i.e. their research tests) were carried out was a time-chart used.[16]

A third important contribution to the debate is made by Gustav Jahoda who, over 40 years later in 1963, believed that it was not until the age of 11 that children understood the implications of historical dates; age 11 is a 'turning point' in this concept development. Yet he also is not entirely pessimistic; 'Gradually around the age of five an ordering of past events into earlier or later begins to emerge.' He thinks that the difficulty of time charts might be overcome by planning them to work backwards in time starting from the child's present.[17] Thus psychologists have been very tentative about the ability of primary school children to understand time. But they are more hopeful than the Gittins Report on the Primary School (1967) which believed that even 11-year-old children could only understand time as far back as their grandparents and that time-lines were useless until children were 13 years of age.

This pessimism and caution of research psychologists has been borne out only to some extent by practising teachers. There is a steadily growing number of teachers who are willing to use time charts in an effort to teach the concept of time gradually during the 5–11 years of schooling. Mary Barnes in her book *Studies in Historical Method* published in 1904 came to the conclusion that children could not understand time because they were not taught properly:

> I think then, that, in teaching History a child should always have by him a chart of centuries, as one has a map of the world, so that the children may place their heroes in time, as they do in space.

She records how one 9-year-old girl in an American school said to her mother:

> I shall always try to keep my History book, because it has something very precious in it. It has a long line running through two or three pages

all marked off in pieces, and each piece is a hundred years, and it tells you just where people are.[18]

Allowing for the Edwardian turn of phrase this child obviously understood the past better when using a time-line; it was her anchor and security in the mass of events and people.

The only full-scale treatment of time charts yet published is Helen Madeley's *Time Charts* (Historical Association pamphlet No. 50, 1921, reprinted five times up to 1954 – now out of print). Although Helen Madeley is mainly concerned with the use of time charts of various types for children aged 10–14, much of her experience is useful to teachers of younger children. She suggests the folding time chart (or card) of pictures of historical events and people put in the right chronological sequence; this 'panorama chart for young children' may be opened at one picture or any number to its full extent and it can stand up on a table. She also emphasizes the need for simplicity and few entries on the time chart, and compares the necessity for the chart in time with the map in space.

Sir Fred Clarke believed that young children could learn the concepts of change, duration, and sequence of events but not dates which could just become 'telephone numbers' if learnt by rote. He also cautioned against children assuming that a later date betokened advances in man's way of life. C. F. Strong is more cautious than many writers before him when he says, 'As to the sense of time, this should not be touched at all', at least until the later junior years when clock time is learnt and then charts should only be related to the child's family. By 1956 R. J. Unstead is not so positive; teachers should certainly use them themselves in their preparation and make them for children to use. He thinks that few juniors like making charts themselves (the skeleton plan) but like using them and adding their own pictures to them in the appropriate places. Probably influenced by Plowden, John Blackie is honest when he says: 'There is no general agreement about what should be done'. Like Strong and Pollard he wants to use a time chart only when related to the child's life and going back about 150 years. As in Strong's book his time charts are varied ones from top to bottom of the page.[19]

More will be said later about the construction of time charts. Michael Pollard agrees with short time charts, starting with the present and going back for not more than 200 years. There should also be constant cross-referencing by the teacher to relate projects, stories, and all parts of the past to the time chart. Michael Pollard writes, 'Presenting a child with a time-chart is like presenting a traveller in an unknown country with a map from which the scale and key are missing.'[20] The implication is that a child must be taught how to use a time chart as he must be taught how to use a map.

Yet these somewhat doubtful words of encouragement are not echoed by those experienced with the 5–7 age-range. Three pieces of research work offer more hope. Professor Ruth Beard believes that Piaget and Sturt are too pessimistic; she found that infants could say the date of the year, and knew the names of the days on which they had arranged to attend parties and go out to play.[21] The authors of a book about language and young children – *Understanding Children Talking* – give a delightful example of 3-year-old Stephen saying to his mother, 'I used to be a little boy years ago'. I am sure that Stephen could easily use time charts with success by the time he reached his eighth birthday![22] F. Dobson found that children aged 5 to 9 years had more advanced concepts of 'time' than 'movement' and 'speed' and believes that purposive training with clocks and time charts can accelerate learning.[23]

Time-lines and charts are best made by the teacher and duplicated for each pupil, or made by older juniors. The commercially-produced time charts are usually overcrowded and confusing. A set of folding time charts (for individual use) or wallcharts (for display) were published by Oxford University Press in 1980. They are *The Unfolding Past* by Patrick Gordon and could be useful to top juniors for reference. There are six books or charts in the series. They may be used as pictorial display and are best analysed *after* work has been taught on home-made charts. Published time charts show a reversion to more traditional practice, and as the particular appeal of time charts is personal, ideally teachers should evolve their own.

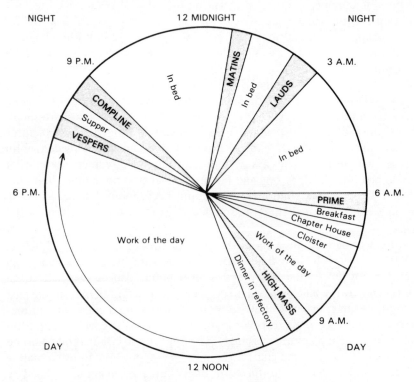

Fig. 3.10   Time clock of a monk's day

Pamela Mays illustrates a time clock in her book from which I have drawn a time clock of a monk's day (Fig. 3.10) using information in various textbooks. In this, 'work of the day' is the time when some monks worked as gardeners, some as farmers, some as builders, some as fishermen, some as teachers, and some copying manuscripts. The names of religious services are in capital letters on shaded parts of the clock face. There were different kinds of monasteries and all monks did not have exactly the same kind of day.

There is no doubt that every classroom should display a large time-line or time chart on one, easily-seen wall and it should be a permanent tool for teacher and pupils to use in all their work. In addition, each child, even from the age of 6, should have a time-line/chart in the middle of his notebook or file, across the double-page spread, for reference in relation to the year's work. Children aged 6–8 will need a duplicated sheet made by the teacher fastened on to the double-page spread. Older juniors can make their own time charts using a ruler and coloured biros. Since time charts have been considered old-fashioned in recent years, inadequate research has gone into the best form of a time chart. As children learn to write on the page from left to right I have found from experience that a horizontal time-line running from left to right is the most effective. The earliest date should start the chart on the left and the present day, or nearer the present day, should be on the far right. Plenty of room should be allowed in the depth of the chart, on wall or book page, for illustrations and writing in the older age ranges.

The use of time charts in the years 5–11 varies very much according to age. Time-lines in the infant school must be linked to the past that is being taught, therefore reference should be made to Chapter 2. Family history in the second year seems to be the suitable time to start using a very short life-line of the child's own life from birth to 7, divided into single years thus:

Pictures illustrating three or four main events of the child's life could be drawn in the appropriate space, which should allow for drawing. For example, a cradle could depict the birth of a brother/sister and an animal the addition of a dog/cat/tortoise to the household. During the second and third term a class time-line could be made by the teacher large enough to include the local topics and visits made. This would be too intricate for each child to have in his book in addition to his own seven years. They could add pictures to the class time-line if there was enough depth to it. In many cases the class time-line will cover only 100 years (1888–1988) since many areas only yield comparatively recent history for local topics and visits. Thus the 7-year-old would enter the junior school with his own life-line to take with him, having learnt his first understanding of time from a large time-line left in the infant school for future use.

In the junior school, where it is to be hoped that one member of staff will be responsible for history/humanities, a more thorough use can be made of time charts. It would seem wise to have a large classroom chart covering the schemes undertaken and accompanying the class through the four years in the school. This should be started simply, but be put on a stout roll of paper large enough to accommodate many additions on its life through the school. In addition, each pupil should have a chart on the double-page spread of his notebook for the particular years of the past studied in one year. During the third and fourth years, pupils themselves might make a classroom time chart to supplement and possibly take over from the one started in their first year and just concentrating on the two years' work. It is important for notebooks from previous years to be kept so that children can refer to them in following years.

Time charts are a practical way to learn and a useful teaching aid, as well as an 'outcome' or record of children's work. But they are only one aid to teaching and are not an immediate cure for lack of time concept. They should be a start to the ultimate aim of the history teacher that her pupils should be able to move freely and easily in time (in the words of Lord Briggs). It should also be remembered that other problems besides time beset the history teacher, and time-concept, which only develops gradually, should not be over-emphasized.

Thoughts on time charts[24]

English primary school teachers have expressed a lack of confidence in the use of time charts. Such has been the effect of minimal research on the classroom. There is, in fact, no reason whatever why a classroom time chart should not prove to be a useful, everyday guide for children at any age from 7 to 13. Indeed, such charts can become a colourful aid to children's learning, enabling them to visualize periods of time, one in relation to another, or assist them to span either long eras or short generations at a glance.

Recent research with children aged 7—11 has demonstrated that primary school children are, even without in-school training, adept at recognizing many historical stereotypes and placing these in an accurate sequence. Teachers will find that most children aged 7—9 and afterwards will fairly easily sequence three separate items in time as first, last, and 'one in the middle'. With practice on a time-line this ability, by the age of 12, can be seen to extend itself considerably to the recognition and accurate sequencing of up to 10 or a dozen selected items. Primary school children can master, first sequence, then duration and even at length, relative scale from one period to another. They are, contrary to popular belief, most able at dealing with aeons of time, 'long long ago', as opposed to more recent, closely-knit generations or centuries. Sequencing tests, easily devised by the teacher, will demonstrate that the average child aged 7—9, with practice, will more readily sequence accurately a fossil, a dinosaur, and prehistoric tools, the pyramids and the Crucifixion, than master, backwards, the events of the past two centuries (for example, Concorde, The Flying Scotsman, a 1914 'Tommy', an antique telephone and Napoleon). The earlier stereotypes are easier to recognize, easier to 'chunk' age by age. It is misleading to assume that children will assimilate a sense of time more confidently if they work backwards, at least beyond the family experience of their grandparents' generations.

When teachers complain that young children 'have no sense of time', this should usually be translated as having 'no sense of *number* associated with time'. The 6-year-old who can accurately sequence ten prehistoric tools from a massive palaeolithic hand-axe to a delicate mesolithic microlith will resort to guesswork if he is asked to estimate their ages or their distance 'ago'. The same faulty mathematics will apply until the age of 13, even though the simple processes of place-order, of subtraction and addition have been well mastered in mathematics lessons. Children take some years to understand the association of number with time. Thus, well-meant time-lines drawn up in rigidly numbered intervals or dated partitions will prove to be misleading. Better by far to introduce and develop in the classroom or along the school corridor, down the length of the hall or across the playground, a time-line which is flexible, changeable, and, above all, verbal. This line should be used for a constant reference, so that all work done with any type of historical evidence, whether it be stories, museum objects, text-book extracts, pictures, or documents can be given its proper place in sequence. Its key points, verbally, should be 'now'; 'then'; 'present'; 'past'; 'remote'; 'long ago'; 'long long ago'; 'in the beginning', etc. To make this type of time-line requires the simplest of materials, preferably a length of clothes line, as long as the dimensions of the teaching space will allow, and some clothes pegs, curtain rings, paper clips, or any device which will permit a symbol or picture to be attached to the line in such a way that it can be easily moved from place to place.

There is a mistaken belief that we can teach chronology by teaching chronologically. Nothing could be further from the truth. Evidence from the past comes at children from all periods and times in a haphazard fashion. No child goes out into the environment and finds houses neatly arranged in chronological order nor sees any other evidence of the past so conveniently ordered. Impressions, anecdotes, pictures, stories, assail him from all parts of the past in random order. His task is to sort and set these into a meaningful chronological sequence; our task is to enable him to do so. The teacher who begins with the earliest item of evidence and painstakingly moves chronologically from period to period fails the child who is absent for a time, changes schools or cannot retain the laborious sequence in his memory. It is far better to offer children short bursts of assorted historical material and require them to practise its rearrangement.

To this end, the most useful device is a ten-picture sequence-card consisting of five to a dozen assorted pictorial stereotypes, each taken from a different historical age. Children can, first, identify each item and discover all they can about it from their history books; second, place each picture in its correct sequential position on the time-line. One such card can best be used among a class divided into five groups of six children each. Each group can then be allocated two of the ten given stereotypes. Their immediate task is simply to order these as 'earlier' and 'later'. Group by group then come to terms with each other on the overall sequence from first to last. If the time-line is conveniently placed along a wall above, first, a length of soft display board and, second, a lower shelf, then as well as placing pictures, the class can add written extracts and solid objects.

The collection of chosen stereotypes should always include at least one very remote item and one very modern article and an illustration from Christ's Life, The Nativity, the Crucifixion, or the Last Supper to establish the 'BC—AD' demarcation. Several pairs of items, which together span almost exactly a century or a millennium, for example, the *Rocket* and the *Flying Scotsman*, Waterloo and Mons, The Crucifixion and Hastings, Hastings and Apollo 13, are also necessary at a later stage. Such intervals can act as markers by which the children will scale their time-line. For example, if from the corner of the room to 'there' takes us to Hastings, then the further distance from Hastings to the Crucifixion must be almost equal. If the distance between the *Rocket* and the *Flying Scotsman* is about a foot, then the distance from 'now' to the Crucifixion must be 20 feet. Given practice, most primary school children will begin to appreciate that there are several ways of scaling the time-line; either we add more and more length at its remotest end or we crowd the recent events more closely together.

The extent to which any teacher involves her class in the essential calculation of age or duration from date is a matter of purely local convenience. Some nine-year-old classes will be ready to undertake the necessary calculations, others will not. Generally speaking, it appears that not enough practice is given in this process, even after the children have mastered the simple rules of mathematics. Primary school children who can cope with the calculations from 100s to units experience insurmountable difficulty if 1000 is added to the place value but the original figures remain the same. (Thus, 980 minus 52 will be relatively easy at 10, 1980 minus 52 may cause confusion.)

Much of the work on time-lines will extend itself into writing, note-taking, individual research, mathematical calculation and the creation of personal time charts, copied into personal notebooks. Some teachers may wish to develop separate lines on different scales; a common feature is to expand one, usually recent, section of the time-line, enlarging it or focusing on to it a separate expansion scale. Similarly, the problems of the past extent of early times, if one once includes a dinosaur, a fossil, or the creation, often leads the teacher into a complex convention of up-scaling the most remote periods at a different level from the recent (copious balls of string, winding tracks and projection beyond the classroom window are some of these devices). One fears that these may only serve to confuse the child; it is better to use a consistent length of wall for all purposes, scaling and re-scaling it as required, rather than endeavouring to make the same scale eternally applicable. Thus, in one term, a 30 foot wall might illustrate the 10-year life time of the child, during the next term might represent the past century and, in the third term, might extend to the life of Christ. During the next school year, one might use the same 30 feet to represent 30,000 years or even three million. Thus, the children will become accustomed to the concepts of time-scale. While it may become convenient in this process to establish certain well-known dates, such as 1980, 1066, AD 33 or 4000 BC such time-marks should not proliferate. Nor should it be necessary for the current time-line to become fossilized and dog-eared by use (this is an argument against the use of lengthy rolls of frieze paper and in favour of the simple clothes line). Children should be encouraged repeatedly to thin out, take down and re-make their classroom line, taking up the most useful time-marks with them to the next class and establishing some of these as the basis for the next year's work.

Frequent discussion of the construction of the line should become a regular part of lessons about the past. Children should be offered their own opportunities to place items as they estimate them; teachers should be prepared to accept some temporary placings in error provided that there are opportunities to discuss and eventually adjust those placings. Oral discussion of the time-line should be a regular feature of the week's work. A glossary of terms such as 'generation', 'decade', 'century', 'millennium', 'before Christ', 'period', and 'age' should be compiled. By the age of 11—13, each child should have become familiar with such terms as 'prehistoric', 'medieval', 'classical', 'modern', and 'geological'. Generally speaking, the time-line should be developed as a linguistic exercise.

John West
Formerly Chief Inspector for Dudley LEA

3.10 Conclusion

How relevant to history that 'time' should be the culmination of a chapter on the classroom operation. Another look at the diagrammatic summary of the chapter in Fig. 3.1 (p. 64) will show that 'time' does dominate half of the two interlinking circles. Primary school teachers seriously interested in teaching the past should spend at least two years in working on the inner circle, the basic methods, building up expertise, resources and generating enthusiasm to colleagues through the excitement and good work done by even an individual class. As the high quality work of this class bubbles out into the rest of the school by display and word of mouth, the second circle may be started. No one teacher or one school will use all the methods in the diagram, but by trial and error the way forward for that school will be discovered. All will be well as long as 'time' and 'evidence' (how do we know?) are of paramount importance in the teacher's thinking.

Notes

1. K. Egan, *Educational Development*, Oxford University Press, 1979.
2. S. Hewitt, 'Becket at Forest Junior – No right answer', in *The Times Educational Supplement*, 11 December 1987 (role-playing of the story of Thomas à Becket).
3. J. Fines, 'Trainee Teachers of History and Infants as Learners' in *Teaching History*, No. 26, February 1980.
4. L. E. Snellgrove, *Storyline History*, Books 1–4, Oliver and Boyd, 1986.
5. R. Unwin, *The Visual Dimension in the Study and Teaching of History*, T. H. 49, Historical Association, 1981.
6. C. B. Firth, *The Learning of History*, Kegan Paul, 1929.
7. G. Evans, *Pilgrimages and Crusades*, The Way It Was, Chambers, 1976, p. 2–3.
8. R. J. Unstead, *Teaching History in the Junior School*, A. &. C. Black, 1956, pp. 56–8 and p. 63.
9. The last two examples are taken from R. J. Unstead, op. cit. p. 83.
10. J. Fairley, *Patch History and Creativity*, Longmans, 1970, p. 79.
11. J. Blyth, 'Archives and Source Material in the Junior School' in *Teaching History*, Vol. 1, No. 1, 1969.
12. J. Salt and R. R. Cumming, 'Follow-up Fieldwork' in T. Corfe (ed.) *History in the Field*, Blond Teachers' Handbook, 1970, p. 37–42.
13. F. J. Johnson and K. J. Ikin, *History Field Work*, Macmillan, 1974, p. 7.
14. P. J. Rogers and R. H. Adams, *Forms of Knowledge, Ways of Knowing and Discovery Learning: Thoughts on 'Discovery Learning'*, Queen's University, Belfast, 1979, p. 2.
15. E. E. Newton, 'An Evertonian Spilling-Over' in *Teaching History*, Vol. 1, No. 4, 1970.
16. E. C. Oakden and M. Sturt, 'The Development of the Knowledge of Time in Children', *The British Journal of Psychology*, Vol. 12, 1922, p. 335–6.
17. G. Jahoda, 'Children's Concepts of Time and History' in *Educational Review*, Vol. 15, No. 2, 1963.
18. M. Barnes, *Studies in Historical Method*, D. C. Heath & Co., 1904, p. 101.
19. J. Blackie, *Inside the Primary School*, HMSO, 1967.
20. M. Pollard, *History with Juniors*, Evans, 1973, p. 8.
21. R. Beard, *An Investigation of Concept Formation among Infant School Children*, Ph. D., University of London, 1957.
22. N. Martin et al., *Understanding Children Talking*, Penguin, 1976.
23. F. Dobson, *A Study of the Concepts of Time, Movement and Speed Amongst Primary School Children*, M. A., University of Southampton, 1967.
24. J. West, *Time-Line*, Nelson, 1986.

4 Sources and resources

4.1 Introduction

In contrast with the materials and procedures appropriate to science, mathematics, art and craft and music, the nature of history lends itself to reading, discussion, and writing, within the confines of the normal classroom. Therefore, it is essential for the teacher of history to younger children to consciously prepare forms of activity through which children can learn. These are the resources to be discussed in this chapter. What is taught (scheme of work) and how it is taught (method) will not be effective without the 'tools of the trade'. 'The classroom operation' is dependent upon at least a minimum of resources.

With money too scarce in the late 1980s even to provide an adequate teaching force in the primary schools, emphasis must be put on the better use of resources already acquired and the creation of new resources from cheap and easily obtainable materials. During the 1960s many schools were provided with more material resources than is now possible, but even then the teaching force was not given much assistance in coping with these resources. Teachers' Centres were established by many local education authorities but these were inevitably at a distance from many schools and often closed in the evenings. It was only the young, fit, and highly motivated teacher owning a car who could 'make it' to the Centre at 4 p.m. to take advantage of the brief remaining time available! Yet dependence on Teachers' Centres was particularly important for primary schools, since even in the 'time of plenty' in the 1960s most primary schools could not accumulate appropriate resources of their own, for they lacked the basic capitation allowance required, and the support which secondary schools could more easily command. As L. C. Taylor has honestly written in *Resources for Learning* (Penguin, 1972): 'The major obstacle in any change from a teaching-based to a resource-based system of learning is the *time* [my italics] it takes to produce, to collect, to arrange the required resources.'[1] I

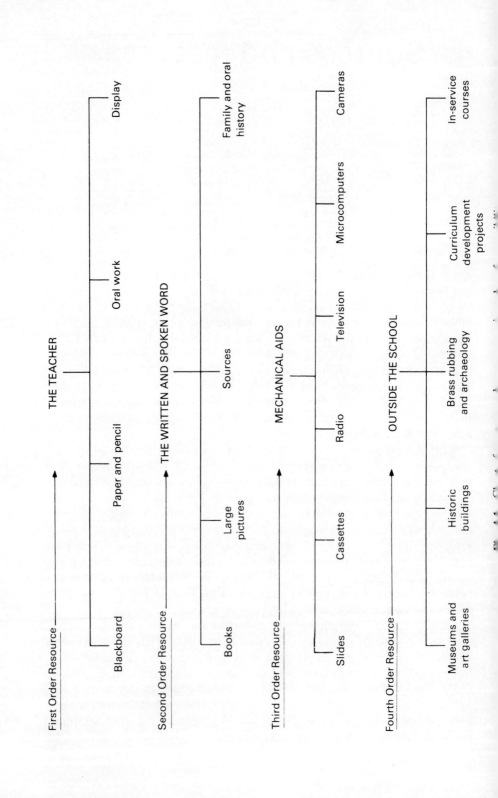

First Order Resource ──────────

THE TEACHER

Blackboard Paper and pencil Oral work Display

Second Order Resource ──────────

THE WRITTEN AND SPOKEN WORD

Books Large pictures Sources Family and oral history

Third Order Resource ──────────

MECHANICAL AIDS

Slides Cassettes Radio Television Microcomputers Cameras

Fourth Order Resource ──────────

OUTSIDE THE SCHOOL

Museums and art galleries Historic buildings Brass rubbing and archaeology Curriculum development projects In-service courses should like to add to this, from personal experience, 'and to care for, store, and check' resources.

Therefore in this chapter I am not going to list in detail the ideal resources for teaching history to 5- to 11-year-olds but to talk about practicalities for the 1980s, remembering that history is only one subject to be undertaken in a crowded curriculum and that all primary teachers carry an excessive load in preparation and marking. Here I must disagree with L. C. Taylor, when in an otherwise excellent book he says of the primary school: 'A single teacher can look after almost all the varied learning activities of a class of children throughout the day and, with enterprise and hard work, supply most of the resources needed.'

How can the past be learnt and enjoyed from slender resources? The outline chart (Fig. 4.1) summarizes my main argument in this chapter. The teacher has a central position as the key resource, in the words of a practising primary teacher: 'In the end, of all the resources at the disposal of a school, the teacher is the most important.' These words start a chapter called 'Human Resources' in A Handbook of Resources in the Primary School by Michael Pollard.[2] Therefore the first order resources are closely dependent upon the well-being of the teacher; blackboard, use of paper and note-books, oral work, and the putting up of displays. Other resources depend upon the teacher but to a lesser extent. The second order resources are books of all kinds, source material in books, documents and packs (units), family and oral history. The third order resources are mechanical aids; slides, cassettes, radio and television programmes, micro computers and cameras. Finally, resources outside school are museums and art galleries, historic buildings, brass-rubbing and archaeology, curriculum development projects and in-service courses. These last two 'orders' of resource depend for implementation upon the teacher who is the prime resource. Relevant books on resources for learning about the past are Teaching History 8–13 by George McBride (published by the Teachers' Centre, The Queen's University, Belfast, 1979), particularly Section III 'Resources for teaching history'; A Handbook of Resources in the Primary School by Michael Pollard (Wark Lock, 1976); and Treasure Chest for Teachers (Teacher Publishing Co. Ltd., 1987).

4.2   First order resource: the teacher

More than most subjects, history demands more from the teacher than from any other resource – which may account for it being taught badly in both primary and secondary schools, and also for many primary teachers opting out of teaching it altogether. As in all areas of the curriculum in the primary school the class teacher has a vital role to play; she must know her children individually and be able to maintain reasonable discipline. In addition, for history, she cannot depend much upon textbooks in class and is unlikely to have had extensive professional guidance in history as such while at college. Thus she must acquire some information about her scheme of work and must be prepared to tell a connected story and explain the events and people of the past in oral exposition and questioning. Therefore, her voice must carry to the back of the classroom and not irritate the children by being monotonous or dull. Many children gain a lifelong interest in the past from the enthusiastic and lively oral work of a primary school teacher. Above all, she must be a good organizer of material to handle the mass of facts of history, selecting the relevant and interesting ones, and to organize to advantage what resources she has collected to use for her lessons.

Closely connected with the teacher, her training and experience, as well as herself, is the blackboard which she has at her disposal. A surprisingly rare mention of this valuable resource is to be found in Pamela Mays' *Why Teach History?* (University of London Press, 1974). She says of individual aids: 'Strangely enough, the most important is the one that is most frequently forgotten. It is the blackboard.' Therefore headteachers should make a practice of providing one or two roller blackboards to every classroom and should do their best to keep them in good condition and washed down regularly to ensure a black rather than a grey board! Careful organization of the blackboards for a morning's lessons, where possible rolling back work required later, is a sure sign of the efficient teacher. The board may be used for difficult words to spell, for summaries of lessons, for rapid drawing to illustrate, or for building up of a chart (Fig. 4.2). Different coloured chalks may be used for different purposes, yellow and orange standing out more

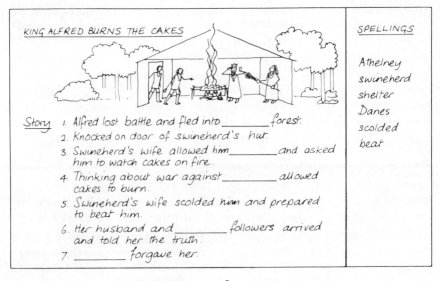

Fig. 4.2   How to use the blackboard

than blue, green, or even red. Although we cannot all work with the dexterity of a Rolf Harris or a Tony Hart our match figures and efforts at ships on the sea evoke appreciative mirth and good learning even if the more artistic children could do better themselves! The teacher can always solicit the help of the artistically-gifted members of the class to fill in her ideas and outline.

Paper and cardboard of all sorts are a staple resource in all teaching and learning. This does not mean that recording by constant writing is recommended but that all children from 5 to 11 should value their history notebooks or files. Children, however young, should not undertake work on pieces of paper to be destroyed or lost. The 6-year-olds I worked with built up some drawings, sentences, or pictures, to be pasted in, about all our topics and took great pride in their large sugar paper 'books of the past'. These consisted of different coloured paper fastened to make a book, the cover of which they decorated with great pride. Pat Raper, a gifted Montessori teacher of infants with a real feeling for and knowledge of the past, was responsible for history in her school and each child in every class had large books entitled 'A yesterday book'. 'A long ago book' and 'I remember book'. These were built up during the two infant years and each child was responsible for the contents and how it looked. The teacher is also responsible for making and duplicating worksheets, 'missing-words' compositions, charts and diagrams, individual time-lines to paste in the centre of notebooks (until the older juniors make their own), and illustrated workcards. An example of work prepared on paper for 6-year-olds is the plan of 'Old Southampton' (Fig. 4.3). The first letter only of each word would be given to the children to complete the word of the building from work done on the 1611 Speed map of Southampton. An example of a workcard prepared for 6-year-olds by Pat Raper is the folding card on a motte and bailey castle (Fig. 4.4). The teacher also uses deep rolls of white paper to prepare classroom time charts, already discussed. Paper is used regularly for drawings; and card, cardboard, and other materials for display purposes. Other uses of paper of all sorts are too many to list and are obvious to all primary teachers. It is essential to keep a well-organized store-room or cupboard with definite rules to which the children must adhere.

A third first-order function of the teacher is oral expression with the help of the blackboard, pictures, and models. Primary teachers are usually careful to use simple words and to check that children understand their meaning. Recent research on language in the classroom has been applied to the additional difficulties encountered in talking about the past. If infants from lower socio-economic groups are likely to understand only a 'restricted code' of language (according to Basil Bernstein), in their normal communication, they will find talk about the past even more difficult. Jeannette Coltham found that some 9-year-olds thought that the 'ruler of a country' was something to do with the ruler on their desk for measuring.[3] Therefore

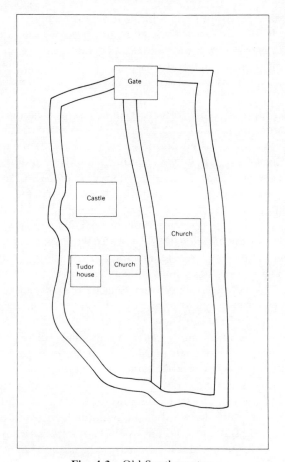

Fig. 4.3   Old Southampton

teachers should explain very carefully the words that they use. As well as talking to the whole class the teacher also uses different methods of talking when helping individual children and groups of children. A teacher who has not been trained to address the class as a whole is very limited as a resource. When teaching history, it is essential to give some stimulus to the class as a whole before starting on individual or group work.

Much has already been said about display as a method and outcome of teaching but in a primary school this depends almost entirely on the initiative of the class teacher. Children should always be encouraged to assist and might take over some displays in the top class, but most ideas and hard work come from the teacher. One cannot imagine a successful classroom without lively and imaginative display using as many children's work as possible. Display should be changed after about two weeks and therefore, if display is an essential resource for learning, the teacher responsible for it is a key factor.

I have emphasized the teacher as a first order resource because all else is pointless without a good teacher. Those who cannot find appropriate other resources or who are irritated by the constant breakdown of the hardware, (not always regularly serviced by the non-existent technician!) need not feel inadequate as teachers of history if they know their work, can handle children, and provide appropriate activity. There has also been a tendency, in spite of the good work of professional associations, to underestimate the importance of the teacher. Michael Pollard believes that class teachers should have outside assistance 'with repairing library books, preparing them for issue, mounting visual aids and making workcards', and 'typing chores in connection with classroom work'. Therefore the other resources that I discuss in this chapter undoubtedly improve the teaching of history, but are not basic essentials. Each teacher must decide what she can manage to do to bring some variety into the teaching of the past. If one method works, keep it and save energy. If you are getting stale, change. You may then find it helpful to try out more of the resources to be discussed later in this chapter.

4.3   Second order resource: the written and spoken word

In history the teacher depends to a large extent on the written word and during the last twenty years she has been given generous support from publishers in the form of textbooks in series, resource books, charts, workcards, historical fiction, and advice about how to use children's families and the spoken words of old people. These all cost money and effort must now be made to use what is already in the school and what can be carefully acquired to complement what is already in possession.

Books

Michael Pollard devotes half of his very useful little book on resources to books. He presumes that primary schools have libraries, though this is seldom true. Some make use of wide corridors to house a library but this is inadequate for quiet reading and selection of books, and unsafe in these days, especially when doors are unlocked and strangers use the school in the evening. Dependence on small class libraries for topic work, particularly in the upper part of primary schools, is entirely inadequate. All children should be trained gradually to use a library for themselves and 7-year-olds should be introduced to the school library as soon as they enter the junior school. Senior pupils in primary schools should be used in dinner hours (usually too long for children's comfort) to take responsibility in the library and help younger children to find and read books. For many bright 7- and 8-year-olds with reading ages well above their chronological age, a class library is usually

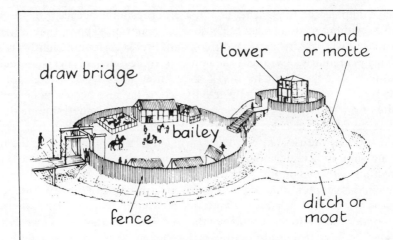

draw bridge

tower

mound or motte

bailey

fence

ditch or moat

this is one of the first castles
the Normans built.
the soil from the ditch was
thrown inwards to form a
mound or motte.
on top of this mound stood
the wooden tower.
this type of castle was called
a motte and bailey castle.
it was very useful because
it could be quickly built.

Fig. 4.4   Work card of a motte and bailey castle (by permission of Pat Raper, Cholsey Infants' School)

1. what is the name of this fortress?

2. can you tell me <u>how</u> they were made and <u>why</u>?

3. why do you think they built towers?

4. can you find a book about castles and see what else you can find out?

5. how long would it take you to make a small castle like this?

6. would you like to live in such a castle?

quite inadequate. Libraries should contain historical fiction, non-fiction and sets of books useful for 'topic' learning. Children should be encouraged to borrow non-fiction and class teachers could borrow sets of books for the class library for a limited period. Is it too much to hope that some day a scale post will be given to a teacher willing to run the library and that time from teaching will be given for this vital work? Michael Pollard devotes several pages of his book to advice on how to build up a reasonable library of history books as a core stock from which to develop as new publications and finances allow. His basic list is 24 topics as follows:[4]

Prehistoric animals	Communications
The ancient world	(perhaps subdivided)
Prehistoric man	Electricity
The Romans	Inventions
The Saxons	Discoveries
The Normans	Explorers
Children in history	Town life
Clothes	Homes
Entertainment	Country life
Farming	Industry
Fuel	(perhaps subdivided)
Local history	Government
Transport	Sport
(perhaps subdivided)	

He believes these to be basic topics and suggests that some books intended for secondary schools and adults can be very useful for their illustrations. Advice about how to judge the suitability of a book will be given in the section on 'Evaluation' in Chapter 5. If a school has a Parent/Teacher Association much can be done to encourage gifts of books no longer needed at home. In these days of shortage, schools, as well as charitable organizations, might as well gain from unwanted books. Michael Pollard gives advice on mending and preserving books as well as a whole chapter on 'the school library' which, unfortunately, is not to be found in every school.

Though better than nothing, a series of four textbooks has serious limitations. In an original and stimulating article, Philip Abrams, as long ago as 1964, questioned the historical value of textbooks and favoured the use of packs of source material.[5] He rightly believes that of all school subjects, history is most bedevilled by the dependence of teachers and children on textbooks, and he lists the 'hazards of excessive authority, of meaninglessness and of bias'. His belief in source material encourages its use 'at any level, for infants or undergraduates'. To dullness may be added the fact that publishers can dictate historical content in a junior school by the sale of large sets of four books (often at a reduced rate for bulk purchase) which saddle a school for many years with one scheme of work. It is to be hoped that the 'national curriculum' in History will not lead from 1989 to the use of four textbooks approved by government, and monopolized by certain publishers. A further limitation of the four textbooks is the idea transferred to pupils that one author or book is the fountain of knowledge in history, an idea more readily gained in schools unable to afford reference books on more detailed topics. A final limitation is that children have to look at one format, style of illustration and type of 'activity' throughout four years.

How does a teacher tackle the problem of a series of books already in school and no money to buy any more? Let us analyse four series specifically written for 7- to 11-year-old children to find out how pitfalls can be avoided. They are R. J. Unstead's *Looking at History* (A & C Black) published in 1953 and frequently reprinted since, Ray Mitchell and Geoffrey Middleton's *Living History* (Holmes McDougall) in five books first published in 1967; the *Oxford Junior History* in five books published from 1980 and also frequently reprinted; and Haydn Middleton's *Living in the Past* (Blackwell) in five books from 1983. The dates of publication show that old or new copies of these books are likely to be in use now. All four series are based on British history and their approach is chronological; all include narrative and illustration, and each series has specific additional features absent from the others.

The narrative story, told in four parts (books), may be used as a resource in various ways. The uninformed teacher may need them for information to form the basis for her lessons and explanations. The children themselves may read them. Children can also use the story to answer questions and carry out tasks set in the last three books. The three more recent series have the text printed in two columns for easy reading. A textbook is always useful for reference by children while the teacher is explaining the topic in her own words; pictures, difficult words, maps and diagrams can be referred to.

Most textbooks have one or two out of four types of illustrations: accurately coloured contemporary reproductions (such as medieval manuscripts on p.30 of *Living in the Past: The Middle Ages*), good photographs (such as a trench in World War I in the *Oxford Junior History* Book 5 p.107), sketches copying contemporary pictures (such as 'Harold is killed' and 'The Normans Chase the English from the Battlefield' on p.8 of Book 2 of *Living History*) and crude reconstructions depicting imaginary people and scenes (such as most illustrations in *Looking at History*). The last type are the cheapest to produce and therefore all too common; they are usually too highly coloured and unreal historically. The illustrations in the selected books are a variety of these four types. In all cases the manuscript sources, photographs and sketch maps are more useful than the imaginary drawings; the latter are particularly unfortunate when depicting people. Yet good illustrations remain a particularly important resource for the teacher.

Three of the four series include activities based on the narrative. Rather too many of these suggestions would involve teachers in more work, providing more source material. The factual texts often try to cover too much ground so that children cannot gain any detailed information from the books. Teachers could forestall attempts to answer some of the vague questions by substituting their own. Therefore teachers should read the activities section very carefully and be selective. Some teachers may prefer the Unstead series as it omits activities, expecting teachers to make up their own.

After the first year in the junior school (7- to 8-year-olds) it is advisable to provide a different textbook, especially if there is a dearth of reading books, to ensure a different approach. This may be done, if two sets are becoming too dilapidated, by selecting two good half sets and encouraging pairs of children to have one each. This can lead to interesting comparisons by the children. But the teacher herself should be careful to know both books. Or, the illustrations in the dilapidated books could be use to make workcards (if ancillary assistance was available) or for children to cut up and paste into their own notebooks. This can also be done with the pictures from old BBC and ITV pamphlets.

Reading books[6] on more detailed topics are not published in profusion for the First School and infant teachers rely on pictures in junior age books to explain the past. Shirley Paice, deputy head of an infants' school, wrote with good sense in the *Times Educational Supplement*, when she showed conclusively that young children do not read non-fiction information books because the books are not suitably written and therefore the children are not helped to do so.

> The aim of much modern education is self-initiated learning. For this one needs an acquaintance, a close friendship even, with books of a particular kind. These can be called reference books, information books, non-fiction of many kinds. This friendship should begin in the earliest years of reading.[7]

She goes on to criticize the inadequacy of information books for this age group, citing Macdonalds' *Starters* as having the monopoly, and to warn teachers to choose books for the 5- to 8-year-olds much more carefully. 'Until we are prepared to insist on a text which is informed, enthusiastic and lucid, matched by attractive format and accurate illustrations, we get what we deserve, a curate's egg!' Yet since 1982 more publishers are catering for the 5 to 7 age-range. I have already listed the best in two previous publications.[8] Five series stand out as 'good buys'. Longman's *Into the Past* concentrates on twentieth century social history; CUP's *Activity Books* provide tasks on such topics as farming, animals, toys and Ancient Egyptians; Usborne *History Books* and *Picture Classics* are highly illustrated but the teacher would have to read them to infants; *Dinosaur* books by Althea are clearly illustrated on every page; and there is a new series, published by Kingfisher, called *Stepping Stones* for 4- to 6-year-olds (e.g. *Looking at a Castle* by Brian

Davison). A sixth series published by A & C Black called *Beans* could be used by older infants and all juniors, or read to younger infants. A few more publishers are breaking new ground in providing small and short topic books for First School children, together with suggestions as to how to make large pictures, story tapes and other teaching materials.

Junior children are more fortunate in their provision of reading books; finance and storage present more difficulties than choice. Again the 7 to 9 age-range has less scope than older juniors who tend to be joined to junior secondary children to form the best-selling 'middle years'. Catherine Firth's *History Bookshelves*, (Ginn) initially published in 1954 and now out of print are well worth borrowing from a library. Each set (shelf) of six small books is concerned with some aspect of a particular period. Each shelf also has a useful teacher's book. The illustrations are black and white sketches, manuscript sources and family trees. *Museum Bookshelves* is a similar series and most relevant to the expanding educational use of museums. Longman's *Focus on History* and *History in Focus* (colour edition) edited by Ray Mitchell and Geoffrey Middleton are a high quality production of topics in English History from Stone Age to 'Our Own Century'. The books have an index (good training for 7-year-olds), are profusely illustrated with large sketches from contemporary manuscripts and photographs, and have a clear text with activities relating to the illustrations. Kingfisher *Explorer Books* boast more pictures than text and a pull-out wall poster. *Knights and Castles* by Jonathan Rutland is particularly well constructed.

Combined resources of books together with work cards, teachers' guide, wall pictures, spirit duplicator masters and model-making books come from CUP in Tom Corfe's *History First* series, and John Platt's *Active History* from Macmillan. A similar combination but less conventional in content is Sue Wagstaff's *People Around Us* (A & C Black), which is used regularly in many ILEA schools. These are multi-racial books with excellent illustrations, a teachers' guide, spirit masters and photographs. It will be sad if lack of money prevents schools from ordering these combinations of resources and the national curriculum throws teachers back onto the one 'textbook' each year in one series.

New emphases on the environment and local history have led to publications such as Allan Waplington's *History Around You* series of five books linked to his popular Granada TV series. A Starter book in this series by Dorothy Morrison has also been published by Oliver and Boyd for infants. W. H. Smith's new venture (1985 onwards) mainly for parents, *Investigating History*, is published by Hodder and Stoughton. Pamela Mays' *Towns and Villages* and Geoffrey Timmins' *Roads, Canals and Railways* in this series are practical small books with one-colour clear sketched illustrations (some amusing); their attractive appearance and scholarly content will appeal to teachers, parents and children. An imaginative, though expensive, contribution has been made by the Lutterworth Press in association with the

National Trust in *Crisis at Crabtree* (1986) by Sally Miles. It is a delightful and amusing story of four buildings in a village coming to life to fight planners aiming to demolish them in order to build a motorway. The buildings are called Norman, Elizabeth, George and Victor and Victoria!

Family history is also a popular and ever-growing 'industry', sometimes used too frequently all the way up the junior school. It is ideal for infants and younger juniors. It would be impossible to write of all the publications in this category, and more are likely to be published. *My Family Tree Book* by Eileen Totton is a large individual workbook to be filled with information and photographs; it is to be hoped that teachers will use it to make cheaper workbooks until copyright laws allow it to be photocopied, or Unwin Hyman publish a cheaper edition. It must be very popular in spite of the cost as it is now in its seventh printing (1986). Richard and Helen Exley's *Grandmas and Grandpas* (Exley publications) is also very popular, having been through thirteen impressions since 1975. It is a compilation of primary children's views and pictures of their grandparents including such statements as 'Grandpas are delightful things they date back to the last century'! A series intended for 9- to 13-year-olds, but very useful to teachers of younger children, is *How do we know? Finding out about History* edited by David Penrose and published by Collins; particularly relevant to family and oral history are John Cockcroft's *In My Time* and Sallie Purkis' *Thanks for the Memory*, both of which emphasize the value of family and oral history as authentic historical evidence.

Older juniors are well catered for in reading books. The *Then and There* series now edited by John Fines started publication in the 1950s and the books are still an excellent 'buy' as value for money. Longmans continue to add new titles and filmstrips to accompany them. They are very scholarly books written by specialists but are not as well illustrated or purposive in activities as the less well-known series, *The Way It Was* from Chambers. This series broadens out to topics in Scottish and European History, has excellent bibliographies, glossaries and indexes. It is a pity that this series is not better known. Black's *Junior Reference* series remain well-illustrated and scholarly books; Alistair Ross' *Going to School* is a very good, more recent addition (1982).

Since 1980 a spate of colourful topic books have erupted onto the market from Wayland, Batsford, Macdonald and Kingfisher. Some are repetitions of older books in content and lay-out garnished with 'glorious technicolour' pictures. But Macdonald's *Camera as Witness* by Penny Marshall is an invaluable series for study of the last hundred years in excellent large photographs. Their *Everyday Life* Series (*A German Printer*, *A Greek Potter*, etc.) has much to commend it for imaginative illustrations interspersed with text, new detailed content, a picture glossary, a bibliography and places to visit. Wayland's *Life and Times* series include dates, new words, further information and indexes, genuine photographs as well as artists' reconstructions. Dorothy Turner's *William Shakespeare* in Waylands' *Great Lives* series is a refreshing and successful attempt to explain the playwright and poet to junior children and encourage primary teachers to introduce children to Shakespearian plays – a much needed task.

Ward Lock Educational have 'put a toe into the water' with their long awaited series *Looking into History*, but only one book so far has appeared. This is Paul Noble's excellent *The Seventeenth Century* (1986), a large format book presenting a scholarly view of this dramatic period in British history. Five topics are considered in depth; coloured photographs, contemporary pictures, time-lines and a centre pull-out picture of Cheapside, London, 'now' and 'then', make it unique in publishing. Each topic is initiated by a picture story of the main events and there are basic dates and information to provide necessary explanation of the narrative. Kingfisher's *See Inside* series make a new contribution in getting children to study a topic in detail; dates, a glossary of terms and an index and bibliography are additional to coloured illustrations and contemporary drawings. *An Ancient Chinese Town* and *A Galleon* are two such books. Oxford University Press has brought out a new series for upper juniors (and lower secondary pupils), *History Source Books*. It starts with four topic books on *The Elizabethan Age* full of splendid black and white and coloured contemporary illustrations; the clear narrative is interspersed by questions and documents. The only surprising omissions are a bibliography, a glossary of terms and an index.

Textbooks and reference books should be regularly used but a third category of the written word demands attention and its use enhances teaching of the past: this is historical fiction. Vivienne Little and Trevor John's *Historical Fiction in the Classroom*[9] is a worthy successor to Catherine Firth's 1924 and Helen Cam's 1961 *Historical Novels*[10] with an additional advantage of how different teachers used particular novels with their classes. Most of the contributions are from teachers of 8- to 10-year-old children. They enthuse about the extra dimensions given to a period by the teacher reading the stories at the end of sessions on the same topic. In the accounts by teachers, some reading led to role-playing and dramatic presentation but few seemed to get the children to read the novels themselves and use them in their writing to illustrate an historical event or to stimulate the writing of imaginative historical work. A novel about the Battle of Edge Hill, *Edge* by Merlin Price, led to visits to the battle site, near the school, the writing of poems inspired by this visit, the examination of artefacts related to a battle, study of biased original accounts of the battle and, finally, a discussion of continuity and change using maps.

Finding large typeface historical novels for younger juniors is difficult; but *The House that Moved* by David Rees (Young Puffin, 1982) comes into this category. Seventy-seven pages of large type, about two boys involved in moving a real Tudor house to another place, fulfill these needs and may be read by the teacher or the individual child. Ian Serraillier's stories of ancient myths in the New Windmill Series (Heinemann) come in hardback, illustrated books and are suitable for 8-year-olds upwards; *The Road to Canterbury* seems particularly useful as it combines the literature of Chaucer with the fourteenth century historical period. Also for older juniors are Penelope Lively's *Astercote* (Puffin), an adventure story about the Black Death in modern form, Dorothy Edwards' *A Strong and Willing Girl* (Magnet, 1982), about a Victorian servant, Nan, who was the author's aunt in real life (a good use for oral and family history), and David Wiseman's *Thimbles* (Puffin, 1985) which brings the 1819 Massacre of Peterloo alive through the experiences of two very different girls of the period. Alison Uttley is thought-provoking, in *Travellers in Time* (Puffin, 1977), in putting into the mouth of a young girl, dreaming of going back to Tudor times, such sentiments as 'I lived in the past with a knowledge of the future', 'his future was in my past' and 'I belong to the future and the future is all around me, but you can't see it. I belong to the past too, because I am sharing it with you. Both are now'. These thoughts on time could well be used in a discussion with top juniors.

I hesitate to over-emphasize the reading of historical fiction by primary school children since reading any full-length book from cover to cover is usually only enjoyed by older and abler juniors and it is most often done at home. It also demands interest from the teacher to read to children, and considerable teaching skill to use a particular novel relevantly in class. The best we can do is to make sure that some 10-year-olds are reading them as their current 'reading books' for odd moments in class, and ask them to tell the class about them in short reviews towards the end of term. Perhaps two children could tackle one book and be responsible for a session together, reading out a particularly amusing or colourful paragraph. A list could be put on the library notice-board relating certain novels to certain periods of history. If teachers can read short extracts and stimulate children to read them privately this is probably the most that can be done. Teachers may want to combine English/History lessons and always make a practice of discussing and reading certain novels relevant to the period of history studied. The outline of the history needs to be given before the novel is understood. 'Children are not less interested than grown ups. The problem is that they *know* less. In particular they know less history.'[11] Historical fiction can bring the past to life for the good intelligent reader but can confuse and antagonize the less able by its intricate detail and specialized vocabulary. Less able children are really better reading a short, clear, and well-illustrated reading book. Older and more able children thrive on historical fiction.

Large pictures

Picture-reading is a good method of teaching History to infants and less able juniors. Bright juniors can also enjoy a discussion of an intricate contemporary picture, such as *The Encampment of the English Forces at Portsmouth in 1545* (showing the sinking of the *Mary Rose* ship).[12] Therefore teachers should start to accumulate large pictures right from the beginning of their careers. Few publishers dare risk trying to sell such resources at the present time and Macmillan's *Class Pictures*, when in print, were garish and inaccurate in many details. *Junior Education* and *Child Education* do publish large pull-out pictures but historical topics are only sporadically included. *Pictorial Charts* of Uxbridge have some useful wall illustrations of buildings but some of their charts are too detailed for junior children; *The Medieval Manor* is an exception and is very simple and clear.

More directly useful are posters from museums and art galleries; 'Thomas More and his Circle', 'Elizabeth I' and 'Richard III' from the National Portrait Gallery, 'Unknown Melancholy Man' (Exhibition of Tudor Miniatures) at the Victoria and Albert Museum and 'Longview of the Thames' (1647) by Nicholas Hollar at the Tower of London. The development of the use of museum education officers in recent years has led to museums providing more teaching materials, including large pictures. One example is a very clear poster called 'The Liverpool Overhead Railway' from the Merseyside County Museum. English Heritage Education Series have produced fine large aerial view posters (680 × 480 mm) of fortifications from Roman times to the nineteenth century with notes for teachers. Ladybird books publish a chart of kings and queens of England which could be put up in the school entrance or library for easy reference for all classes. 'One-off' national historic events usually lead to a plethora of well produced and cheap wall pictures; The Norman Conquest of 1066 in 1966, the coronation of Elizabeth II in 1953, the Silver Jubilee in 1978 and the royal weddings in 1981 and 1986 are examples already behind us. The Spanish Armada of 1588 will enjoy the same fame with support from the National Maritime Museum. Teachers should be quick to collect such occasional illustrative material.

These pictures should be backed and preferably kept flat in a plan chest or hung vertically in a suspender clip if there is nowhere else to keep them unfolded. For these aids to be really useful it is best to have beaver boarding at the front of the classroom to use while teaching and to put up pictures on beaver boarding round the classroom when the particular topic is completed so that children can refer to them in small groups or individually. An earlier part of this book has been concerned with display (Chapter 3) which is mainly children's work, but a good beginning is made if the teacher can provide a centre piece of a large picture to encourage children to contribute their own pictures and those they have found outside school. An ideal form of large picture is a brass-rubbing of a figure of figures from a church brass (Fig. 4.5) or stone-rubbing of information on a tombstone done by the children themselves (Fig. 3.9).

Small pictures can become large pictures when slides and projector are used either for a class lesson or for children in small groups looking at

Fig. 4.5   Henry Norris, and Clemence, his wife, 1524 (from *Monumental Brasses of Lancashire and Cheshire*, J.L. Thornely, W. Andrews, 1893)

illustrations of a particular part of a larger class project. John West used this technique in his own research into children's awareness of the past. Most museums, 'stately homes' and English Heritage and National Trust properties sell slides which can be enlarged for class use. The old-fashioned epidiascope proved more useful to teachers of History than the modern overhead projector. The greater use of video-recordings from television programmes themselves constitute another form of well researched historical material in large pictures. Large contemporary maps will be discussed later in relation to the written and spoken word.

Original sources

The uses of textbooks, reference books, and novels is the first way to learn about the past. But the nature of history closely involves time and evidence; therefore teachers should want their pupils to question what they read in textbooks and should encourage them to seek reassurance from original sources, archives, or documents. Since the establishment of national record offices after 1945, and particularly since 1960, publishers, teachers, advisers, HMI, and archivists have co-operated to produce documents for use in schools in one way or another. This use, starting in the secondary schools, has gradually percolated down the age range so that a single challenging and pictorial old map has been used for teaching the past to 6-year-olds (Fig. 3.4, p. 74). The natural classification of sources is into printed sources and archival sources. The latter differ from the former in that they remain in their contemporary handwriting and in some cases (before about 1700) need 'transcribing' (or translating) into present-day handwriting to be understood. A small selection of these archival sources, being more difficult to find and understand, have been selected and made into archive teaching units or history packs.

Printed sources

Primary teachers are likely to overlook compilations of printed documents as being too difficult for 5- to 11-year-olds. Yet there are several very useful collections with introductions and explanations. Basil Blackwell started a series *They Saw It Happen* in the mid-1950s in three volumes of original sources of illustrate English history. They are subtitled 'Anthologies of eye-witness accounts and events in British history' and select key events – 'the magic moment' – which altered the course of history in some cases. The short eye-witness accounts are introduced by a concise explanation, and reference to further reading is given in many cases. The influence of eighteenth-century coffee-houses is shown in an extract from a book by a French visitor given in the 1689–1897 volume.

> I have had pointed out to me in several coffee-houses, a couple of lords, a baronet, a shoe-maker, a tailor, a wine-merchant and some others of the same sort, all sitting round the same table and discussing familiarly the news of the court and town. The government's affairs are as much the concern of the people as of the great. Every man has the right to discuss them freely.[13]

A similar compilation, in paperback, is a series called *Portraits and Documents* (Hutchinson). Again they illustrate English history and are helpful to primary teachers because they have good, clear photographs/pictures of important personalities in the centre pages. The extracts are short and are also commented upon by the editors. In the medieval volume, *The Early Middle Ages 871–1216*, Derek Baker includes an extract from the Annals of

St Neots giving one version of the words of the swineherd's wife in scolding King Alfred for burning the cakes – 'Look man, the cakes are burning, and you do not take the trouble to turn them; when the time for eating them comes, then you are active enough'. The hunger of King Alfred during his wanderings in the marshes of Athelney may well be understood by children when this extract is read to them. A third printed series is the *Picture Source Books of Social History* edited by Molly Harrison and Margaret Bryant (Unwin Hyman), each book covering a century. They have the advantage of using contemporary illustrations, and furniture from the Geffrye Museum, as well as accounts.

For those who feel restricted by these selected extracts and want to see and use an actual printed original source, there are some very useful easily-obtainable books from which suitable extracts can be taken. J. M. Dent's editions of *The Anglo-Saxon Chronicle* and *The Ecclesiastical History of the English Nation* by the Venerable Bede, a monk of Jarrow Monastery, are simple accounts of English history up to 1066 and include many vivid accounts of colourful actions through which children can see for themselves what life was like in those far-off days. The martyrdom of St Alban (at Verulamium, now named St Albans in his honour) nearly failed several times through downpours of rain. King Ethelbert of Kent 'sitting in the open air' with his Christian wife Bertha received Augustine and his monks sent by Pope Gregory 'bearing a silver cross for their banner, and the image of our Lord and Saviour painted on a board'. Coifu, the high priest of Northumbria, newly converted to Christianity, mounted King Oswald's stallion to literally strike down with his spear the pagan idols that he had worshipped. These and many other small gems of narrative bring the past to life and can be easily dramatized.

The history of the eighteenth century can be illustrated from *The Journeys of Celia Fiennes* edited by Christopher Morris (Cresset Press, 1959) and Daniel Defoe's *A Tour Throughout the Whole Island of Great Britain*, two volumes (Dent, 1966). These two acute observers give detailed descriptions and their views of localities and so provide wonderful source material for the study of local history. Celia Fiennes' journey by horse from 'Leverpool' (Liverpool) to 'Prescote' (Prescot) is described in this way:

> Thence to Prescote 7 very long miles but pretty good way mostly lanes; there I passed by Mosel (Knowsley), the Earl of Darby's house which looked very nobly with many towers and balls on them; it stands amongst tall trees and looks like a pleasant grove all about it; its an old house runs a large compass of ground; the town of Prescote stands on a high hill, a very pretty neate market town, a large market place and broad streets well pitch'd.[14]

Children in schools on this road can understand the 'then' and 'now' of their local area through this. In 1724 Daniel Defoe published his well-known contemporary 'guide-book' describing economic and social conditions in England and Scotland before the Industrial Revolution. Teachers can select any area in which they are teaching and find some paragraph of interest with the 'then' and 'now' comparison so helpful to children in starting a discussion. Here is an account by Daniel Defoe of Southampton having lost her medieval trading predominance by the beginning of the eighteenth century:

> Southampton is a truly ancient town, for 'tis in a manner dying of age; the decay of the trade is the real decay of the town: and all the business of moment that is transacted there, is the trade between us and the islands of Jersey and Gurnsey, with a little of the wine trade and much smuggling. The building of ships also is much stop'd of late: however the town is large, has many people in it, a noble fair High Street, a spacious key, and if its trade should revive, is able to entertain great numbers of people. There is a French church, and no inconsiderable congregation, which was a help to the town, and there are still some merchants who trade to Newfoundland, and to the Streights with fish: but for all other trade, it may be said of Southampton as of other towns, London has eaten it up.[15]

For children in Southampton, innumerable questions may be asked and much useful discussion can arise.

Other well-known travellers' records can similarly illuminate the local scene in different ages: John Wesley's *Journals* for the eighteenth century when industrialization was beginning; William Cobbett's *Rural Rides* for the early nineteenth century; and J. B. Priestley's *English Journey* for the years between the two World Wars.

Archival sources and packs
By these are meant first-hand information on paper or parchment such as letters, diaries, posters, maps, old books, parish registers, inventories (i.e. lists of property at the end of a person's will), school log books, and old newspapers. Other archival material such as parliamentary papers, legal documents, and those involving Latin and very difficult palaeography (i.e. old handwriting) are not so useful to primary teachers. They are found in Record Offices (both city and county offices), libraries, museums, newspaper offices, and even in the attics of teachers and pupils. Although using archives presents teachers with storage problems and is very time-consuming, the work is rewarding and the older junior years (and secondary years) seem the ideal time in which to experiment with it as a class activity. The teacher has to be careful to relate the documents to her syllabus and not to get too involved in detail at the expense of seeing the document as illustrating the work as a whole. Later in this chapter, Carol Wilson and Kenneth May show how source material can be used well in teaching the History of Liverpool.

Four ways of using archival material may be highlighted as valuable in the 5 to 11 age-range. The first is the use of old maps. The usefulness of the 1611 Speed Map of Southampton with 6-year-olds has already been discussed. More advanced work was done in 1968 by J. M. Salt at Green End Primary School, Burnage (a residental suburb of Manchester), with 8-year-old children using nineteenth and early twentieth-century maps of Burnage to show the age of and presence of different buildings in the area. Here is Mrs Salt's account of their work.

Visits to Manchester Central Library

A group of 8-year-old children went with their teacher to the Manchester Central Library. Arrangements had been made previously for the original maps of Burnage in 1820, 1845, 1848, 1900, 1926, 1934 and 1960 to be available in the Manchester Room, and for photocopies to be made for further work in the classroom. Each child had cyclostyled sketch maps of the area to be studied, with the present buildings marked.

From the 1820 map, notes were made of the buildings then appearing in the area. These were coloured red on the cyclostyled map. Next the children looked at the 1845 and 1848 maps and noted the buildings which had appeared since the 1820 map. These were filled in on another cyclostyled map in green. The same was done with each map until the children had six maps completed. Finally, on a photocopy of the 1960 map the various colour codes were brought together to show the ages of the different buildings in the area under a colour key. This gave the children the opportunity to handle and use original documents at the library and to record their findings in a simple form.

It became apparent that Burnage was a small rural community until as late as 1934. The houses were strung out in a ribbon development along Burnage Lane, backed by fields. Until 1900 Burnage did not support a church. The children found that present-day street names related to old farms and features which have since disappeared. The children were enthusiastic and were stimulated by this visit to make their own enquiries from the few elderly inhabitants who remembered Burnage when it was still farmland. Old books and pamphlets were lent to the children.

A further visit to the library was arranged at which the 1900 map, 25 inch scale, with fields marked, and the tithe schedule, were available. The children took the field numbers from the map and by referring to the schedule were able to find out who owned the land, who used the land and for what purpose, and the rent paid. Most of the land was pasture, meadow, and gardens (conflicting with an old inhabitant who spoke of the fields of corn). The old maps were of differing scales. This led to a group of children making a scale map of a section of Burnage Lane.

The children thus gained experience in:

1 Use of source material

2 Making simple records of findings:
  (a) Age of buildings
  (b) Lane use
  (c) Place names
3 Seeking information from library, school reference books, and local inhabitants on their own initiative.
4 Interpreting their findings in various media:
  (a) Map making
  (b) Individual booklets
  (c) Class books
  (d) Model making
  (e) Pictorial representation in variety of materials.

J. M. Salt
Green End Primary School, Burnage

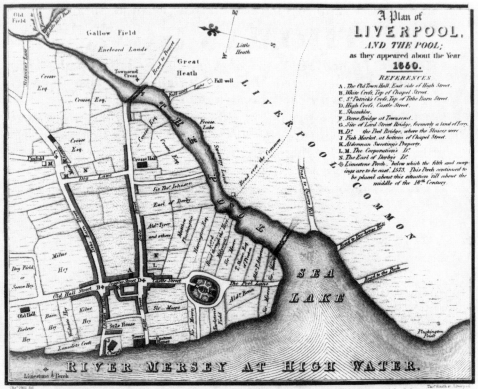

Fig. 4.6 Liverpool in 1650 (by permission of Liverpool City Libraries)

Two Blue Coat Boys.

Absconded,

From Christ's Hospital, Newgate Street, London, on Wednesday last, June the 18th. 1817,

Two Blue Coat Boys,

Answering the following Description :

WILLIAM MASON,

Between 13 and 14 Years of Age, about 5 Feet high, pleasant open Countenance, dark Complection, dark Eyes, round Face—his Two Eye Teeth very prominent, project over the other, so as to appear like Two Tusks when he speaks.

THOMAS HOW,

Between 15 and 16 Years of Age, about 5 Feet high, florid Countenance, has a red Mark on his right Cheek Bone, and his right Arm (when he left London) in a Sling.

Their Shoes and all their Clothes have their respective Names marked on them, they have Two silver Badges on their left Shoulder, as belonging to the KING'S WARD, their Shirts and yellow Stockings, have a large letter K marked on them.

It is supposed they are gone to Exeter, Tiverton, or Plymouth.

Their disconsolate Friends earnestly request any one seeing them will detain them, and give immediate Notice to Mr. HUGGINS, Steward of the Hospital; or to Mr. JOSEPH COOPER, 73, Borough, Southwark—when all reasonable Expences will be thankfully paid by either of the above.

June 23rd. 1817.

ANN KEMMISH, **Printer,** 17, KING STREET, Borough, London.

Fig. 4.7 Runaway schoolboys, 1817 (by permission of the Postmaster General)

Liverpool Record Office owns a large-scale original plan of Liverpool in 1650 (Fig. 4.6). This is an excellent aid for teaching local history to 9- to 11-year-olds either as a wall map or, preferably, as a slide. It shows the Pool (hence Liver*pool*), now built over to form the main shopping street, the simple H plan of the main streets (still called by the same names), and the land owned by different Liverpool 'worthies'. In other words, in 1650 Liverpool was a small town dependent on the trade provided by the River Mersey. Original maps of this quality, used as visual aids or as smaller versions for children to use in pairs, provide endless interest and develop the comparison of 'then' and 'now' in an area known to the children. Sylvia Wheeler used a map of the field system for Bushey in 1800 and the 25 inch OS map of Bushey for 1871 in her work on the social life of Bushey when it was just a Hertfordshire village.[16]

Maps are a particularly valuable original source for children of 8 years upwards but pictures from source material are good learning resources for children from the age of 6. Advertisements for children's magazines are amusing and interesting 'starters' for discussion. Although the poster refers to boys of 13, older juniors may be sympathetic with the two boys who ran away from Christ's Hospital School in 1817 (Fig. 4.7). Many such advertisements are a source not only for discussion but for drawing and art work as well as creative writing. Old photographs are always wonderful pictures and more will be said about their use later when discussing family history.

Documents in original handwriting are difficult to handle in junior schools when they are dated before 1700, but work has been done successfully with older juniors. For example, the letter from Charles I to Sir William Norris in 1625 demanding a 'forced loan' from him is almost a copperplate hand sent to all those wth money, the amount and collector's name being inserted in another hand (Fig. 4.8). There is an ironic address on the back of the document 'To our trusted and well-beloved Sir Wm. Norris' and a request for quick payment 'with such alacrity and readiness as may make the same so much more acceptable'. There is much here to throw light on the character of Charles I and his lack of intention to repay the loan 'within eighteen months'. This document is easy to transcribe and throws a great deal of light on local and national affairs on the accession of Charles I in 1625.

A seventeenth-century inventory should be tackled one room at a time. Work on the 1700 inventory of 'The little nursery' at Speke Hall can be started by the seven items in the nursery being read without help, then a transcription read as a check (Fig. 4.9). After that the plan of an empty room can be given to each child to draw in the seven items (Fig. 4.10). Practical, imaginative, and even numerical work develops from this one small piece of source material. A final single document I have used with older juniors is a letter of 1705 from Kathryn Norris of Speke Hall to her son Richard, an apprentice in London. In those days envelopes were not used, the letter was folded and the address written on the back of the letter for the messenger – 'This for Mr Richard Norris at Mr Alexander Caine's, a merchant in London'. This letter is easy to read without a transcription. The blackboard could be used for comparison of ways of life in 1705 and the 1980s, evidence coming from this letter. Finally, each pupil could write out the letter using

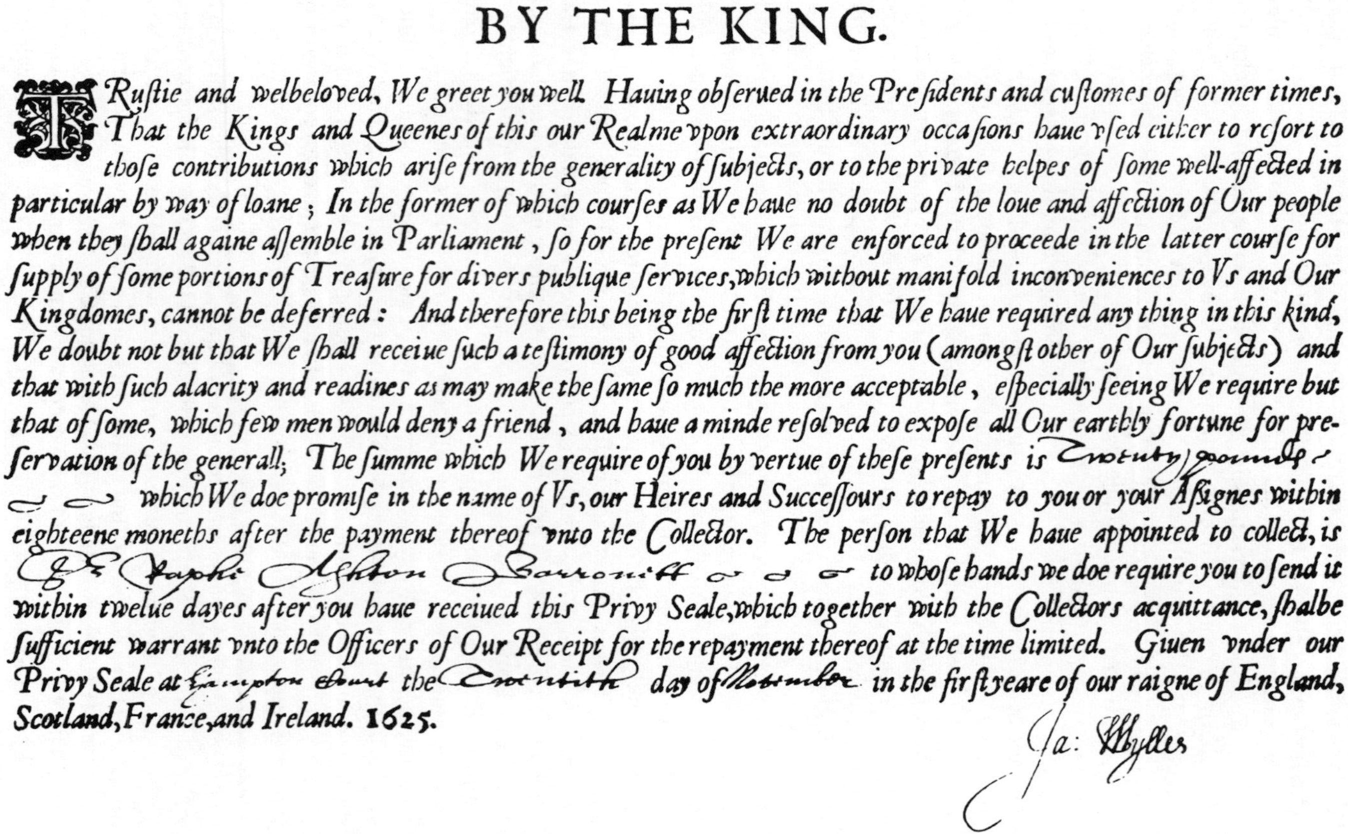

BY THE KING.

Ruſtie and welbeloued, We greet you well. Hauing obſerued in the Preſidents and cuſtomes of former times, That the Kings and Queenes of this our Realme vpon extraordinary occaſions haue vſed either to reſort to thoſe contributions which ariſe from the generality of ſubjects, or to the priuate helpes of ſome well-affected in particular by way of loane; In the former of which courſe as We haue no doubt of the loue and affection of Our people when they ſhall againe aſſemble in Parliament, ſo for the preſent We are enforced to proceede in the latter courſe for ſupply of ſome portions of Treaſure for diuers publique ſeruices, which without manifold inconueniences to Vs and Our Kingdomes, cannot be deferred: And therefore this being the firſt time that We haue required any thing in this kind, We doubt not but that We ſhall receiue ſuch a teſtimony of good affection from you (among ſt other of Our ſubjects) and that with ſuch alacrity and readines as may make the ſame ſo much the more acceptable, eſpecially ſeeing We require but that of ſome, which few men would deny a friend, and haue a minde reſolued to expoſe all Our earthly fortune for pre-ſeruation of the generall; The ſumme which We require of you by vertue of theſe preſents is twenty poundſ which We doe promiſe in the name of Vs, our Heires and Succeſſours to repay to you or your Aſſignes within eighteene moneths after the payment thereof vnto the Collector. The perſon that We haue appointed to collect, is G'Chypli. John Brrow to whoſe hands we doe require you to ſend it within twelue dayes after you haue receiued this Priuy Seale, which together with the Collectors acquitance, ſhalbe ſufficient warrant vnto the Officers of Our Receipt for the repayment thereof at the time limited. Giuen vnder our Priuy Seale at Weſtmr. in the firſt yeare of our raigne of England, Scotland, France, and Ireland. 1625.

Ja:

Fig. 4.8   'By the King': request for a forced loan by Charles I, 1625 (by permission of Liverpool City Libraries)

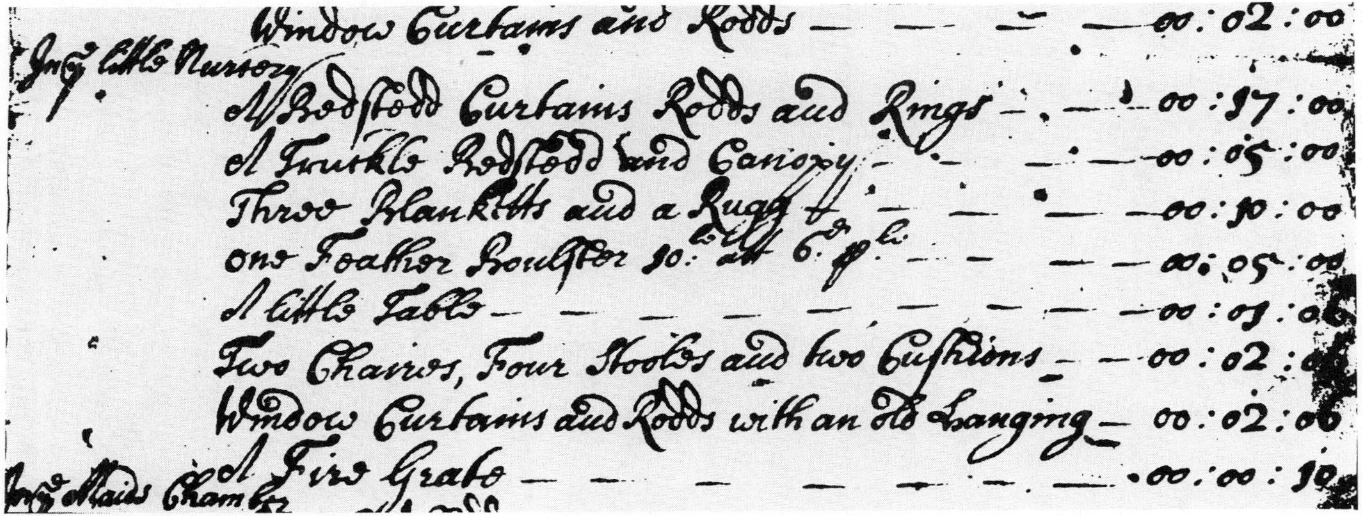

Fig. 4.9 Inventory of the Little Nursery, 1700 (by permission of Liverpool City Libraries)

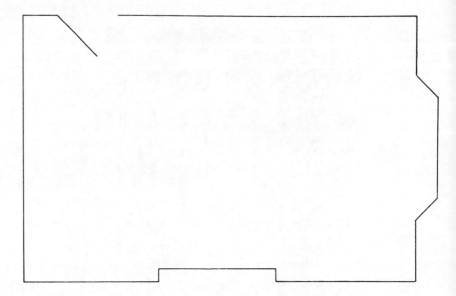

From the 1700 inventory for the Little Nursery, find out the items of furniture and draw them in this plan. Label your items. Add up the items' value and give your final sum.

Fig. 4.10   Plan of the Little Nursery, 1700

present-day punctuation and spelling in order to understand the meaning. Kathryn Norris did not punctuate at all! (Fig. 4.11).

A very suitable topic for all 5–11 children is classrooms of the past and the most accessible and understood period is the late nineteenth and early twentieth centuries. School log books, inspectors' reports, work done by children, and descriptions of old school buildings abound in record offices and they are usually easy to read, being written in copperplate. The Museum of the History of Education at the University of Leeds, started by W. E. Tate, one of the pioneers of teaching local history, possesses the original of a most enlightening essay written by a 13-year-old girl in 1897. It has such relevance today for those interested in ending discrimination against girls and women, that I shall quote it in full:

> I do not like boys. They are so rough and noisy. They think themselves much cleverer than girls but they are mistaken. Girls are much more useful to their mothers than boys. If you see a boy nursing a baby, he

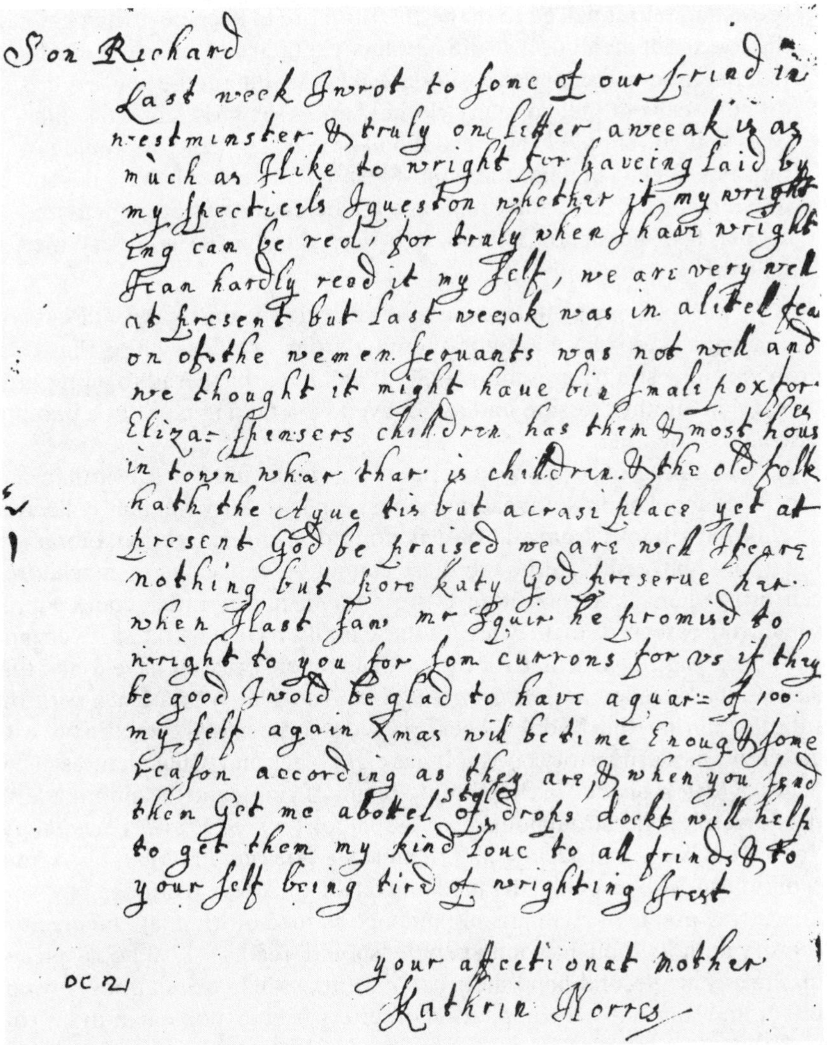

Son Richard

Last week I wrot to sone of our friad in
westminster & truly one leter aweeak is as
much as I like to wright for haveing laid by
my specticels I question whether it my writ
ing can be reed, for truly when I have wright
I can hardly reod it my self, we are very well
at present but last weeak was in a litel fear
on of the wemen servants was not well and
we thought it might haue bin smalpox for
Eliza: spensers children has them & most hous
in town whar thar is children & the old folk
hath the Ague tis but a crasi place yet at
present God be praised we are well I heare
nothing but fore Katy God preserue her.
when I last saw mr Squir he promisd to
wright to you for som currons for us if they
be good I wold be glad to have a quar= of 100
my self again Xmas will be time Enough for some
reason according as they are, & when you send
then Get me a botel of droos dockt will help
to get them my kind loue to all frinds & to
your self being tird of wrighting I rest

OC 2

your affectionat mother
Kathrin Norres

Fig. 4.11 Kathryn Norris's letter to her son, 1705 (by permission of Liverpool City Libraries)

does it so clumsily you think all the time he is going to let it drop. Boys make their sisters do all sorts of things, such as clean their boots, brush their clothes, put their playthings – bats, balls, and marbles safely away. When a boy has a toothache he makes a deal more fuss about it than a girl would, and mother has to do a deal of things to make him quiet. The boys are so fond of play that they cannot find time to come to their meals, and if they are not ready just when they want they make a row about it. The best thing to do is to let them go without, and you may be sure that they will come to the bread and butter, before the bread and butter will go to them. It costs more to keep boys than girls, they wear out their boots so quickly and tear their clothes so dreadfully that the shoe-maker and the tailor are always calling at the house. Girls do not wear out half so many clothes. Folks say girls talk more than boys, but you should hear them at ball or marbles then you would not think so. Well, I suppose there must be boys or we should have no-one to build houses, shoe horses, plough the fields, look after gardens and shops. The nicest boy I know is Willie Murphy, he is a very nice fellow.[17]

This very articulate and mature piece of work may be the basis for discussion in a mixed class of top juniors coming from families where the same problems may still be present in 1988. It would perhaps lead to a prepared 'debate' in another session and might even be a talking point at a parents' association meeting.

A fourth area of archival material often under-used is Edwardian and pre-1945 school books and reading books. A particularly valuable collection of children's books from the past is housed in the Education Library at Liverpool University. Although these cannot be duplicated many children can bring them, teachers often possess them, and libraries could supply some from reserved stock. Many of these books have illustrated covers and gilt-edged pages, particularly if they are old school prizes. I have found that an 1892 book called *Stories from English History* by Maria Hack with the subtitle 'during the Middle Ages' provides interesting comparison with children's modern history books. It has eight black and white pictures in 263 pages of text, is divided in chapter into reigns of kings, and the author adopts the narrative style throughout. Two 1890 books – *Tom Brown's Schooldays* 'by an old boy' and *Henry M. Stanley the African Explorer* by Arthur Montefiore also provide detailed narrative and few pictures, but very interesting points of comparison, and a good idea of what late nineteenth-century authors thought young people 'should' read. A 1793 book, picked up cheaply in a second-hand shop in York, throws light on relations between father and son as it is a compilation of letters from a 'nobleman to his son' with the father telling a *History of England in Letters* to his son, a student at Oxford University. This was before the time when a student could study history at Oxford. These letters, which go as far as 1680 in Volume I, can be used in small extracts as the parts of history are learnt in school. They are clearly printed on parchment, easily read, and discussion about family relationships can come from them. This particular book is leather bound. One or two expeditions to second-hand bookshops, particularly in old towns, enables the teacher to build up an adequate resource library of ancient books as sources, to be used as a topic on 'Old books' with a time chart for dates.

So far I have looked at archival material in the form of maps, pictures, and single documents but since the mid-1950s universities, local authorities, record offices, one branch of the Historical Association, and commercial publishers have found a ready market in selecting and editing certain archival materials supported by other materials, and selling them as archive teaching units, history packs or just compilations of documents on certain topics. For about ten years from 1965 to 1975 groups of teachers in schools, teachers in record offices, and authors produced units of materials fitting into folders and therefore more easily carried, used, and stored. But there was still the difficulty of checking each folder for innumerable documents of different sizes, therefore the third stage of development was the A4 folder containing all A4 size documents, pictures, handbooks, and transcriptions. The Essex Record Office has initiated this in its Seax Series of Teaching Portfolios. Since financial difficulties have curtailed many new publications, Teachers' Centres are trying to publish local materials in paperback form. As the printing is usually done at the Teachers' Centre, the booklets are not expensive and schools can buy enough copies for shared class use. This has been done for many years by the Staffordshire Record Office under the leadership of R. A. Lewis, Inspector for Schools. The advent of the photocopying machine has also enabled teachers to use specific materials in one booklet for duplicating enough copies for educational purposes. Care should be taken to adhere to the copyright laws of the day.

So much work has gone into the production of archive units and there have been so many good ones for sale that it would be impossible to describe and analyse even half of them. Many are too difficult for primary children and should be used in the 11–16 age-range and even beyond. Yet primary teachers can be selective of those intended for 9–13 use. The teacher should select a unit title within children's understanding and then select certain documents from the unit. One of the most attractive I have seen is *Some Kent Children 1594–1875* (Kent Record Office, 1972) edited by Margaret Phillips, the Teacher Adviser in Kent Record Office at Maidstone. The material is divided into separate folders according to the source of the documents; so there is, for example, 'The accounts child', 'A schoolgirl diarist' and 'The inventory child'. Written and visual documents are treated in a most imaginative and lively way, and no child however young could fail to respond to some part of the unit. It also suggests in outline what work could be done with the materials and provides an excellent bibliography. If all record offices could appoint a teacher/archivist of such calibre, records would be used much more in primary schools.

Archive units more structured for teaching purposes than those already discussed have been published by the Manchester branch of the Historical Association, the only branch in the country to undertake this from its own funds and due to the initiative of Dr Alys Gregory, then chairman of the branch. Three units have been published and can be used for the 9–11 age range because the topics chosen are of perennial interest to children. They are *Orphan Annie* edited by Constance Francis (1969) and *The Princes of*

Loom Street edited by Muriel Rosser (1972), both concerned with deprived children and their families in an industrial town in the nineteenth century, and *Quarry Bank Mill and Samuel Greg* edited by Muriel Rosser and Peter Spencer (1982).[18] Reference to information books of historical quality are included and both units use documents which can easily be read. *Orphan Annie*, about a London orphan Ann Saunderson aged 10, apprenticed to James Pendleton a Manchester tape-weaver, is more useful to the teacher than to the children, as little activity is given for children to undertake from the unit. But the *Handbook* gives excellent information, explaining the documents and the *Research* booklet leads the teacher along with suggestions of how to make workcards appropriate to the documents. Muriel Rosser's unit has one *Handbook* of information but six different coloured cards as 'research cards' from which children can work. These cards cover transport, family living conditions, population and overcrowded towns, education, wages and food, work and leisure. Each card stipulates which documents should be consulted to answer the six questions and Mrs Rosser has cleverly used each particular document only once so that children will not be competing for the same documents to answer their particular workcard. This unit is also the only place where I have seen a clear sketch of 'back-to-back' houses, this time a sketch of two houses in Chorlton-on-Medlock, Manchester. All these units are scholarly, imaginative, and can be used practically by teachers of 9–11 primary children.

Packs of material have been published without specific intention of being used for teaching purposes. These are collections of information with no handbook for teachers. The most famous are Jackdaw folders, first produced by Jonathan Cape in 1963. Most of them are not suitable for juniors unless they are carefully edited, but they are useful as display and stimulus material rather than learning material. Margaret Devitt wrote a useful companion to Jackdaws – *Learning with Jackdaws* (Cape, 1970) – and she shows in a flowchart how they can be used to relate to each other. Two of the most useful Jackdaws for 5- to 11-year-olds are *The Development of Writing* by Carol Donaghue (No.47) and *The Tower of London* by David Johnson (No.62). They are useful resources to be used by all children and both contain very good large wall pictures.

The years 5–11 and on to 14 are the ideal ones in which to concentrate on the real stuff of the past before it is subjected to the limitations of examinations. In these years real enjoyment can be experienced by both teacher and children in using different types of source material. This 'involves the ability to steep the class completely, and for protracted periods of time, in the very words and deeds of the subject' comments John West. To do this the teacher needs help from archivists, in-service training, and assistance in school or, where possible, the local Teachers' Centre to handle the necessary source materials. Teachers should try to familiarize themselves with *one* area of source material for each of the 5–11 years, from old photographs in the infant school to turnpike road accounts in the top class of the junior school. This should be related in some way to the scheme of work for that year. In the following two accounts, Carol Wilson and Kenneth May make skilful use of source material with older juniors in teaching the history of Liverpool.

How I teach the history of Much Woolton in the seventeenth century to 9- to 11-year-olds

I have developed a scheme for teaching local history which could be applied to many areas. The period I cover for Much Woolton, where the school is situated, is from the early seventeenth century to the twentieth century. The work occupies two terms, the first concentrating on the seventeenth century. Just over one hour a week is spent on the basic teaching.

It is possible to discuss only one of its sections here, the introductory one, which involves an examination of local life during the seventeenth century. Of the many sources available for this period I concentrate on Probate and Quarter Sessions records; ten probate inventories and four Quarter Session petitions are used.

A most important task is first of all to motivate the children and to create an interest and curiosity in the subject which will be maintained. A successful way I have developed is to request that the children bring into school objects of any kind which they regard as being 'old'. This always produces a great variety of items ranging from some only a few years old to several of genuine antiquity. They promote discussion and, eventually, classification into categories — 'fairly new', 'old', 'very old' and 'very, very old'. We then comment upon how difficult it is to determine whether objects are 'old' or not and usually decide that those not in common use today can be easily recognized as 'old'.

Having developed interest in ideas associated with chronology and change I then show the children photocopies of wills of people who lived in Woolton in the seventeenth century. As with the objects, initial reaction is not directed; pupils are encouraged to examine and draw their own conclusions about age and origin. This leads naturally to a study of palaeography so that they can read the documents for themselves. Each child has a copy of every document and, later, transcriptions of them. Reading the wills leads to a great deal of discussion about spelling, literacy, and writing styles. It is at this stage that the children try to write with quill pens. They appreciate how difficult it is to form modern letters with them and write about this experience. They find the exercise both enjoyable and instructive. Next the children are asked to write their own wills, deciding which possessions they would bequeath and to whom they would leave them. These serve as extremely useful comparisons between past and present values and customs.

Once they are reasonably proficient at reading the wills — four class lessons — the children examine inventories. This is after they have made an inventory of their own bedroom, noting all the items belonging to them. We look at these, deciding how useful they could be as evidence to people who found them in a hundred years' time. What would they learn about children in 1980? The pupils then consider which things would not have been included in their parents' day and grandparents' day. It is surprising how acute their observations about change can be. Following this, groups of children study the inventories, two inventories per group, making lists of things relating to agriculture and 'occupations'. This involves much group discussion and open-ended questions about the way of life of people at the time. The group work lasts for four sessions. Each group is asked to look at both the will and the inventory and explain how they thought that the person maintained his or her family. This leads to creative writing about life in the seventeenth century. They are able to build up a reasoned picture of what life was probably like for particular family units in Woolton.

To see a little of how the family units fitted into the larger community, a further source is introduced, i.e., the Quarter Sessions Rolls. In particular we look at petitions made by distressed people in a variety of circumstances, which gives rise to discussion about the causes of poverty and how the community functioned as a caring society.

Pupils respond to these materials in a number of ways. Imaginative writing and their own dramatic creations are among the rewarding work they produce. I feel that by using this approach children exercise a number of skills which they will extend and develop in later years. The concepts, so important to any study of history, of time, change, similarity, difference, etc., are dealt with in a meaningful way. They gain an impression of the scale of life in a previous age and are given a more vivid insight into seventeenth-century England than textbooks could provide.

Carol Wilson
then at Woolton County Primary School, Liverpool

A study of 'Castlesite' in an urban area with 9- to 11-year-olds

Children's enjoyment of history is enhanced when they know it is real, when they can see where it happened, when romanticism is illustrated with true facts, and when the understanding of the subject under study is within their comprehension. It is for these reasons that I find local history, the more local the better, makes a great contribution to the teaching of the subject, though it is important that it is not isolated from national or international history.

Some 400 metres from the school in Liverpool where I worked for thirteen years is a small open space with the evocative name 'Castlesite'. Today the area is bounded by houses on three sides but reserved as an open space because a castle was erected here about the time of the Norman Conquest. National history of the eleventh century conditioning land use in the twentieth century! An ideal subject for a local history study.

A visit to the City of Liverpool Record Office produced some useful information concerning the castle. The VCH* supplied important material concerning the location and environment of the castle, some details of its history

* VCH = Victoria County History (in this case for Lancashire).

and a useful map which included the school, so that by tracings and use of the OS map scale 1 : 2500 the exact position of the castle could be located. This book was also of obvious use for information and transcriptions of Domesday Book. Another useful booklet which described excavations undertaken at the site in 1927 provided a plan of the castle, a cross-section of the excavations across the inner and outer ditches, diagrams of timbers found lying at the bottom of the ditch and believed to be from a drawbridge, a conjectural drawing of the drawbridge, and a list of other finds including pottery, the leather sole of a shoe, metal, horn, and bone objects found in the ditches.

From the information obtained I planned a work unit on the castle and related subjects for children aged 9+ to 11+. It seemed to me that time can be wasted and efforts frequently duplicated in the research and preparation of teaching materials; I therefore planned to put together a unit of work which would be valuable to teachers over a number of years. My aim was to provide background information which teachers could use to plan lessons and pupils' worksheets which would include basic information, maps, diagrams, and tasks to be completed on site or in school. Time required for the work would vary according to the amount of integration with other subjects and the number of aspects covered by each group of children but I considered a minimum of two hours per week for a term to be required. For practical organization at the site and the economical use of resources in school, the work was planned for children to work in groups. I found four groups of from six to eight children to be a workable arrangement but this did not preclude the use of class teaching when appropriate. By using the study during a long period of teaching practice it was possible to have an extra adult to assist and stimulate the children. In the school, which is of open plan design, materials and resources were available to the children on a 'help yourself' basis thus saving children time and teacher frustration.

The materials produced for study consist of pupils' worksheets and a teachers' guide enclosed in a ring binder which includes background information on the building of the castle, the excavation of 1927, maps and diagrams, information regarding the Domesday survey, a list of relevant books in the school library, and of slide sets and film strips, and a 'Domesday pack'. It was not intended that the worksheets should be used in their exact form. An enterprising teacher would wish to direct the work to suit the composition of the class.

Before the worksheets were used adequate class teaching about the Normans was given and introductory information explaining the purpose and method of compilation of Domesday Book before this section was undertaken. I found the book *Domesday Rebound* (HMSO, 1954) to be helpful and useful for this work.

Teachers will be aware of the problem of children slavishly copying from reference books, which is undoubtedly an unprofitable exercise. A technique I found useful and used in the worksheets was to ask children to use accurate factual information obtained from resource materials in imaginative story writing. Pupils used several books to collect the information but used their own composition and ideas to produce the final piece of work.

THE CONTENTS OF THE WORKSHEETS IN BRIEF

Worksheet 1 (four A4 sheets)
Information provided: Location and building of the castle; scale plan of the castle; sketch of a typical motte and bailey castle; film strips. Normans, Bayeux Tapestry.
Work by children: Use of reference books to study motte and bailey castles and Normans in the mid-eleventh century, use of the information to make sketches of a castle and to write a story about a serf or villein who helped to build the castle, and of a Norman soldier who lived in it; use of the scale plan to mark the dimensions of the outer and inner bailey and the width of ditches in the school playground. (Could the outer bailey be enclosed in our school playground?)

Work Sheet 2 (three A4 sheets and copy of local OS plan (1 : 2500)) †
Information supplied: Plan showing position of castle and school, cross-section of fosses.
Work by children: Position of castle and school to be traced from plan and superimposed on current OS plan to locate position of castle in relation to road and houses adjacent to site today; use of information discovered to find the exact position of the castle on site; writing of poems about walking on the land where Norman soldiers had tramped; work concerning streams indicated on the map and possible interviews with local residents about any evidence of archaeological remains in the gardens.

Work Sheet 3 (four A4 sheets)
Information supplied: Detailed list of finds; maps and diagrams of dig in 1928.
Work by children: Work related to thirteenth-century pottery; imaginative work with correct historical detail derived from the finds of a leather shoe, antler and bones of fourteenth century; plasticine or papier mâché model of castle.

Work Sheet 4 (three A4 sheets)
Information supplied: Details of discovery of timbers from the base of a drawbridge; conjectural drawing of bridge.
Work by children: Further study of finds given in teachers' notes; full-size diagrams to show beams unearthed; model of drawbridge in balsa wood; imaginative story or poem of battle for the possession of drawbridge; further study and work on life in a Norman castle, shields, armour, and weapons.

THE DOMESDAY SURVEY (This could be done in a class group)

Information supplied: A children's 'Domesday pack' including a copy of the relevant page from Domesday Book; transcript from the VCH; map of the West Derby hundred in 1086; details of Domesday survey; vocabulary; slide set.
Work by children: Study and discussion of Domesday documents; matching present day names of districts of the City with names of manors in the

† may only be done under licence.

survey; discovering the services rendered by thegns and villeins to the king; listing crimes and punishments: a Domesday survey of children in the class.

Kenneth May
then Headteacher of West Derby Church of England Primary School,
Liverpool

Family and oral history

A great deal of time has been spent on 'the written word' so far in this chapter and this is one of the problems in the primary school. So many children have reading difficulties that history must be viewed as a spoken/ oral subject as well. If emphasis is placed on reading and writing the majority of children will not enjoy the past. In recent years oral history has become a respectable area of historical research and much of it consists of the reminiscences of old people during the last century. This has given the study a natural link with family history which also depends on using source material, mostly of the last hundred years. Suitable books for children to use have been discussed earlier in this chapter. Therefore, in this section we consider how primary teachers can use family and oral history in the classroom as an acknowledged professional method of historical enquiry. Oral and family history may be used effectively throughout the 5–11 age-range, but not in every year.

Work with 6-year-olds has already been described in an earlier part of this book; in this instance 'life-lines', family trees, and artefacts were used to help the children to reconstitute their families backwards about 60–70 years, to the time of their grandparents. Susan Lynn has continued this work in a London school and describes her experiment in the following way.

How I teach history to five-year-olds

Teaching history to young children means, in my view, introducing them to the skills of historical thinking as well as learning to enjoy the past. These I would define as, first, distinguishing between reality and makebelieve (at the common sense rather than at the philosophical level that concerns academic historians); second, ordering a sequence of events; third, relating the sequence to a time scale; and finally, seeing events, people, and their surroundings from the perspective of another point in time.

The problem is to find work that develops these skills and, at the same time, matches the level of development of 5-year-olds. When I made the attempt with a group of five children (average age, 5.10), in the second year infant class of an outer-London suburban school one day a week for four weeks, I chose, as the topic, the children's own past lives. Here, I thought, the distinction between reality and make-believe would be meaningful to the children, for they could use their own memories, and incidents reported at home, as well as their observations of their own and friends' younger brothers and sisters (all the children in the group had younger brothers and sisters). Interest in the past could be generated by displays of family photographs, the children's own pictures and cut-out illustrations of babies and young children, tape recording children's memories, and making family trees. I knew that the children could order a sequence and it followed that the sequence in this case would be their own physical growth, and landmarks in their lives, such as the acquisition of skills like walking and talking, the birth of younger brothers and sisters, and so on. I anticipated that relating the sequence to a time scale would not occur spontaneously to the children and that they would have to construct it actively themselves. Each child had a sheet of paper with an 18-inch line drawn horizontally across it. Using a three inch square card, the children marked out six squares below the line, each square representing a year of their lives. Each square was then numbered as shown below.

1	2	3	4	5	6

Above each square they drew a picture of themselves to show how they grew bigger each year. To help them grade the heights of the pictures, I gave them a card marked in six sections, the bottom section serving as the height for the baby, the second as the height for age one, and so on.

6
5
4
3
2
1

By writing in each year square something that had happened in that year (or dictating to me when their enthusiasm for putting pencil to paper flagged) they were not only ordering a sequence in relation to a time scale, but also looking at their lives from the perspective of earlier points in time.

How successful was my attempt? The sequence of landmarks in their lives came readily, though it required some initial prompting, especially for years three and four. The time scale did, indeed, prove more difficult. They could not accept that the number at the left of the line of squares should logically be 0 and settled instead for one month. However, they understood that the number at the right end should be six, since, as they said, 'You are five all the time until you are six.' Much more difficult for one of the children was the problem of recording the birth of her one-year-old sister. She could not see that this should go into the 4—5 square and insisted for a time on recording it in the 1—2 square. One source of her difficulty was clearly her fixation on the present age of her sister. However, her subsequent behaviour alerted me to the presence of another problem: an inability to distinguish past and present, compounded by a confusion of identity between herself and her baby sister, which possibly stemmed from a more fundamental inability to distinguish between her own situation or viewpoint and that of another person. Having introduced her baby sister into the scenario, she then began to attribute to herself at age four and five events like teething and having a nappy changed. The other children seemed to have no such difficulties, since they intervened with comments, such as, 'You're talking about Louise (the baby sister), not you', and did not show any confusion after correctly recording the birth of their own brothers or sisters.

To sum up, I believe that the general approach here described could be a useful addition to the repertoire of historical activities in infant classes. It takes a context in which the distinction between reality and make-believe is meaningful to children, and, by concentrating on the skills of historical thinking, it serves as a guide to what might be called historical readiness. It allows particular strengths and weaknesses to be identified and taken into account when planning history-based work. For example, all the children in the group would benefit from more work on time scales, and the weakest member seems to need more practice in distinguishing between different people's situations, without which no real understanding of other people in time or place can occur. The approach is undoubtedly teacher-directed, but I make no apology for that, since, without such direction the practice of skills and diagnosis of difficulties might not have taken place. As far as the children were concerned, the amount of relevant conversation sparked off recall of past events connected both with themselves and with members of their families, and speculation about the future. These results suggest that the children both enjoyed the experience and became more aware of the time dimension in their lives.

Susan Lynn
Polytechnic of the South Bank, London

Help may also be gained by junior teachers mainly from three published sources. One is the work of Sallie Purkis who experimented with children of 7–8 in a Cambridge primary school, another is the work of Brendan Murphy of Wigan working with 10- to 11-year-olds, and finally the extensive work of Don Steel and Lawrence Taylor described in some detail in their book *Family History in Schools* (published by Phillimore, 1973). Sallie Purkis had

Fig. 4.12   The Craven family c. 1900

a mixed-ability class including five remedial readers and most children found writing more difficult than reading. She started from an old photograph of their school in 1908 found in the local library. In this photograph schoolgirls aged about 13 were gardening as part of the curriculum and the purpose of the project was to find out how these girls, the great grandmothers of the class, lived in the same area in Edwardian days. Therefore Sallie Purkis sent the children's grandmothers and elderly friends a short list of questions called 'Ask grandma'. The replies enabled the class to build up a picture of Edwardian clothes, washdays, schooldays, shopping days, and general life style. The grandmothers lent artefacts and letters of all sorts and by half term the walls and tables of the classroom were so busy with information and relics of grandmother's day that these ladies were invited to school to talk to the children and look at the display.[19]

In the same way, a photograph of my maternal grandparents and their four children (the eldest boy had died of meningitis when a baby) taken about 1900 (Fig. 4.12) could form the basis of a family history project with the initiative coming from the teacher and her family. The photograph throws into stark relief the social life of a lower middle-class Edwardian family living near Manchester. The 'best' clothes, particularly of the parents, make this an important and expensive family occasion. My eldest aunt (in the middle) always made the girls' clothes and had put a great effort into her mother's spotted dress. As eldest daughter (given considerable status) she allowed herself a more fancy outfit than her younger sisters (my mother on the right-hand side) and had piled her hair 'on top'. My uncle, in his Eton collar and with a handkerchief suitably placed in his top pocket, has a place of honour near his mother as 'the only son'. He always got more pocket money than his sisters! All look solemn for this splendid occasion although they were a jolly family from my recollections. This may be contrasted with informal family slides in the 1980s: 'then' and 'now'. So much of the past can come out of one good photograph, particularly when supported by 'oral' evidence which I can well remember being told me by my mother. Children are intensely interested in their class teacher and her family. This photograph could lead to children bringing family groups of more recent years, time charts could be made and a topic of 'Family groups – old and new' could be started.

Brendan Murphy experimented mainly with top juniors and therefore more archival work could be undertaken than in Sallie Purkis's class. This involved mostly independent work by children on their own families from oral evidence, documentary records (family bibles, birth certificates, parish registers, and school log books), other records (letters, newspapers), material exhibits, pictorial records, and professional evidence from the record office. In the case of these children, four years older than Sallie Purkis's class, great-grandmothers were traced, maps made showing where relations had gone all over England and local maps showing workplaces of relations in the past and present. Children made their own scrapbooks of their families. In this scheme, as Brendan Murphy points out, the teacher has to be very well organized and systematic with so many precious resources about the classroom for a considerable time.[20]

Don Steel and Lawrence Taylor undertook a large-scale research programme on family history in schools near Reading in the late 1960s. The children worked back in three stages through five generations to 1860 starting from 'Who am I?' The second stage involved parents, and the third 'Generation 3, 1918–45', 'Generation 4, 1890–1930' and 'Generation 5, 1865–1900'. They used documents, evidence through tape recordings of old people's descriptions, and many artefacts. Out of 700 children using the scheme only 30 found it difficult to participate because of tensions at home. These children worked on the teacher's family, helped others with their families or collected information from local old people not related to them. The second chapter of Steel and Taylor's book shows how family history may be used as a unifying factor in interdisciplinary work. The natural integration of English, art, drama, geography, mathematics, social studies, and family history is illustrated. One sentence is very encouraging for non-specialists in primary schools:

Thus history is the natural focal point for work in many subjects, and the reason that it is often taught more interestingly at the Primary level

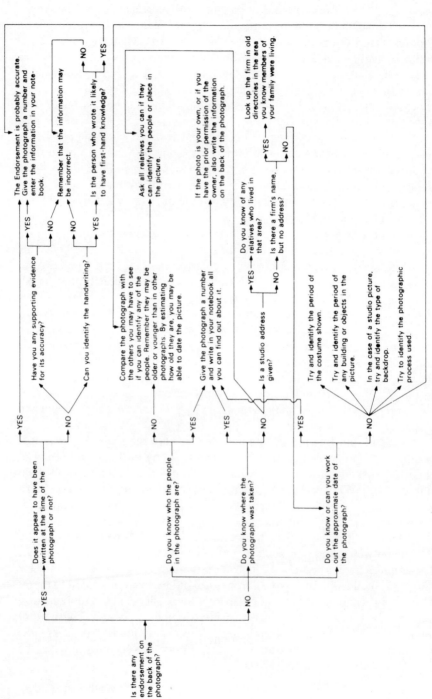

Fig. 4.13 Family history: techniques of photo analysis (from *Family History in Schools*, D.J. Steel and L. Taylor, Phillimore & Co. Ltd.)

may be that there the teachers are not history specialists. The history they teach is, therefore, more related to other areas of human knowledge and, above all, is concerned not with parties, policies and the balance of power, but with people.[21]

Most of this research was done with children over 11 years of age but four parts of the book are particularly useful to primary teachers. One is the letter sent to parents to show that the work is serious and to guide them in lending artefacts. The second comprises the two accounts by teachers of work done with 7- to 8-year-olds and 8- to 9-year-olds on the 'Who am I?' project and with 9- to 11-year-olds on interdisciplinary work using patches of history at the points 1945, 1914, 1870. These may be found on pp. 153–160 in *Family History in Schools*. The third useful reference is to training primary children to use tape recorders for them to read information found in parish registers which they have not time to write down when visiting a church or record office. Steel and Taylor also suggest applying the family history techniques to families in other periods of the past. For example, the Cecil family from the Tudor age to the present day may be studied quite easily from *The Cecils of Hatfield* by David Cecil (Constable, 1973). If old photographs are the main evidence, teachers will find *Techniques of Photo-Analysis* very useful (Fig. 4.13).[22]

All these examples of family and oral history have the great advantage of depending upon human resources in the community, therefore they are cheap in comparison with other resources. They also involve speaking rather than writing which is always an advantage to younger children. They give children pride in their own environment and link them purposefully with other generations. However, this method can be overdone and a whole scheme based on family history should be avoided.

4.4   Third order resource: mechanical aids

So much development has taken place in this area to help (or hinder!) teachers in the last five years that a whole booklet could be written usefully. In the context of this revised edition I am going to highlight only certain 'aids' which are a good investment. Publishers' catalogues, information from the BBC and ITV, from computer software firms, museums and organizations such as the National Trust, give details which change as the years go by, therefore advice in 1988 would not be worth reading in 1990. Yet two comparatively new inventions, the video-recorder for television programmes and the photocopier, are here to stay, and most schools either have them or plan to buy them as essential pieces of equipment. The first enables teachers to make television programmes their servants rather than masters and the second gets rid of the drudgery of using a spirit machine for duplication of A4 sheets for children's activities. The second is more important than the first, provided that the current copyright laws are strictly observed.

I propose to look at six different aids. The first is a slide projector, which has taken over from the filmstrip projector by now. Slides presenting the still picture are cheap and accurate and can be a useful introduction, conclusion or way of giving more detailed information to children. In many schools children are entrusted with using viewers and machines in small groups on specialized topics. On some occasions two children in turn tell the rest of the class about their particular task undertaken during a class visit, with the help of slides. This is a good beginning to 'public speaking' as the slides give a sense of security. By the fourth year of the primary school, children should be expert at this method of presentation. Slides can be made by teachers and children (or converted from their photographs) as well as bought from publishers, museums, the National Trust, English Heritage, private 'stately homes' visited and the BBC. It is important to keep slides in proper containers carefully labelled and in the correct order to avoid loss and confusion in showing them.

The second aid which has been much developed by commercial firms during the last five years is the cassette recorder which produces comparatively cheap tapes. In addition to radio programmes, cassettes, easily used by quite young children, are a way of teaching young children to listen, as an alternative to watching. Cassettes, like slides, are easily stored and kept in order in special boxes. Rachel Redford lists five good cassette series, some with books and activity cards and all with teachers' notes.[23] Topics such as Mary, Queen of Scots, Bonnie Prince Charlie and Edwardian Stories figure in this series. If you are involved with a Victorian/Edwardian schools topic, why not let a cassette tell the children period stories instead of the teacher telling them modern stories? Or better still, why not simplify an involved story yourself and tape it as a five-minute story to be used many times? I found that quite an involved story of the 'Massacre of Peterloo' in Manchester in 1819 could be understood by 6-year-olds if the tape was played twice. Thus cassettes can form an activity for children, make them responsive to listening carefully, and relieve the teacher of the burden of imparting all the information.

The third mechanical aid is the radio programme. So many changes have taken place since the never-to-be-forgotten Eileen and Rhoda Power stories of the 1930s.[24] In this age of multi-media communication, children have not been schooled in listening as they once were. Yet still the radio programme has its place in schools, especially as programmes can be tape-recorded and replayed more cheaply and easily than using a video-recorder, which some primary schools still lack (or find stolen). Programmes change as the years go by but *History Long Ago* (BBC) for 8- to 12-year-olds has been a firm favourite supported as it is by the Oxford Junior History Series of books by Ray Burrell and Peter and Mary Speed. A new programme in 1987–8 is *Lost and Found* (BBC) devised by Elizabeth Cleaver and written by Sallie Purkis. It runs each week for two terms and has a slide pack of artefact photographs, teachers' notes and background material to support it. Intended for 9- to 11-year olds, it is concerned with evidence including oral history and artefacts. The content of the programmes is the twentieth century, mainly from the point of view of social history, and one wonders whether this material would not be more useful for younger children who study themselves and their families more naturally.[25]

The fourth type of aid, and the most used, is the television programme which too often determines the scheme of work in primary schools and leads to overdemand upon local libraries on the same topic. Programmes which have endured are *Watch* (BBC) for 6- to 8-year olds and *Zig Zag* (BBC) for 8- to 10-year-olds. Both these programmes are on inter-related Humanities though the *Zig Zag* autumn term 1987 is concerned with the Vikings in a dramatized form. *History Around You* (Granada) continues to be a favourite programme through which to introduce local history particularly as Allan Waplington, the lively presenter, edits the series of textbooks by the same name. *How We Used to Live* (Yorkshire Television) remains an excellent dramatized series extending from 1874–1953; two video packages, 1874–87 (Victorian) and 1936–53 (World War II) may now be bought, though they are rather expensive for primary schools. *Now and Then* (BBC) is a programme for 9- to 11-year-olds to complement the geographical programme *Near and Far*. It is a topic-based series using building materials (e.g. wood from the Weald and Downland Museum at Singleton, West Sussex), voyages of discovery (e.g. the *Golden Hind*), travel and transport to help children to understand change and continuity, and to use basic skills. Unfortunately, *The Domesday Project* (BBC), ably televised by Michael Wood to introduce Norman England, may be used by few schools, although many participated, since the cost of the videodisc is so great.[26] How much medieval life is learnt from a contemporary sociological study is questionable although it is good to see 1086 recognized as important. The excellence of these programmes tempts teachers to rely too heavily on them; it is to be hoped that the national curriculum will guide schools into constructing their own schemes of work to use such programmes as tools, only appropriate in small doses at convenient times.

The arrival of the microcomputer in the primary classroom heralds a new technological age for History teaching as well as for most other areas of the curriculum.[27] One of its prime virtues is of course its value for pupil-initiated learning. Yet one machine has to be carefully managed in a class of thirty junior children; therefore at present it cannot be advocated as a continuous agent of learning. Two student teachers of infants show the success of a computer for non-readers and non-writers when studying a small nineteenth-century cottage in Lancaster.[28] Work has also been done with top juniors by Cottia Howard on the *Mary Rose* pack; her work is summarized below.

Other experiments by primary teachers in London Schools and on the study of local and fairly recent history seems to have been most successful but we must guard against the tail wagging the dog, only selecting parts of the past which lend themselves to the use of the microcomputer (e.g. Census Returns). Chris Drage summarizes and assesses many of the new computer packs relevant to History.[29] He favours those he writes about but warns teachers to prepare the class thoroughly both before and after the use of the micro. Some of the packs are purely descriptive and social (e.g. *Viking England* and *Norman England*), others are simulations needing empathy and understanding from children (e.g. *Cateby Manor*, *Archaeology* and *Wagons West*) and a third type are linked to television programmes (e.g. *How We Used to Live*). Chris Drage particularly recommends 'Making Ends Meet 1902–6' in *How We Used to Live*. He believes that such work stimulates much discussion between children and between teacher and class.

The *Mary Rose* Computer Project

The *Mary Rose* Computer Project developed from work second year children in a large 9—13 middle school were undertaking on the Tudors. The school's schemes of work for history and geography had recently been revised, and the integration of these subjects under the heading 'social studies' and the following of termly or half-termly projects was a feature of the teaching, particularly of the younger children. Much new resource material had been purchased, and the *Mary Rose* computer package, published by Ginn, seemed a promising resource. The program simulates the discovery and subsequent exploration of the wreck of Henry VIII's warship, the *Mary Rose*. The computer software is in two parts, the first of which involves a search of the Solent to locate the wreck, and the second concerns the removal of mud and silt from the ship, recovery of artefacts and the recording of archaeological details.

My class of 33 ten and eleven year olds was divided into groups of three, and for three double lessons a week we involved ourselves in the project. An earlier science topic had been 'floating and sinking', and had linked with the actual recovery of the *Mary Rose*. We had all followed this event with great interest in newspapers and on television, and our experiments, and the conclusions we had drawn, were constantly referred to and provided us with useful background knowledge.

Each group of children was required to find the position of the wreck using the first 'survey' part of the program before proceeding to part two. It soon became obvious, however, that 'survey' itself would take the entire term unless the children developed their own strategies for systematic searches of the Solent. Their excitement at using the computer was such that they were quite happy to continue navigating their boat haphazardly around the area without necessarily achieving success. However, after one or two groups had been successful, the mood of the class changed as an element of competition crept in, and systematic searching began to be developed. The children were all very enthusiastic about the work and the excitement generated was quite infectious. Once the children had completed a survey, they wrote up their log books, and when all the groups had succeeded in finding the wreck and had worked out its latitude and longitude from the bearings they had been given, we were ready for part two.

For the 'diving' program the children adopted the titles 'controller', 'operator', and recorder swapping roles for each dive. They researched into the equipment needed for underwater exploration, read accounts of underwater archaeology and made lists of the equipment they would have to check off before they were allowed to proceed with the program. As this section of the project was more difficult than the first, with accurate plotting on charts to be carried out, and with the idea of moving around underwater to be firmly grasped, two class demonstrations were undertaken first. Following these, the groups worked in turn, diving down to the wreck, plotting their movements in a team record book, and engaging in discussion of possible strategies. After each dive the children would transfer their group record to the class record which covered the whole of the wreck, and they would also write up their log books. The 'de-briefing' or discussion sessions after each day's diving served to highlight any problems the children were experiencing. All the details of mud clearing and of 'finds' discovered were also recorded on the program disc by the computer. This meant that although we had several computers available, only one could be used for the project as the disc was updated with new information by each group.

The *Mary Rose* project had so far, even in its very limited and controlled form, been successful in creating enthusiasm for a period in history, and in developing communication skills sometimes neglected in the classroom. It was therefore decided to develop it further during the following year with all second year classes. This coincided with the introduction of more flexible staffing arrangements in the school which had implications for the organization of the project. The 'year head' was released from her class responsibility and could now work with small groups of children and the computer in the central work area outside the classroom, whilst another teacher co-ordinated the background and follow-up work in the classroom itself. The school year was divided into blocks of nine or ten weeks, each second year class to take over from where the previous one had left off, thus producing a *year* disc of information rather than a *class* one.

The school's new history guidelines, based on the work of Lally and West (1981), meant that the staff were conscious of the need to develop skills of reference and sequencing, and concepts of time, change, evidence, empathy, and cause and effect. The *Mary Rose* project, therefore, had a central role to play within the social studies curriculum. As well as providing a starting point and a means of motivating children, it was also required to support the aims of social studies teaching in the second year with reference to specific skills and concepts from both history and geography. By this time we had begun to build up a collection of resources to accompany those provided with the computer software. The *Mary Rose* Project Pack from BP provided us with slides and an audio cassette, together with worksheets, teacher's notes and a

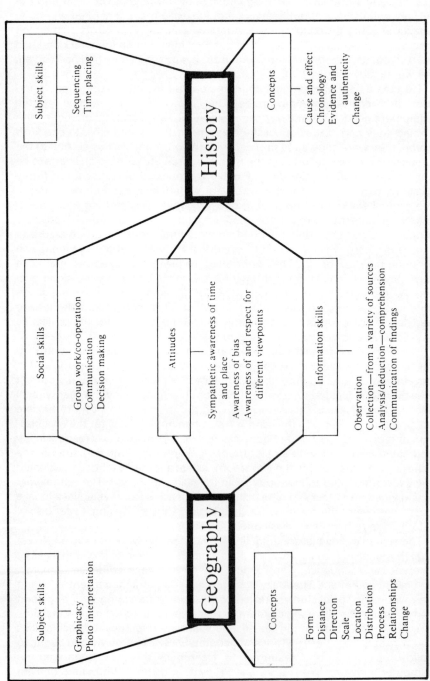

Fig. 4.14 *Mary Rose*: elements of history and geography

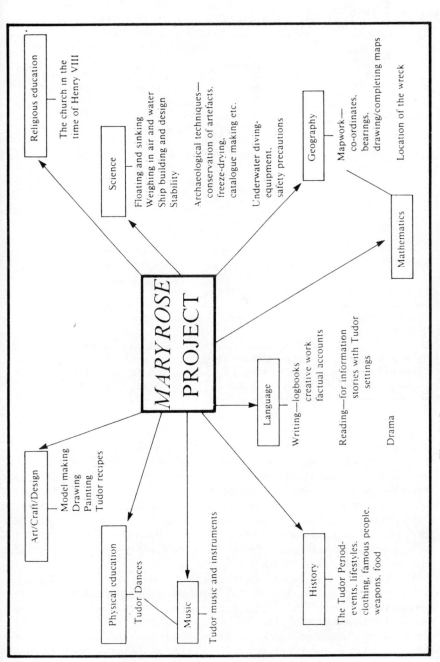

Fig. 4.15 Activities in the *Mary Rose* project

SKILLS AND CONCEPTS ENCOURAGED AND DEVELOPED THROUGH THE USE OF THE *MARY ROSE* COMPUTER PROGRAM			
SUBJECT SKILLS/ CONCEPTS:	HISTORY	GEOGRAPHY	LANGUAGE
	Examination of evidence: observation, organization, classification, speculation, prediction,	Direction: north, south, east, west; port, starboard; up, down.	Reading and following instructions
			Note writing
		Location: co-ordinates,	Discussion
	Empathy	bearings, latitude and longitude.	Vocabulary
		Distance	
SOCIAL SKILLS:	Group co-operation Decision making Communication		
COMPUTER SKILLS:	Interpretation of screen messages Typing		
NB This diagram refers to those skills and concepts developed and encouraged by the computer program directly. Many more skills and concepts were developed by those activities detailed in Fig. 4.15			

Fig. 4.16

colouring book. Authoritative accounts of the archaeological exploration of the wreck by Alexander McKee and Margaret Rule were used for reference, and additional interest was generated amongst children, staff and parents when the Parent Teacher Association invited Malcolm Cockell of Babcock Engineering to give an illustrated talk on 'The Raising of the *Mary Rose*'. During this event the parents were given an opportunity to see the children at work on the programs and to look at some of the work produced for the project, as well as hearing a first hand account by one of the people involved in bringing the wreck to the surface.

With a program such as the *Mary Rose* it is important to bear in mind that it is the undertaking of the project that is important and of value, rather than reaching any definite 'finishing point'. Although at the conclusion of the third year of the project only 23 of the 95 artefacts had been found, and there was some feeling of disappointment amongst children and staff that we had not discovered a major find such as a cannon or the ship's bell, when we assessed the project as a whole it was considered to have been a success. Figs. 4.14, 4.15 and 4.16 show the elements of history and geography in the project, the activities of the project and those skills and concepts which we felt were encouraged and developed through the use of the computer software.

Cottia Howard
Naunton Park Primary School, Cheltenham
(This work was carried out at Franche Middle School and formed the basis for an article in *Educational Review*, Vol. 39, No. 2, 1987)[30]

The last, but not least, mechanical aid is the camera which is owned and used effectively by many primary age children, including infants. The camera is particularly useful when field work is being undertaken. Polaroid cameras, though not cheap to operate, can be bought by the school to develop and print photographs instantly, and this provides an immediate source of evidence to be shown and discussed in class. Prints from personal cameras are an addition to any work, especially if family and oral history is undertaken. Any teacher who is a photographer finds her hobby very useful in preparing work for children. Thus the camera can become a link between teacher and class.[31]

As mechanical aids are expensive, commercial firms and the BBC and ITV only produce what schools will buy and use. Teachers should formulate their own schemes of work and refuse to be influenced by winds of change and fashion, only buying what is really useful to them. As long ago as 1968 Michael Wynne of the BBC wrote 'History broadcasts, then, move with the changing curriculum, sometimes following, sometimes leading, and contributing at these points where the special resources of broadcasting seem likely to be most usefully deployed'.

4.5   Fourth order resource: outside the school

Although resources outside the school are placed as fourth in importance in this chapter, in some ways the teacher has more support from outside the school than inside. Most large museums and art galleries have excellent education officers, efficient ancillary services, and sometimes an archivist, therefore teachers are helped very practically by their personal assistance, booklets and worksheets as well as the actual exhibits. Provided that the necessary legal conditions are fulfilled and cover negotiated, taking children out from a primary school is much less contentious than taking pupils out from a secondary school, because the class time-table is the class teacher's business and there is no examination fever. However expense may now be a difficulty. This part of the chapter will consider how museums, art galleries, 'stately homes', brass-rubbing, archaeology, curriculum development projects and in-service courses can help the teacher.

The greatest development in the last five years has been in activities of organizations trying to exploit the wonderful historic heritage of Britain, to preserve the buildings and make money from tourists for their upkeep. The National Trust, English Heritage and individual owners of 'stately homes' have noticeably developed their help to schools and several theatre groups are doing useful work in old houses and in the classroom. Archaeology is being fast developed as an educational interest in primary schools, with great success.

Museums and art galleries

These are the most easily accessible outside agencies and much has been written about them. The overall quality of their educational facilities is so good that it is impossible in a brief space to do justice to their work. More has been written about museums than art galleries, which have developed their educational facilities more recently. General books on museums are more plentiful than books specifically relating museums to the teaching of history, especially where primary schools are concerned. This in itself shows how much museums and art galleries are integrating agencies in the curriculum and how well they may be used for topics and projects. Two names of curators stand out from the point of view of publication as well as other work. One is Molly Harrison, famous for her work at the Geffrye Museum in Shoreditch, London, and the other is Barbara Winstanley of the Derbyshire Museum Service. Molly Harrison has published widely and her books include *Changing Museums* (Longmans, 1967) and *Museums* ('On Location' Series, Mills and Boon, 1973). The second book is copiously illustrated and perhaps more use for primary teachers. Barbara Winstanley's *Children and Museums* (Blackwell, 1967) is a sound, well-documented book giving illustration and worksheets and much helpful reference material about museums all over the country. The most comprehensive and specifically historical book is John Fairley's *History Teaching through Museums* (Longmans, 1977) in which he analyses types of museums (comprehensive, specialist, folk, open-air, ship, etc.), discusses how visits should be organized and 'work directives' planned, and finally outlines what services the School Museum offers nationally.

As all exhibits in museums are genuine no one collection can be completely comprehensive. Museums now have replicas of some of their collections for educational purposes and to lend to schools. An outstanding example of this is Derbyshire's Blue Time Box Project of artefacts to be placed on an actual clothes line with pegs (provided) in true John West style. This is due to the imaginative work of Harry Butterton, History Adviser, and the Derbyshire Museum service made famous by the work of Barbara Winstanley. The large city museums such as Merseyside County Museum, Liverpool, exhibit a variety of materials ranging from dinosaurs to the Liverpool–Manchester railway engines and coaches. Examples of specialist museums are the Geffrye Museum (English homes), Platt Hall Costume Gallery, Manchester, the Grosvenor Museum at Chester (mainly Roman), the National Portrait Gallery (Old Masters), the Bethnal Green Museum of Childhood, London, the Jorvic Museum at York (Vikings), Wigan Pier (industry), the Armley Mill Museum at Leeds, the Judges' Lodgings Museum at Lancaster, the Bosworth Field Museum and the British Schools Museum at Hitchin.[32]

Examples of open-air museums are Fishbourne Roman Palace, Clarke Hall at Wakefield (a seventeenth-century yeoman's house), Ironbridge Gorge Museum in Shropshire, and Singleton Open Air Museum near Chichester. Examples of folk-museums are the Castle Museum at York, the American Museum at Claverton, near Bath, and the Abbey Museum, Kirkstall near Leeds. Among ship museums are the *Cutty Sark* at Greenwich, Buckler's Hard Maritime Museum, Hampshire, and of course the *Victory* and *Mary Rose* at Portsmouth. All of these are most suitable for primary children.

The organization of visits requires planning some way ahead, visiting the museum to meet the Education Officer, planning the visit, and buying relevant material for preparation. Most education officers are so efficient that the teacher only has to do as she is told once the museum has been reached. All the usual precautions should be taken for the safety and well-being of the children on a journey. All children should know what their tasks are from preparation in school beforehand and come with clip board (with waterproof cover when not in use) and pencil(s). They should be reminded that all exhibits should be treated very carefully as handling is often allowed in the museum teaching rooms. After an introductory talk by the Education Officer or teacher, the children should be divided into groups, each with a child group leader, to look round. It is usually better to limit viewing to one room or area. Infants are capable of doing this if suitable groups are formed, tasks are simple and few, and one area is selected.

The workbooks provided for children are an example of quality content and production and they certainly ease the teacher's life and are comparatively cheap to buy. The Geffrye Museum provides and sells many teaching resources, one being several worksheets on 'Food and drink', with spaces for drawings of objects found in the period rooms in the museum. The Open Air Museum at Singleton, West Sussex, excels in its help to teachers. A Museum Teaching Kit includes a *Handbook for School Teachers*, and *Wander Around Trails* may be bought on 'Windows and doors', 'Medieval frame construction' and 'Walling materials and roofs'. In each of these trails, primary teachers are warned that the trails 'are not considered suitable for handing out to children of a junior age in this form' yet the information, diagrams and map of the site for each one are so clear that teachers could quickly prepare a trail shortly before the visit. The Singleton Open Air Museum materials are imaginative and provide scholarly information, and the exhibits include a real reconstructed market hall. Durham has a similar type of museum in the Beamish Open Air Museum. The City of Bristol Museum produces cheap resource packs suitable for all primary children, including *People in Prehistoric Times* and *Meet the Housekeeper at a Georgian House*. The British Museum has now an active Education Service making important national exhibitions appeal to younger children, and producing reasonably priced Activity Booklets on for example *The Egyptians, The Romans*, and *The Ancient Olympic Games*. The Royal Academy of Arts has a free booklet *Background Material for Teachers* to help children to view the exhibition 'The Age of Chivalry: Art in Plantagenet England 1200–1400'; this is an illustrated information book for the teacher and there are no worksheets. The Tate Gallery has published Gallery Explorer Packs for Young People, two of which are suitable for 8- to 12-year-olds; each pack of ten A4 sheets has a large coloured picture of a famous painting, information and follow-up work. There is also a booklet *Tate Trails*. Nothing but good can come from this interrelationship between art and history. The Museum of East Anglian Life at Stowmarket, Suffolk, provides work books on various topics; an interesting one is on the Steggal Family, a specific local farming family of 1900, their home, work and implements. These are only a very small sample of educational resources provided by museums and galleries and many more have been initiated in the last five years.

Museums and art galleries not only provide visits and materials for children and teachers, they also encourage children to spend time in them in school holidays. At the Bethnal Green Museum of Childhood, children can play the alphabet game and look for exhibits listed according to letters of the alphabet. At the National Portrait Gallery a day's Elizabethan music-making has already been described. Here children use the portraits as clues to make puppets and portrait blow-ups. Bradford Industrial Museum even organized a family project on photography called 'Snap happy'. The Museum of London runs four-day courses for 40 children at a time on 'Covent Garden market'. In these imaginative enterprises the education officer takes a step beyond objects and worksheets. In the same way the Sudbury Hall Museum, Derbyshire, sells a compact colourful guide for children which opens out into a board game – 'The Entertaining and Moral Game of Pitfalls and Praises' – to be played with dice and counters. On a visit to Sudbury Hall I found a room packed with parents and children playing 'bygone' games on an antique table. Although holiday time is not classroom time the interest children gain from these activities outside school rubs off onto their work in school.

Museum loan services are invaluable. In 1884 the Merseyside County Museum at Liverpool had the first loan service. An exhibition bus now tours Liverpool schools showing a particular display of artefacts devised by Education officers. The National Museum of Wales, based at Cardiff, lends material out for a term, taken and collected by a van. The City of Leeds

Museum has now built up a large loan collection reflected in the good work done in History in their first and middle schools. The Imperial War Museum in London lends materials on the two World Wars, and the American Museum, near Bath, lends exhibitions connected with North American history to all parts of the country unless they are too fragile to go by rail. Some museums also sell replicas of exhibits which children buy for their collections and some of the more expensive items, such as a cuneiform tablet from the British Museum, can form the basis of a school museum. It is these artefacts that can be used as suggested earlier in work with 6-year-olds before they bring their own 'old things'.

So far I have discussed what regular help museums and art galleries can give schools. But recently new initiatives have been taken, as much to interest tourists as to help children: The Battle of Hastings, Domesday Book and the Armada have led to special exhibitions in relevant places for a period of time. They all provide materials for schools; the Royal Academy 'Age of Chivalry' exhibition is an example. 'Letts Keep a Diary' at the Mall Galleries, London (1987), advertises free entrance to schools and shows original diaries borrowed from famous libraries from Edward VI to Sir Hugh Casson. The innermost thought of diarists through the ages help children to be empathetic towards people in the past.

This short account of museums and art galleries as resources for teaching and learning history is quite inadequate in comparison with the tremendous support they are to teachers in primary schools. Teachers who join GEM (Group for Education in Museums) find the annual *Jem* journal, meetings and contacts invaluable. It is almost possible to structure a history syllabus around local museums and art galleries and it is here that original sources so suitable for 5- to 11-year-old children may be found in abundance. This is a safer syllabus than one geared to changing radio and television programmes or family history. From these small beginnings an understanding of history is developed in later years.

The National Trust, English Heritage and private 'Stately Homes'

Buildings and landscapes owned by the National Trust and English Heritage are kept in a first class state of repair and schools are encouraged to visit them. Much effort is put into providing materials and suitable guided tours for primary schools. All schools should be members of both, and receive their journals, in which all buildings are listed with times of opening and facilities.

The National Trust celebrated its ninetieth birthday in 1985 and much advance has been made in educational facilities even since then. An obvious function of the Trust is to open its buildings to schools, but it also provides age-related resources, a teachers' newsletter and films on Yorkshire Tele-vision showing children enjoying some of the properties. Teachers will not fail to notice large well-established houses such as Hardwick Hall (Der-byshire); Petworth House (Sussex); Longleat, with the lions (Wiltshire); Montacute House (Somerset); and Tatton Hall (Cheshire). Smaller, less well-known and more unusual buildings are sometimes overlooked: Little Moreton Hall (Cheshire) is one of the 'finest specimens of sixteenth century half-timber work'; Wilderhope Manor (Shropshire) is so remote from civilization that 'it remains to a remarkable extent as originally built in the sixteenth century'; East Riddlesden Hall (West Yorkshire) is an early seventeenth century family house; an Erddig (Clwyd) is one of the few large houses showing servants' quarters as they used to be and naming actual servants and their work. Quarry Bank Mill, Styal, is a working museum of the eighteenth century with an Apprentice House in the grounds. Much is known of the owner, Samuel Greg, and many schools incorporate work on these buildings as a regular part of the curriculum. Similar work is carried out elsewhere, including the remarkable Higher Mill textile museum at Helmshore, Near Accrington.

During the last five years, role-playing and drama have become an increasingly important way for children to empathize with the past. The Young National Trust Theatre is a professional group taking dramatization into Trust properties for children to participate. In 1985 Knole House (Kent), Charlecote Manor (Warwickshire) and Montacute House (Somer-set) were visited by the theatre group to re-enact a visit to the house by Queen Elizabeth I. The professionalism and authenticity of such produc-tions are a tremendous 'highlight' of any work in school on the periods concerned. A recent programme for top juniors has been on the First World War – 'A Blighty One' – played in the actual mansions used as hospitals during the period 1914 to 1918.

The Historic Buildings and Monuments Committee for England has taken on a new look since it became English Heritage in 1984 under the chair-manship of Lord Montague of Beaulieu. It competes with the National Trust for educational visits and has a very firm educational interest and service. The properties in its charge vary from Hadrian's Wall to castles, stately homes, monasteries, windmills, graves (Grimes Graves near Thetford, Nor-folk) and stone circles (Stonehenge). In August and early September, 1987, an army of enthusiasts crossed from the USA to dramatize stirring military events in Britain's history, such as a medieval combat at Pickering Castle (North Yorkshire), Walmer Castle (Kent) in the Tudor age and an English Civil War garrison at the keep of Framlingham Castle (Suffolk). English Heritage has a magazine for schools, called *Remnants*, published twice a year and *English Heritage News* quarterly. It advertises courses for teachers, videos, teaching packs,[33] aerial view posters, books and new developments in the facilities owned by English Heritage. Royal palaces in the London area and the Tower of London are ever-useful large buildings with which English Heritage helps teachers to help children. As in the case of the National Trust, English Heritage arranges special role-playing days with schools in certain areas; for example Northamptonshire children with special needs from several schools enjoyed the preparation, day and follow up at Kirby Hall 'in 1600'. Role-playing in Suffolk properties has been well recorded.[34]

The input and output of a huge organization such as English Heritage cannot be matched by individual owners of houses who find it difficult to finance the maintenance of their buildings in any case. Large buildings such as Leeds Castle, Berkeley Castle and Haddon Hall do not cater for school parties specifically, but teachers familiar with preparation and follow up for any visit and prepared to find out about the building and family may prefer to plan their own work and provide their resources. In this same category of privately-owned historic buildings are The Priory, Lavenham (Suffolk) and Hedingham Castle (Essex). Both have the advantage of being comparatively small buildings which primary children find easier to conceptualize. The owners of The Priory, a grade 1 listed building and one-time home of Benedictine monks, have restored the building and made it their home; they are developing a school clientele and are at hand to give children first hand experience of historical detective work. What remains of Hedingham Castle is three storeys of the square keep built in the twelfth century; the lack of furniture enables children to appreciate the very fine stone architectural features inside the keep. A real find for busy parents and teachers is the bookstall, set out on the second floor, of up-to-date cheap and expensive books for children on castles and medieval life. The businessman owner has taken the initiative to provide most suitable reading material.

Brass rubbing and Archaeology

Both these influences from 'outside the school' are attractive 'ways in' to an understanding of the past. Both require activity on the part of the children in relation to concrete objects, all of which are genuine historical artefacts. The first became a popular pursuit in the 1960s and 1970s but curators of brasses, mainly in churches, had to limit the use which could be made of their treasures to prevent them from being rubbed away by zealous enthusiasts. In several areas centres have been established where replicas are assembled and schools can pay for permission to do rubbings. They have also become a commercial concern, and completed brass rubbings may be bought as classroom 'aids'. I have found that the rubbing of the Childwall brass depicting Henry and Clemence Norris in the fifteenth century and their connection with Speke Hall, Liverpool, has brought the study of a Tudor house to life (Fig. 4.5). Two of the most useful publications on brass-rubbing are *Brass Rubbing* by Malcolm Norris (Studio Vista, 1965) and *Discovering*

Brasses and Brass-Rubbing by Malcolm Cook (Shire Publications, 1968). The first is a beautifully-produced book fully illustrated and with clear instructions on how to rub brasses as well as specialized information about British and European brasses. Malcolm Norris includes a picture of a brass rubbing of a friar of c 1440 found at Great Amwell, Hertfordshire; it is 16 inches tall and particularly appropriate for young children to rub. He also provides a very full bibliography and a gazeteer of outstanding brasses in Britain. A useful practical article has been written on brass-rubbing from their own teaching experiences by Mary Buckles and Brian Scott.[35] As brasses are immovable they are of restricted use to teachers.

During the last five to ten years, archaeologists have made great efforts to link their work with primary schools. In 1976 Francis Hill announced the formation of an education committee of the Council for British Archaeology.[36] Since then, much has been achieved, conferences have been held (University of Southampton), artefacts from digs packaged at reasonable cost (University of Sheffield)[37] and books written for teachers.[38] To prove that archaeologists are 'hands-on' people with an understanding of children, and not just academics, the University of Manchester Archaeology Unit has initiated *Archaeology Alive*, a theatre group, with the help of M.S.C. funds. This group goes round local schools taking on the role of 'war correspondents' in ancient times and dramatizing the death of 'Pete Marsh' the Lindow Man, who was murdered in Wilmslow two thousand years ago and whose mummified remains are held by the British Museum, which does however sometimes allow Peter to travel elsewhere. This is good work, so long as the finds of archaeology are related to other parts of the past on a school sequence/time line. Like family and oral history, local history, the two World Wars and handling Victorian artefacts, it can be overdone if the same topics and methods are repeated during the six years of primary schooling.

Resources from curriculum development projects

Nearly all of the materials from research and development projects concerned with primary history were produced under the aegis of the Schools Council. The projects mentioned in Chapter 2 have given rise to substantial resources, some of which are still available for purchase, though at a price to encourage careful choice and systematic use, while others survive in libraries and teachers' and resource centres. *Environmental Studies 5–13* devised materials mainly for local geographical study; its historical publications *Environmental Studies 5–13: the Use of Historical Resources* (Schools Council Working Paper No. 48, 1973) has already been mentioned in Chapter 2. Owing to a change in publication policy, the *Place, Time and Society* materials are no longer handled by their original publishers, but some of them can be obtained from SCDC Publications, School Curriculum Development Committee, Newcombe House, 45 Notting Hill Gate, London W11 3JB, and it is hoped that the successor body, the National Curriculum Council, may continue this service. The publications available include the basic handbook *Place, Time and Society 8–13: Curriculum Planning In History, Geography and Social Science*, the booklet on *Evaluation, Assessment and Record Keeping* mentioned in Chapter 5, and pupil materials on *Clues, Clues, Clues: Detective Work in History, Life in the 1930s*, and (with less historical emphasis) *Money, People on the Move, Shops*, and *Rivers in Flood*. The lively *World Studies 8–13 Teachers' Handbook* (Oliver and Boyd, 1985), mentioned in Chapter 2, includes a useful set of references to sources.

Of the two sets of Bayeux tapestry materials referred to in Chapter 2, the one from the *Curriculum Enrichment for Gifted Children* was published in 1980, under the title *Schools Council Curriculum Enrichment Packs: Discovering History*, obtainable from Special Education Co. Ltd, and distributed by Globe Education, Houndmills Basingstoke, Hants RG2 2XS. The other set is the Bayeux tapestry pack of materials and *Teachers' Handbook* from the *Listen, Think and Speak* project published in 1984 by Holt, Rinehart and Winston for the Schools Council. Mention may also be made of the *Cambridge Schools Classics Project*, supported by the Schools Council and the Nuffield Foundation. Although mainly concerned with secondary-school work, this project did produce materials (in English) on both Greek and Roman history that are well worth considering in relation to topics for older juniors. They include, for example, packs on *The Gods of Mount Olympus* and *Greek Festivals*, which would also be relevant to integrated work including religious education in a multicultural perspective. The materials from this project were published by Cambridge University Press.

Some schools and LEAs have also developed very useful local projects,[39] some of them supported by small grants from the Schools Council of the School Curriculum Development Committee, and any teacher planning historical work in primary schools would be well advised to enquire whether any such local initiative has been taken.

In-Service Courses

The new GRIST (Grant Related In-Service Training) regulations in relation to in-service work are altering the provision of courses for the Humanities subjects. Schools are more likely to ask for courses on mathematics, language, disadvantaged children, multi-cultural issues and microcomputers than courses in primary Humanities. At the time of writing, there seem to be few courses on History in the primary school, especially as the few History Advisers who exist are concentrating on the new GCSE examination in the secondary school. More in-service work is being done after school, in schools and by teachers themselves. An example of this is the course on History in the Primary School run by Robin Lane, Headteacher of Lostock Hall County Junior School, Preston, on five days of consecutive weeks.[40] Bruce Weston, Humanities Adviser in Liverpool, has developed a three-term in-school course for primary teachers after school hours. This course starts with a term on the place of Humanities in the primary curriculum, moves on to specialist contributions on historical, geographical and multi-cultural needs and ends with a term on how to manage changes in the curriculum in the primary school. One piece of work is done by each teacher, related to her own school, after which she gains an LEA certificate of proficiency in the teaching of Humanities.

DES regional courses have come to an end, but the DES do run occasional courses for History and Geography together. The Historical Association has just initiated a one-day annual conference in London (at present) which is held in an historic building when possible. It is supported by London museums and BBC radio and television organizations. Chester College has also initiated a weekend History conference for primary teachers. It is to be hoped that such courses will be offered by more institutions of higher education in the future. Teachers who have experienced limited help in their own teacher training can gain from day, weekend or week-long intensive courses when they may listen, read, try out activities and discuss. In a recent regional survey we read that 'the overwhelming demand was for the increased provision of long and short in-service courses for primary school history teachers with a particular focus on local history'.[41] 'Outside the School' – a fourth order resource – has endless possibilities but requires teachers to have time to make contacts and arrange visits from school and to school from outside. This means that teachers need to be stable in their jobs and able to develop a repertoire of those special occasions which should be built into the syllabus and repeated to improve their approach. It is a sad reflection that recent changes in teachers' contracts and conditions of service are not likely to encourage them to venture into new approaches involving much work for them outside school hours. History, above all, is an area of the curriculum which depends upon wide reading and extra-curricular activities to feed enthusiasm in pupils.

4.6 Conclusion

In any primary school, resources should ideally be in the care of a member of staff with the assistance of at least a part-time technician-cum-secretary. Even if the teacher in charge of History-Humanities has not that responsibility, it is as well to keep all historical resources in one place and for teachers to list their requirements in a notebook for the following week. The teacher responsible for history should work out priorities through looking at the notebook and discussing with colleagues how resource needs can be fulfilled for each term. This is another reason for having a scheme of work for all years known to colleagues: their scheme should be flexible enough to allow for changes in the use of resources. Whenever resources are used they need to be checked and mended at the end of the year. The maintenance of adequate sources and resources for the teaching of history is no mean task and must be built up gradually, but the teaching of the past in the primary school is impossible without them.

Notes

1. L.C. Taylor, *Resources for Learning*, Penguin, 1972, p. 236.
2. M. Pollard, *A Handbook of Resources in the Primary School*, Ward Lock Educational, 1976, p. 9.
3. J.B. Coltham, *Junior School Children's Understanding of Historical Terms*. Ph.D. University of Manchester, 1960.
4. M. Pollard, ibid. p. 21.
5. P. Abrams, 'History without Textbooks' in *Where?* August 1964, p. 15.
6. R. Lavender, 'Children Using Information Books' in *Education 3–13* vol. 11 No. 1, Spring 1983.
7. S. Paice, 'Teaching Children Not to Read' in *The Times Educational Supplement*, 1 February, 1980.
8. J. Blyth, *Place and Time with Children 5 to 9*, Croom Helm 1984, also *History 5 to 9*, Primary Bookshelf Series, Hodder and Stoughton, 1988.
9. V. Little and J. John, *Historical Fiction in the Classroom*, T.H.59. Historical Association, 1986. V. Little et al. 'Historical Fiction and Children's Understanding of the Past' in *Education 3–13* vol. 14 No. 2, 1986. Also A. Low-Beer, 'Imagination and the Use of Historical Fiction in School' in R. Fairbrother (ed.), *History and the Primary School*, Special Issue No. 6. Greater Manchester Primary Contact, 1986. Also T. Hastie, 'Just a Pack of Lies: A Selection of Historical Fiction for use in Schools', in M.J. Corbishley (ed.), *Archaeological Resources Handbook for Teachers*, Council for British Archaeology, 1983. Also G. McBride (ed.), *A Catalogue of Children's Historical Novels*, Queen's University, Belfast.
10. H. Cam, *Historical Novels*, G48 Historical Association 1961.
11. H. Burton, 'The Writing of Historical Novels', in *Children and Literature*, Bodley Head, 1973.
12. Obtainable from the City Museum and Art Gallery, Museum Road, Old Portmouth, PO1 2LJ.
13. T. Charles-Edwards and B. Richardson, *They Saw It Happen 1689–1897*, Blackwell, 1958, p. 21.
14. C. Morris (ed.), *The Journeys of Celia Fiennes*, Cresset Press, 1947, p. 184.
15. D. Defoe, *A Tour Through the Whole Island of Great Britain*, vol. 1. Dent, 1966, p. 141.
16. S. Wheeler, 'Young Children, Documents and the Locality', in *Teaching History*, vol. 1. No. 3. 1970.

17. Quoted in W.B. Stephens, *Teaching Local History*, Manchester University Press, 1977, p. 130–1.
18. Obtainable from Dr F. O'Gorman, Historical Association, Department of History, University of Manchester, Oxford Road, Manchester M13 9PL.
19. S. Purkis, 'An Experiment in Family History with First Year Juniors', in *Teaching History*, vol. 4, No. 15, 1976.
20. B. Murphy, 'History in the Family', in *Teaching History* vol. 2, No. 5. 1971.
21. D.J. Steel and L. Taylor, *Family History in Schools*, Phillimore, 1973, p. 16.
22. D. Steel and L. Taylor (ed.), *Family History in Focus*, Lutterworth Press, 1984.
23. R. Redford, 'Listen with Mog', in *The Times Educational Supplement*, November, 1987. *Mary Queen of Scots*, Whigmaleerie, Main Street, Balerno, Edinburgh EH4 7EQ. *Bonnie Prince Charlie*, Drake Educational Associates, St. Egam Road, Fairwater, Cardiff CF5 3AF. *Pickwick's History Series*, Ladybird Books Ltd., P.O. Box 12, Beeches Road, Loughborough, Leicestershire LE11 2NQ. In 'Literature Leaps to Life' in *The Times Educational Supplement*, 12 December, 1987, she recommends Penelope Lively's *The Ghost of Thomas Kempe* (4½ hours) from Cover to Cover, Dene House, Lockeridge, Marlborough, Wiltshire.
24. E. and R. Power, *Boys and Girls of History*, C.U.P. 1927 and *More Boys and Girls of History*, Cambridge University Press, 1953.
25. The radio programme *Lost and Found* (BBC) has a pack of slides (twentieth century artefacts) and *History of Britain* (Radiovision) has a filmstrip.
26. A. Ross, *The Domesday Project*, A and C Black, 1987. E. Hallam, *The Domesday Project Book*, Hodder and Stoughton, 1986.
27. There are five articles on micro-computers in R. Fairbrother (ed.) ibid., also H. Cooper, 'Monitoring the Past' in *Junior Education*, vol. 11, No. 2, December 1987 (The Iron Age with 8 to 9 year olds).
28. J. Blyth, *History 5 to 9*, ibid., pp. 87–9.
29. C. Drage, 'Historic Decisions' in *Acorn User*, 1987, pp. 155–75, *Viking England* and *Norman England*, Fernleaf Educational Software, Fernleaf House, 31 Old Road West, Gravesend, Kent DA11 0LH. *Cateby Manor*, Resource, off Exeter Road, Doncaster DN2 4PY. *Archaeology*, Cambridgeshire Software House, Town Hall, St Ives, Huntingdon, Cambridgeshire PE17 4AL. *Wagons West*, Tressell Publications, Lower Ground Floor, 70 Grand Parade, Brighton, East Sussex BN2 2JA.
30. Resources for the *Mary Rose* Project:- *Mary Rose*, Ginn Microcomputer Software, 1983. E. Bradford, *The Story of the Mary Rose*, Hamish Hamilton, 1982. E. Cooper, *The Mary Rose*, Macmillan Education, 1984. A. McGowan, *The Ship: the Development of the Sailing Ship 1400–1700*, H.M.S.O. 1981. A. McKee, *How we found the Mary Rose*, Souvenir Press, 1981. J. Nichol, *Evidence in History: the Tudors*, Blackwell, 1981. T. Pashey, *Living History*, Wayland, 1985. M. Rule, *The Mary Rose: the Excavation and Raising of Henry VIII's Flagship*, Conway Maritime Press, 1982.
31. Y. Davies, 'Primary Questions' in *The Times Educational Supplement*, 25 April, 1986. She also mentions a Diploma course in Media Studies for primary teachers at Llay, Clwyd.
32. N. Cruickshank, 'Victorians valued' in *The Times Educational Supplement*, 20 November, 1987. This article is a tribute to the work of Mrs Jill Grey who collected books and educational artefacts from the seventeenth century and

became the curator of a private museum in Hitchin, Hertfordshire. Since Mrs Grey's death a private trust is being planned to preserve this outstanding collection and enable it to tour the country.

33. e.g. Osborne House (seaside home of Queen Victoria) resources: *A Practical Handbook for Teachers; Life on a Royal Estate – a Document Pack for Teachers*; and *Osborne House Slide Pack*, English Heritage, 1986.
34. J. Fairclough and P. Redsell, *Living History*, English Heritage, 1985.
35. M. Buckles and B. Scott, 'A Patch Study in a Junior School, Using Monumental Brasses' in *Teaching History*, vol. 3, No. 11, 1974.
36. F. Hill, 'In its Own Right' in *The Times Educational Supplement*, 12 March, 1976.
37. J. Blyth, *History 5–9* ibid., for details of Sheffield resources.
38. F. Dale (ed.), *Archaeology in the Primary School*, and M.J. Corbishly (ed.), ibid., Council for British Archaeology, 1982 and 1983.
39. Essex Education Department, *Curriculum Extension Project: Infant Series (5–7 years) No. 2. Working with Early Man.*
40. Robin Lane, *History in the Primary School* and *Project Work in the Primary School*, Preston Curriculum Development Centre, 1987.
41. R. Swift and M. Jackson 'History in the Primary School' in *Teaching History*, No. 49, 24 October, 1987, p. 34.

5 Assessment, evaluation and record keeping

5.1 Introduction

If teachers are purposefully concerned with history in primary schools, it follows that they need to know whether their teaching is justified and effective. Now that some kind of official assessment is likely to be introduced, in relation to a national curriculum, this need will also become an official obligation. It is not yet certain what this obligation will entail, or how far it will imply 'benchmarks'. What is virtually sure is that teachers will need to engage in three related activities: assessment, evaluation, and record keeping. It is important that the teaching profession should prove its capacity to carry out all three responsibly and effectively, rather than leaving the way open for others to lay down procedures for them to follow.

These three activities are not easy to implement, especially in the social subjects where aims and objectives are subtle and complex: but all three are important, and all of them need to be approached in a way that teachers can manage in the time and with the facilities at their disposal. In defining them, I follow quite closely the terminology used by Keith Cooper in *Evaluation, Assessment and Record-Keeping in History, Geography and Social Science* (Collins/ESL Bristol, 1976).[1]

Assessment covers how teachers appraise their pupils; how pupils assess themselves and each other; how they assess their teachers; and how the world at large assesses those same teachers. All these are interrelated: children can hardly be learning much if they are unable to say whether they are succeeding. Teachers are aware of all four, and not surprisingly prefer the first two to the last two, though if the first two are effectively carried out, the last two should give rise to confidence rather than to apprehension. It is however the first kind of assessment, of pupils by teachers, that will be considered in this chapter.

Evaluation ranges more widely. It is concerned with how far and how well the aims of a scheme have been achieved. It takes account of assessment, but also of curriculum processes, teaching methods, and the materials which teachers purchase or devise. If it appears, after honest reappraisal, that a programme is not effectively matched to children's capacities, or that worksheets appear to promote copying rather than thinking, then some re-casting of scheme and materials may be needed. Chapter 4 and Section 5.5 in the present chapter embody some suggestions about evaluation of materials for history teaching; the whole book is intended to help with the evaluation of schemes of work.

Record keeping monitors assessment and forms a basis for evaluation. It comprises both the informal records kept in order to mark out children's week-by-week development in basic skills, judgement, and empathy, and also the more formal, cumulative records of progress from year to year which eventually constitute some evidence about individual children that may be passed on to a secondary school.

Assessment, evaluation and record keeping apply of course across the whole curriculum. They will now be considered in relation to history in the successive age-phases of primary education.

5.2   The infant years: 5- to 7-year-olds

During these early years, all children's work is interrelated more firmly even than in later primary education, so minimal assessment of awareness of the past is needed at this stage. The basic skills of reading, writing and mathematical work are essential to all development and most infant teachers try to make their children curious to find out from books, eager to imagine the past through role-playing, and able to discuss with the teacher and with other children the ideas that they form. Tape recording children's discussions in small groups is an easy form of assessment if one knows the voices of individual children well enough; children also enjoy it immensely. The scheme of work suggested in Fig. 2.3 (Ch. 2) is very flexible and the large books made each year will contain mainly drawings, crayoned pictures, short sentences, a time-line, a simple map or plan, and possibly a short family tree. These books can be prepared for a certain day at the end of the year to be discussed in groups, with the teacher moving from group to group, and the children in each group giving a vote for the best one. Then the teacher could show the class as a whole the books selected, and ask for reasons why these have been chosen. This is a combination of teacher with pupil assessment, and the teacher need only keep a record of the best ones by putting H (for History) on the child's record card in question. (Similarly for Geography, Science etc.) Thus, by 7 years of age, two books will have been made, and more children are likely to have an H by their names.

Figure 5.1 may help infant teachers to keep their eye on assessment throughout the two years or so of the infant school.

Concepts	Skills
1. Age of objects and age of people	1. To observe and gain evidence from pictures, maps, plans, buildings, artefacts
2. Sequence of events	2. To find out and use knowledge of his own family as far back as possible
3. Changes in time	3. To communicate by telling, drawing, or making a plan or map
4. Relationships between people and events	4. To begin to understand the point of view of others

Fig. 5.1 Concepts and skills as objectives in the infant school

Therefore, from the years 5–7 assessment is ongoing, and yearly assessment is minimal and a part of class activity. As so few materials are available in this age range for the past, the only need for evaluation is of pictures and other visual material. Record keeping is also confined to the few children who are particularly interested in the past at this stage. Joan Tough's work, *Communication Skills*, has shown that the best way for teachers to assess children's progress is through talking to them individually or in small groups.[2] It is, however, important to ensure that the new Hs are added where they are deserved, and not just where they are expected. Anyone may develop a liking for history.

5.3 Incidental assessment in the junior school

Although it is possible to assess more comprehensively in the 7–11 than in the 5–7 age range, much of what goes on from day to day and the type of task set by teachers throughout the year is a form of ongoing assessment which is seldom proved wrong, even if supplemented by more formal methods at the end of the year. In *Recording Children's Progress*, Joan Dean writes: 'The outstanding teacher has a highly developed intuitive ability to find clues'[3] (i.e. to children's progress) but it is better, where normal teachers are concerned, to have records from several teachers on one child. More recently, in his comprehensive introduction to assessment and evaluation, Marten Shipman has summarized the issues involved in assessment in the primary curriculum and has stressed the values of continuous, systematic, diagnostic appraisal as an integral part of the strategy of teaching.[4] In their practical handbook, *What Primary Teachers Should Know About Assessment*, Aileen Duncan and William Dunn illuminate the general issues and lay particular emphasis on the place of distinctive 'assessment activities' in the curricular programme as a whole, but they pay little direct attention to the assessment of historical understanding.[5] There has been a dearth of other publications actually designed to assist teachers with their appraisals, though this has been attempted more positively in some other areas of the primary curriculum and is now being developed in some schools and LEAs, while some interesting and significant work is going on in institutions of higher education. Some of these developments are to be reported in a forthcoming publication on assessment in Primary Humanities.[6]

The impossibility of separating genuine appraisal from the classroom operation itself, a point to which Shipman refers, is entirely in tune with the approaches recommended in the present book. It remains to be seen how far this fairly obvious aspect of teaching can be reconciled with the expectations about testing that are to figure in primary education after the new legislation. The following observations are based on the assumption that incidental assessment will receive at least some measure of official recognition and encouragement.

'Systematic planning' of a framework has already been discussed in Chapter 2, and the necessary activities and materials for its implementation in Chapter 4. Before incidental assessment can be attempted throughout the year, it is necessary to find out a particular teacher's aims (general, long-standing, overall ones) and objectives (specific skills carried out by pupils in relation to the scheme of work, showing that they have made progress). All the schemes discussed in Chapter 3 could be said to have the aims of helping children:

1 to enjoy the past;
2 to understand the importance of a sequence of events, especially in English history;
3 to begin to understand concepts such as those of time, power, change/ continuity, similarity/difference, then/now, old/new;
4 to begin to use the language of history;
5 to begin to understand people.

Aims 1, 4, and 5 are usually 'caught' from the teacher rather than 'taught' by her. Her use of correct historical language, her explanation, if necessary by use of the blackboard, of the meaning of the more usual words (e.g., century = 100 years), and her sympathetic but dispassionate views about historical characters (e.g., King John and Richard III) will foster aims 4 and 5. The work as a whole and the enthusiasm of the teacher will promote the first aim. Constant discussion and use of time charts will help the second. Concept-formation and concept attainment are fostered by discussion and questioning, e.g., What did Henry VII, Henry VIII, and Elizabeth I have in common? What did the Romans, the Saxons, and the Normans have in common? In what ways were the Romans different from the Saxons and the Normans? These long-standing aims should be assessed incidentally all the time, and cannot be measured only at the end of the year.

Objectives, or specific skills exercised by children, must be conveyed to children before they undertake a task, and one of these could even be stated by the children at the top of a piece of work. They will be employed throughout the 7–11 years in progressively more difficult tasks, especially in written work and the use of original sources. Here are some objectives to be pursued throughout the junior school. They are arranged in an appropriate order of increasing difficulty.

1 to read a suitable history book from cover to cover;
2 to get information on a specific topic from a history book(s);
3 to make a model, graph, diagram, or sketch-map from written instructions or by looking at a picture;
4 to identify artefacts as to possible use and age;
5 to use evidence of the past from a picture, map, artefact, building, or document;
6 to write a narrative history story;
7 to ask questions systematically;
8 to tell a story orally;
9 to talk analytically about the past.

These skills are practised and improved if the teacher introduces suitable resources into the classroom, sets and marks a variety of written work at the end of each topic in the syllabus, and always encourages sensible discussion at some point in each session. In the later junior years oral assessment may involve entering a different topic on a card for each child, who, after preparation, will talk about that topic for up to five minutes and be prepared to answer questions from the class. I should never favour factual tests, however short, in the junior school since knowledge is a handmaiden of the concepts, skills and attitudes needed by the historian. The year's work, if taught with variety, will provide enough motivation, feedback, and ongoing assessment until a longer-term check is made at the end of the year.

5.4 Long-term assessment in the junior school

The ongoing assessment of children undertaking a variety of tasks must be considered in relation to long-term assessment of achievement, another issue to be considered in the forthcoming publication mentioned in the previous section. Henceforth, some more formal, periodic, assessment will become an element in a programme of national testing intended, at the least, to afford a measure of children's progress perhaps at the beginning, certainly at the end, and in practice during the whole span of the junior years. Irrespective of the actual pattern of assessment that may come to be required, it appears likely that some kind of informed comment on each child's progress will be expected at the end of each of the years from 7 to 11.

This is where assessment can be closely linked with children's own cumulative record making (Section 3.5). Books of the past, or history notebooks, could have the centre double-page spread used for a time-line or chart of the period of the past covered during the year. As the four years pass, this will become more detailed. If a thematic approach is the basic one, the time chart should be constructed accordingly. The rest of the notebook will represent the work first in the form of drawings, charts, and maps, all labelled, and if possible a full sentence written about them. Second, several sentences put together to form a paragraph on one topic, or story told by the teacher, should be another type of work. According to the ability and progress of each child, the written work will vary, but by the final year in the junior school most children should have attempted some of the following types of written work:

1 a short paragraph or account of a past event or person;
2 a longer imaginative eye-witness account from the point of view of one of the participants in an event, e.g. Francis Drake describing how he sent fire-ships into Gravelines harbour to burn the Spanish Armada;
3 a two-paragraph account of a historical character, one paragraph being biased in favour of the character and one against, e.g. Mary Tudor;
4 a comparison of conditions in a past age with present conditions – the 'then and now' approach, e.g. 'A Victorian schoolday' and 'My day at school';
5 a paragraph about a historical character gained from a short contemporary account, e.g. Samuel Pepys from an extract from his diary;
6 a short piece of documentary evidence to be 'translated' from the period concerned into modern English;
7 a short description of one history book (biography or novel) read during the year, the child writing why he liked it.

Assessing these books made by the children in small groups could take place through the teacher discussing them with the children and making a comment to be recorded on her record card for the year. That comment should be more concerned with the actual profile of qualities shown in the work than with its standard in relation to the work of other children. Such work would draw upon the child's linguistic attainment, though that would anyhow be measured by other means too. For the rest, its *historical* quality could not be so readily captured by one overall measure. A parent wishing for evidence of progress would necessarily be presented with evidence of a range of qualities, together with demonstration from the children's own books of palpable differences in quality shown over a period of time. If that kind of reporting is to be effective, a teacher must be clearly aware of the qualities which a scheme of work is designed to develop. Meanwhile, a system of this kind has the advantage of children discussing each other's work in the teacher's presence, and in the process learning the essential art of self-assessment, which was referred to earlier as one of the basic aspects of assessment as a whole.

All the four comments from the four junior years would then be inserted on the final record card. It is important to avoid formal tests 'taken in and marked', questionnaires, or too much 'paper work' for the teacher. It must be reiterated that assessment should not be external to the children's work, as secondary school examination papers often are. It should relate, like a GCSE project, to the work itself.

5.5   Evaluation of schemes of work

The first form of evaluation in primary history is fundamentally important, but is easier to write about than to undertake. As already indicated, it concerns the reconsideration of the suitability of courses. Having struggled to the end of the year, probably concerned with the whole curriculum, teachers are not always bursting with zeal to plan anew, this is particularly true in relation to work with a considerable knowledge content, as history has. So there is a very understandable temptation to repeat, substantially, what has already been achieved. After all, it was not too disastrous, was it? Or alternatively, and perhaps more insidiously, there may be a tendency to abandon parts of it in favour of something apparently enterprising but in fact rather trivial and unproductive. Yet in practice there is a curb on both these tendencies. Teachers do have a fund of common sense which prevents them from indulging in manifest absurdities of the second kind, while it also enables them to make minor adjustments, guided by the outcome of pupil assessment, to their established syllabuses. What is required is a means by which these adjustments can be made systematic.

It seems to me that this can be achieved quite quickly when planning a new year's work if the following questions are honestly answered:

1 Which one (or two) pieces of work were least satisfactory with my class in history this year? Why was this? What can I do to remedy it? Or should I abandon this (these) and substitute something better calculated to attain my aims and objectives? And how can I most economically prepare this new work?
2 What do I know (from formal records and informal contacts) about the class that I am to inherit? What history have they already encountered? Are they likely to respond differently when compared with last year? If so, will this involve making any further changes additional to those suggested under point 1?
3 Who can I consult about the changes I think it necessary to make in response to my thinking about points 1 and 2? Is there a Humanities consultant with whom I can share that thinking?
4 What additional equipment shall I need for this new work?
5 What modifications shall I need to make in my methods of teaching in order to carry out the changes arising from my decisions about points 1, 2, 3 and 4?

Put together, this simple evaluation checklist does not involve unrealistic change, not even if it is set alongside comparable changes in the rest of the curriculum. At best, it affords a stimulus; at worst, an investment of effort that may well be more rewarding than the tedium and frustration of unprofitable repetition.

However, this process of evaluation is not something which a teacher should conduct in isolation. It is the responsibility of a head teacher to coordinate the collective evaluation of a school's programme, taking account of a number of related factors. One of these is variety of teaching styles, in view of the work of Neville Bennett[7] and of the ORACLE project.[8] If Mrs Brown's incisive questioning is followed next year by Mr Black's powers of narrative and then by Miss White's flair for drama and role-playing, a fair balance is likely to result. The outcome is less happy if they all enact rather undemanding, uninspiring, and unrelated variations on the same basic information-giving theme. Again, there is the question of progression in skill acquisition. Suppose that Mrs Brown asks her 7-year-olds: 'And do you think they went to town in cars in those days?' then it is reasonable to expect that, two years later, Miss White's role-playing 9-year-olds will be grappling with something subtler, such as the pros and cons of building a railway through a village a century ago. If instead they are enacting elementary themes as at 7 years and merely changing to a different topic, such as housing, then the whole history sequence calls for some re-evaluation.

How a headteacher can alter such situations is a complex question, beyond the scope of this book. It depends on human relations skills and staff development and may not always be popular with everyone. However, pooling of ideas can only be beneficial and it must be valuable for each teacher to be obliged, even once in a year, to consider his or her own particular schemes of work as a part of a larger whole, a component of children's developing experience. The system of official record keeping is habitually regarded in this way. Ideally at least, the same should apply to the evaluation of the curriculum and of its component parts.

5.6 Evaluation of materials

The re-evaluation of the scheme leads necessarily to re-evaluation of materials. The chief value of this second form of evaluation to the primary teacher is to help her to decide which of the existing stocks to use, and which new books or materials to buy. For few resources are so fruitful that they are applicable to every piece of work, or, for that matter, so bad that they cannot be used profitably for any purpose, even if it is only a means of sharpening children's powers of criticism. Some help for this purpose can be derived from reviews, though these are not much help when the books were

Author		Price	Level	Use of book: Library – Text – Topic –
Title		Date	Bibliography	Contents page
Publisher		Date of Evaluation	Glossary	Index *

1. TITLE	– Suitability					
2. FORMAT	– Attractive layout – Durability – Printing	BOOK AS A WHOLE				
3. LANGUAGE	– Sentence flow – Word difficulty/ease – Explanation – Imaginative stimulus – Beginning and ending chapters					
4. ILLUSTRATIONS (plus maps)	– Clear – Related to text – Varied – Used as evidence	TOOLS				
5. EXTRACTS FROM WRITTEN SOURCES	– Suitability – Variety – Used as evidence	CONTENT				
6. CONTENT	– Accuracy – Suitability for existing syllabus – Detail generalization					
7. VIEWPOINT	– Bias/objectivity – Point of view	TOOLS FOR THE CLASSROOM				
8. HISTORICAL CONCEPTS	– Change/continuity – Time/duration/sequence					
9. HUMAN ELEMENTS	– People and their type – Empathy – Power – Conflict/consensus					
10. QUESTIONS AND PUPIL ACTIVITY	– Open – Closed – Skills – Attitudes – Concepts					
11. FURTHER WORK	– Helping other subjects – Using other resources – Using locality – Bibliography					
ADDITIONAL CRITERIA						
FINAL EVALUATION						

* G = Good   M = Moderate   P = Poor

Fig. 5.2 Evaluation scheme for history books

published before the teacher was a pupil in a primary school! In such circumstances the help of experienced and knowledgeable colleagues is indispensable, and is one way in which the role of Humanities consultant or its equivalent can be effectively performed. One historian on a staff, whether or not this is the headteacher, can be of great value for immediate consultation.

However, individual teachers may be thrown back on their own resources and may find it helpful to use a ready-made instrument for evaluating what is available. An exhaustive evaluation scheme for books for primary and middle schools is given in Fig. 5.2, to be used as a whole or in parts. The blank spaces are left for the teacher to insert either just a tick or a crossed tick, or a cross, and to add comments. The final column on the right-hand side is for the letter G (good), M (moderate), or P (poor), to be decided as a result of the ticks and crosses. Thus, in format, a book might have an attractive layout (tick), poor durability in the form of a paper cover (cross), and printing clear but not large enough for the age group (crossed tick). The format would therefore have M in the right-hand column. All the letters would add up to the final evaluation and letter. This evaluation scheme could be kept by the teacher responsible for history, and used by all class teachers for a particular series of books.

Pictures, maps, and wallcharts are also used constantly by teachers, and if time allowed, schedules could be made jointly by all class teachers. These might all equally well apply to other areas of the curriculum. The head-teacher, or the teacher responsible for history in a primary school, should try to build up useful schedules and to evaluate the main resources used with the help of colleagues and the children themselves. All of this should constitute an essential part of the evaluation, and re-evaluation, of history teaching in the school.

5.7   Record keeping[9]

Assessment and evaluation naturally lead to record keeping if they are to be of use in the future. The important side of this exercise is that it must be simple, efficient, and speedy to execute. Three teachers writing on this topic are well aware of the time this can take. Keith Cooper writes: 'Keeping records takes time. Until the day dawns when teachers have adequate secretarial help, teachers will have to find time from all their other tasks so that their records are adequate and useful'.[10] Joan Dean agrees with this sentiment when she writes: 'Record keeping is very much the art of the possible, and teachers will vary in the degree to which they find it helpful to make observations on paper.'[11] May Cooper adds to the refrain with: 'Teacher recording uses a tremendous amount of time, which might be

	Reference and information-finding skills	Skills in chronology	Language and historical ideas
By the age of 8	Can scan pictures and simple books. Can read simple accounts. Can use page references.	Can use basic vocabulary (e.g. 'now', 'long ago', 'then', 'before', 'after'). Begins to understand the chronology of the year (e.g. seasons); and begins to record on a wall chart sequence of stories heard. Can put some historical pictures and objects into sequence.	Can 'use' terms commonly used stories of past (e.g. hero, heroine, king, queen, nobleman, sheriff). Begins to use words such as 'the past', 'myth', 'true'.
By the age of 10	Knows which books supply information (e.g. topic, encyclopaedias). Can use contents, index and glossaries of books; and can read different passages to select information relevant to a topic. Can use visual sources (e.g. pictures, filmstrips, slides, artefacts); and oral sources (talk, tape, radio). Can list main points from one or more sources using teachers' questions	Knows terms BC and AD. Understands 'generation' in a family context. Knows sequence of prehistoric, ancient times, middle ages and modern. Can put a wide range of historical pictures and objects in sequence. Can make a simple individual sequence chart	Can use an increasing number of terms that arise from topics studied (e.g. knight, peasant, emperor, bishop). Knows words such as 'history', 'archaeology'.
By the age of 12	Can use a library catalogue (subject). Can read textbooks and topic books in conjunction. Can make more detailed notes under supplied headings using several sources. Can use abbreviations such as e.g. i.e.	Understands 'century' and how dating by century works. Can put dates in correct century. Knows sequence of Roman, Saxon, Viking, Norman, Tudor, Stuart, Victorian. Is aware of some historical period terms (e.g. Reformation). Can make a time chart using scale.	Can use an increasing number of terms that arise from topics studied (e.g. keep, lateen, sail). Can use common terms of greater degree of abstraction (e.g. ruler, subject, parliament).

Fig. 5.3   Some objectives for pupil progress in historical skills 5–12

Use of analysis of evidence	Empathetic understanding	Asking historical questions	Synthesis and communication using basic ideas
cribe the main features of evidence of the past (e.g. artefacts, buildings) and size as to their use. ar with the question 'How do v?'.	Can say, write or draw what they think it felt like in response to some historical story that has been heard.	Begins to become aware of basic historical questions, e.g. ● What happened and when? ● Why did it happen? ● How do we know?	Using memory and recall, can describe orally and in writing some past events or story in narrative or dramatic form. Can make a pictorial representation.
ne in simple terms 'source' dence'. erstand and make ns from documentary as well ete evidence e.g. pictures,). cribe the main features of aps, diagrams or graphs. ngly asks the question 'How ow?'.	Can make a simple imaginative reconstruction of a situation in the past and how it appeared to some of the people in it, using the evidence available to draw, model, dramatize, write or tell the story.	Becomes used to asking of any historical period studied question about the main features of everyday life, e.g. ● When and how did people live and how did they feed themselves? ● What was the available technology? ● What were the life styles of different social and gender groups? ● What are the differences between now and then?	Can describe orally and in writing some past events or situations recognizing *similarities/differences* with today. Can state information in a graph, diagram or map. Can support an account or conclusion with some evidence.
of variety of historical at different periods of time. nguish between primary and ry sources; and can nd and make inferences nary and secondary (text-books, fiction). gnize 'gaps' in evidence. rpret simple graphical	Can make an imaginative reconstruction that is not anachronistic of a past situation based on several pieces of evidence, including historical fiction, and exploring some of the feelings participants might have had at the time.	Becomes used to asking of any historical period additional questions of increasing difficulty, e.g. ● Who governed and how and with what results? ● What did they worship and what values did they live by? ● What was their art, music and literature?	Can put together orally and in writing a narrative of past events or situations showing evidence of *continuity* and *change* and indicating simple *causation*. Can make accurate diagrams or maps based on several pieces of evidence.

better spent in preparatory work.'[12] Joan Dean also warns teachers that assessment and record keeping can encourage the teacher to expect too much from children. Yet with more individual work done in schools, vertical grouping, mixed ability teaching, co-operative teaching units, and now falling numbers necessitating teaching different age groups together in many schools, there is more need than ever for effective records.

Individual record keeping is not to be recommended in history beyond the rough selection of the letter H on the normal record card near the names of children who are good at history. But two ideas may be considered, which are not too time-consuming. One is a record card for the whole class in history, so that with the scheme framework (Fig. 5.3) in mind, teachers will know at a glance what skills have been mastered (or not) as a whole. The other idea is that children should help the teacher by keeping their own records, thus reinforcing their own learning of self-assessment. This is supported by both Joan Dean and May Cooper. Joan Dean knows one school where each child keeps her own record of what work has been done each week, and with which part of the work she needs particular help. Other schools which she mentions keep records of what content of work has been covered, but this is not so necessary if there is a history scheme. May Cooper starts her 8-year-olds writing their own records for all areas of the curriculum during the last period of each day. From a list on the blackboard, the child selects the work done and adds details about how far she has got with it. She then writes shortly about her feelings in respect of the work, and assesses her own performance. The children like doing this, and feel more involved with the work as well as providing the teacher with valuable information about the feelings of individual children. This method could be applied to history as one subject, once a month, if the teacher did not want it to cover the whole curriculum.[13]

A combination of a good scheme of work, class record card of skills attained, and individual records made each month by each child, may seem the best. If this were done systematically for four years, a very adequate profile of history teaching and learning would emerge by the time the children were 11-years-old. It is to be hoped that this profile could be transmitted to secondary schools, and that the head of the history department there would take notice of it. For if history is adequately considered in primary schools, its outcome should be taken seriously into account by those who plan what is to follow. In this way, it should prove possible to develop and monitor, within the framework of a national curriculum from 5 to 16, the development in historical understanding that is, we all agree, desirable.

Notes

1. K. Cooper, *Evaluation, Assessment and Record-Keeping in History, Geography and Social Science*, Collins/ESL Bristol 1976 (obtainable from School Curriculum Development Committee).
2. J. Tough, *Listening to Children Talking*, Ward Lock, 1976; *Talking and Learning*, Ward Lock, 1977; *Focus on Meaning*, Allen and Unwin, 1974.
3. J. Dean, *Recording Children's Progress*, Macmillan, 1972, p. 7.
4. M. Shipman, *Assessment in Primary and Middle Schools*. Teaching 5–13 Series, Croom Helm, 1983.
5. A. Duncan & W. Dunn, *What Primary Teachers Should Know About Assessment*, Primary Bookshelf Series, Hodder & Stoughton, 1988.
6. W.A.L. Blyth, *Making the Grade: Assessing Humanities in Primary Schools*, Open University Press, forthcoming.
7. N. Bennett, *Teaching Styles and Pupil Progress*, Open Books, 1976.
8. M. Galton, B. Simon & P. Croll, *Inside the Primary Classroom*, Routledge & Kegan Paul, 1980.
9. P. Clift et al., *Record Keeping in Primary Schools*, Macmillan, 1981.
10. K. Cooper, op. cit. p. 40.
11. J. Dean, op. cit. p. 57.
12. M. Cooper, 'Children as Assessors' in *The Times Educational Supplement*, 21 July, 1978.
13. ibid.

Select Bibliography

Most of these books have been published in the last ten years. Articles and pamphlets are not included as they are in end of chapter references.

General
DES (1978). *Primary Education in England*. HMSO.
DES (1982). *Education 5 to 9: An Illustrative Survey of 80 First Schools*. HMSO.
Donaldson, M. (1978). *Children's Minds*. Fontana.
Egan, K. (1979). *Educational Development*. Oxford University Press.
Elliott, G. (1976). *Teaching for Concepts*. School Curriculum Development Committee.
Heeks, P. (1981). *Choosing and Using Books in the First School*. Macmillan.
——(1982). *Ways of Knowing: Information Books for 7–9 Year Olds*. Thimble.
Treasure Chest for Teachers (1987). (12th edition.) Teacher Publishing Company.

General History
Blyth, J. (1984). *Place and Time with Children 5 to 9*. Teaching 5–13 Series. Croom Helm.
Blyth, J. (1988). *History 5 to 9*, Primary Bookshelf Series, Hodder & Stoughton.
DES (1985). *History in the Primary and Secondary Years: An HMI View*. HMSO.
Faculty of Community Studies and Education (1986). *History in the Primary School*, Special Issue 6. Greater Manchester Primary Contact, Didsbury School of Education, Manchester.
Low-Beer, A. and Blyth, J. (1983). *Teaching History to Younger Children*, T.H. 52. Historical Association.
Mays, P. (1974). *Why Teach History?* University of London Press.
McBride, G. (ed.)(1979). *Teaching History 8–13*. Queen's University, Belfast.
Nichol, J. (1981). *What is History?* Blackwell.
Noble, P. (1985). *Curriculum Planning in Primary History*. J.H. 87, Historical Association.
——(1986). *Understanding History*, Help Your Child Series. Hodder & Stoughton for W.H. Smith.
Northern Ireland Council for Educational Development (1984). *History: Guidelines for the Primary School*.

Reeves, M. (1980). *Why History?* Longmans.
West, J. (1966). *History Here and Now*. Teacher Publishing Company.

Topic Work (including History)
Bassey, M. (ed.) *Concept Ladders in Primary School Topic Work*, Trent Papers in Education, 84/2. Trent Polytechnic. Nottingham.
Bradley, H., Eggleston, J., Kerry, T. and Cooper, D. (1984). *Developing Pupils' Thinking Through Topic*. Longmans for School Curriculum Development Committee.
Gunning, S., Gunning, D. and Wilson, J. (1981). *Topic Teaching in the Primary School*. Croom Helm.
Kerry, T. and Eggleston, J. (1988). *Topic Work in the Primary School*. Routledge & Kegan Paul.
Wiltshire County Council (1987). *History-based Topic Work*.
——(1983). *Topic Work in the Primary School*. Both from Education Department, County Hall, Trowbridge, Wilts.
Wray, D. (1988). *Project Teaching: Bright Ideas*. Scholastic.

Stories, Role-playing and Imaginative Work.
Best, A.M. (ed.) *Story telling: Notes for Teachers of History in the Junior School*. Historical Association.
Fairclough, J. and Redsell, P. (1985). *Living History*. English Heritage.
Farjeon, E. and H. (1983). *Kings and Queens* (poems). Dent.
Fines, J. and Verrier, R. (1974). *The Drama of History*. New University Education.
Johnson, L. and O'Neill, C. (eds.) (1984). *Dorothy Heathcote: Collected writings on education and drama*. Hutchinson.
Little, V. and John, T. (1986). *Historical Fiction in the Classroom*. T.H. 59, Historical Association.
Snelgrove, L. (1986). *Story-line*, role 1–4. Oliver & Boyd.
Wagner, B.J. (1979). *Dorothy Heathcote: Drama as a Learning Medium*, Hutchinson.

Activity in the Classroom
Hall, L. (1987). *Bright Ideas: History*. Scholastic Publications.

Oral and Family History
Doherty, B. (1987), *Granny was a Buffer Girl*. Methuen and Heinemann (New Windmill Series).
Exley, R.H. (1984), *Grandmas and Grandpas*. Exley Publications.
Gifford, G. (1986), *Too Many Grans*. Hodder & Stoughton.
McLauchlin, E. (1985). *Interviewing Elderly Relatives*, Federation of Family Histories (from E. McLauchlin, Varneys, Budds Lane, Haddenham, Nr. Aylesbury, Bucks).
Purkis, S. (1987). *Thanks for the Memory*, How do we know Series, Collins.
Steel, D. and Taylor, L. (1973). *Family History in Schools*, Phillimore.
——(1984), *Family History in Focus*, Lutterworth Press.
Steel, D. (1980). *Discovering Your Family History*. BBC.

Taylor, L. (1984) *Oral Evidence and the Family Historian*. Federation of Family History Societies.
Totton, E. (1983). *My Family Tree Book*, Unwin Hyman.

Going out of school – churches, museums, art galleries, abbeys, castles and 'stately homes'.

Dobson, J. (1978). *Children of the Tower*, Heinemann.
Hudson, K. and Nichols, A. (1987). *Cambridge Guide to Museums of Britain and Ireland*, Cambridge University Press.
Pluckrose, H. 1984. *Look Around – Outside*, Heinemann.

Publications of The National Trust, English Heritage and many museums and art galleries have replaced books to help the teacher, e.g. Richardson, J. (1984), *Inside the British Museum*. British Museum.

Books on specific buildings soon go out of print. A recent series (1987) from Franklin Watts is *Great British Castles, Houses, Churches* and *Monuments*.

Appendices

I Articles from *Teaching History* from 1980 to 1987

On understanding and concept-formation
J. West, 'Primary School Children's Perception of Authenticity and Time in Historical Narrative Pictures', No. 29, February 1981.
J. West, 'Testing the Use of Written Records in Primary Schools', No. 32, February 1982.
J. Fines, Review Article, 'Go West, Young Man', No. 34, October 1982.
J. Lally, 'Writing History, 8–13', No. 37, October 1983.
M. Pond, 'School History Visits and Piagetian Theory', No. 37, October 1983.
H. Cooper, 'From Marbles to Murder', No. 36, June 1983.
J. West, 'The Dudley Project: "Children's Awareness of the Past" ', Comment, No. 40, October 1984.

On sources as evidence for teaching
I. Mason, 'The Records Road Show or Documents in Essex Classrooms', No. 31, October 1981.
B. Dix, 'Down among the Deadmen: Graveyard Survey', No. 31, October 1981.
A. Ross, ' "Faction" and History: Solving some Problems in Primary Children's Understanding of the Past (Kelly's Street Directory)', No. 34, October 1982.
H. Glendinning and G. Timmins, 'Population History with Juniors', No. 36, June 1983.
G. Rogers, 'The Use of Primary Evidence in the Junior School Classroom', No. 38, February 1984.
J. Davis, 'Artefacts in the Primary School', No. 46, June 1986.

On curriculum planning
P. Noble, 'Primary History: What Guidelines are Needed?', No. 33, June 1982.
P. Sudworth, 'An Analysis of History Teaching in the Primary School since 1960', No. 33, June 1982.
T. D. Cook, 'Towards a Nationally Agreed Framework for the Teaching of Primary School History', No. 42, June 1985.

G. Batho, 'History: A Most Crucial Element of the Curriculum (LEA guidelines)', No. 42, June 1985.
N. Procter, 'History, Geography and Humanities: a Geographer's Interpretation', No. 48, June 1987.
R. Swift and M. Jackson, 'History in the Primary School: a regional survey', No. 49, October 1987.

On microcomputers
J. Gent, 'A Primary School's Experience with a Microcomputer', No. 30, June 1981.
R. Jones, 'Primary Schools: Humanities and Microelectronics', No. 33, June 1982.
A. Ross, 'Microcomputers and Local History in a Primary School (1861–71 Census Returns)', No. 35, February 1983.

On projects
A. Blake, 'Who was John F. Kennedy? A Project for Juniors', No. 30, June 1981.
J. Standen, 'Place, Time and Society 8–13, with Top Juniors', No. 31, October 1981.
A. Dilks, 'Time Travellers: Teaching Tudor History to Young Children', No. 43, October 1985.

On role-playing, drama and imagination
V. Little, 'What is Historical Imagination?', No. 36, June 1983.
T. May and S. Williams, 'Empathy – a Case of Apathy', No. 49, October 1987.

On teaching the past to infants
J. Fines, 'Trainee Teachers of History and Infants as Learners', No. 26, February 1980.
C. Taylor and J. Allmark, 'A Castle in the Classroom (Portchester)', No. 26, February 1980.

On archaeology
D. Wright, 'A Small Local Investigation (Archaeology and the First School)', No. 39, June 1984.
R. David, 'Taking Advantage of Tollund Man (Sheffield and Archaeology)', No. 46, June 1986.

On museums
G. Pearson, 'Jorvik – Inside the Museum Case', No. 41, February 1985.

On oral history
A. Hall, 'Rose's Life', No. 26, February 1980.

On textbooks
S. Purkis, 'The Unacceptable Face of History (a viewpoint of R.J. Unstead's work)', No. 26, February 1980.

Teaching History is published four times a year by the Historical Association through Blackwells, the publishers, Oxford. Copies of the journal may be obtained from the Historical Association, 59A Kennington Park Road, London SE11 4JH, and from

Basil Blackwell, Broad Street, Oxford. *Education 3–13, Junior Education, The Teacher, Primary Teaching Studies* and the *Greater Manchester Primary Contact* also publish articles on History in the primary school.

II Places of historic interest referred to in the text

Museums

Abbey House (Kirkstall), part of Museum of Leeds. (Tel: 0532–637861)

Andover Museum (Iron Age), 6 Church Close, Andover, SR10 1DR. (Tel: 0264–66283)

Armley Mills Industrial Museum, Canal Road, Armley, Leeds, LS12 2QP. (Tel: 0532–797326)

Beamish Open Air Museum, Nr Chester-le-Street, Co. Durham. (Tel: 0207–231–811)

Bethnall Green Museum of Childhood, Cambridge Heath Road, London, EC9 9PA. (Tel: 01–980–2415)

Bosworth Field Museum, Sutton Cheney, Market Bosworth, Leicestershire, CV13 0AD. (Tel: 0455–290429)

Bradford Industrial Museum, Moorside Road, Eccleshill, Bradford. (Tel: 0274–631756)

British Museum, Education Service, Great Russell Street, London, WC1B 3DG. (Tel: 01–636–1555)

Bucklers Hard Maritime Museum, Beaulieu, Hampshire. (Tel: 059–063203)

Castle Museum, York. (Tel: 0904–53611)

City of Leeds Museum, Municipal Buildngs, Leeds, LS1 3AA. (Tel: 0532–462465)

Clarke Hall Educational Museum, Aberford Road, Wakefield, Yorkshire. (Tel: 0924–375–598)

Cutty Sark Clipper Ship, King William Walk, Greenwich, London, SE1. (Tel: 01–858–3445)

Derby City Museum, The Strand, Derby, DE3 6JH. (Tel: 0322–31111)

Friargate Wax Museum, Lower Friargate, York, YO1 1SL. (Tel: 0904–58775)

Gallery of English Costume, Platt Hall, Platt Fields, Rusholme, Manchester. (Tel: 061–224–5217)

Geffreye Museum, Kingsland Road, Shoreditch, London, EC8 8EA. (Tel: 01–739–8368)

Grosvenor Museum, Grosvenor Street, Chester. (Tel: 0244–21616)

Higher Mill Textile Museum, Helmshore, Accrington, Lancashire. (Tel: 0706–226459)

Imperial War Museum, Lambeth Road, London, SE1 6HZ. (Tel: 01–735–8922)

Ironbridge Gorge Museum, Ironbridge, Telford, Shropshire, TF8 7AW. (Tel: 0952–45–3522)

John Judkyn Memorial Museum, Freshford Manor, Claverton, Bath, BA3 6EF. (Tel: 022–122–3312)

Jorvic Viking Centre, Coppergate, York. (Tel: 0904–643–211)

Judges' Lodgings Museum, Church Street, Lancaster. (Tel: 0524–32808)

Mary Rose Trust, 48 Warblington Street, Old Portsmouth, Hampshire, PO1 2ET. (Tel: 0705–750521)
Mall Galleries, The Mall, London, SW1Y 5DB. (Tel: 01–930–6844)
Merseyside County Museums, William Brown Street, Liverpool. (Tel: 051–207–001)
Museum of East Anglian Life, Stowmarket, Suffolk, IP14 1DL. (Tel: 0449–612229)
Museum of History of Education, Parkinson Court, University of Leeds, Leeds. (Tel: 0532–431–751)
Museum of London, 150 London Wall, London, EC27 5HN. (Tel: 01–600–3699)
National Maritime Museum, Park Row, Greenwich, London, SE10 9NF. (Tel: 01–858–4422)
National Portrait Gallery, St Martins Place, London, WC2 0HE. (Tel: 01–930–1552 Extension 249/273)
Portsmouth City Museum and Art Gallery, Museum Road, Old Portsmouth, PO1 2LJ. (Tel: 0705–827261)
Science Museum, Exhibition Road, South Kensington, London, SW7 2DD. (Tel: 01–589–3456)
Sudbury Hall Museum, Nr. Derby. (Tel: 028–378–305)
Tate Gallery, Millbank, London, SW1 4RG. (Tel: 01–821–1313)
Tudor House Museum, St Michael's Square, Southampton, Hampshire. (Tel: 0703–24216)
Weald and Downland Open Air Museum, Singleton, Chichester, Sussex, PO18 1OE. (Tel: 0243–63–348)
Wigan Pier, Wallgate, Wigan, Lancashire, WN3 4EU. (Tel: 0942–323666)

Houses
Berkeley Castle, Dursley, Gloucestershire. (Tel: 0453–810332)
[1]Charlecote Park, Wellesbourne, Warwick, CV35 9ER. (Tel: 0789–840277)
Chatsworth House, Bakewell, Derbyshire. (Tel: 024–688–2204)
[1]Erddig, Nr. Wrexham, Clwyd, LL13 0YT. (Tel: 0978–355314)
Haddon Hall, Bakewell, Derbyshire. (Tel: 062–981–2855)
[1]Hardwick Hall, near Chesterfield, Derbyshire. (Tel: 0246–850–430)
Hinchinbrooke House, Brampton Road, Huntingdon, Cambridgeshire. (Tel: 0480–51121)
Kensington Palace, Educational Bookings, London, W8 4PY. (Tel: 01–930–3141)
[2]Kirby Hall, Corby, Northamptonshire. (Tel: 0536–203230)
[1]Knole House, Sevenoaks, Kent, TN15 0RP. (Tel: 0732–450608)
Leeds Castle, Maidstone, Kent. (Tel: 0622–65400)
[1]Little Moreton Hall, Congleton, Cheshire, CW12 4SD. (Tel: 0260–272018)
Longleat House, Warminster, Wiltshire. (Tel: 0985–213507)
[1]Montacute House, Montacute, Somerset, TA15 6XP. (Tel: 0935–823289)
[2]Osborne House, Isle of Wight. (Tel: 0983–200022)
[1]Petworth House, Petworth, Sussex, GU28 0AE. (Tel: 0798–42207)
[1]Speke Hall, The Walk, near Liverpool, L24 1XD. (Tel: 051–427–7231)
[1]Tatton Park, Knutsford, Cheshire, WA16 6QN. (Tel: 0565–54822/3)
The Priory, Water Street, Lavenham, Suffolk, CO10 9RW. (Tel: 0787–247417)
[1]Wilderhope Manor, Easthope, Much Wenlock, Shropshire, TF13 6EG. (Tel: 069–43–363)

Castles
[2]Deal Castle, Deal, Kent. (Tel: 0304–372762)
[2]Framlingham Castle, Framlingham, Suffolk. (Tel: 0728–723330/724189)
Hedingham Castle, Castle Hedingham, Essex. (Tel: 0787–60804/60261)
[2]Pickering Castle, Pickering, North Yorkshire. (Tel: 0751–74989)
[2]Tower of London, Tower Hill, London, EC3 4AB. (Tel: 01–709–0765)
[2]Walmer Gate, Walmer, Kent. (Tel: 0304–364288)

Religious Buildings
Canterbury Cathedral, Canterbury, Kent.
[2]Rievaulx Abbey, near Helmsley, North Yorkshire. (Tel: 04396–228)
[2]Westminster Abbey (Chapter House, Pyx Chamber and Abbey Museum). (Tel:
   01–222–5897)

Record Offices
Essex Record Office, County Hall, Chelmsford, Essex, CM1 1LX (Tel: 0245–492211
   Extension 20070)
Merseyside County Record Office, William Brown Street, Liverpool, L3 8EN. (Tel:
   051–327–1946)
Staffordshire Record Office, Eastgate Street, Stafford, ST16 2LZ. (Tel: 0785–3121
   Extension 8380)
Kent County Archives Office, County Hall, Maidstone, Kent, ME14 1XH. (Tel:
   0622–671411 Extension 3363)

Miscellaneous
Fishbourne Roman Palace, Fishbourne, Chichester, Sussex. (Tel: 0243–785859)
Kingswood Nursery/Infant Centre, Albrighton, Wolverhampton WV7 3AW. (Tel:
   090–745787)
[2]Ludlow (castle – streets – church) and Stokesay Castle, Shropshire.
[1]Quarry Bank Mill, Styal, Wilmslow, Cheshire, SK9 4LA. (Tel: 0625–527468)

III Useful addresses

Archaeology
Archaeology Alive, University of Manchester, Oxford Road, Manchester, M13
   9PL.
Archaeology in Education, Department of Archaeology and Prehistory, University
   of Sheffield, Sheffield, S10 2TN.
Council for British Archaeology, 112 Kennington Road, London, WC1B 3QQ.
Young Archaeologists' Club, United House, Piccadilly, York, YO1 1PQ.

Associations to join
English Heritage Education Service, 15/17 Great Marlborough Street, London,
   W1V 1AF.

[1] = National Trust
[2] = English Heritage

GEM (Group for Education in Museums) Jeni Harrison, 389 Great Western Road, Aberdeen, AB1 6NY.
Historical Association, 59A Kennington Park Road, London SE11 4JH (*Teaching History* is a journal of the Historical Association).
National Trust, PO Box 30, Beckenham, Kent BR3 4TZ

Drama
Unicorn Theatre for Children, 679 Newport Street, London WC2.

Field Work
British Rail Education Service, PO Box 10, Wetherby, Yorkshire, LS23 6YY.
Heritage Education Trust, St Mary's College, Strawberry Hill, Twickenham, TW1 4SX.

Local Education Authorities
Essex Education Department, Threadneedle Street, Market Road, Chelmsford, Essex, CM1 1LD.

Microcomputers, Films and Videos (in addition to the references at the end of Chapter 4).
BIGPRINT, Barbara Maines, South House, Yatesbury, North-Calne, Wiltshire, SN11 8YE.
Cambridge Micro Software, Cambridge University Press, The Edinburgh Building, Shaftesbury Road, Cambridge, CB2 2RU.
Department of the Environment, Bookshop, Hampton Court Palace, East Molesley, Surrey KT8 9AU. *Tudor Palace of Hampton Court* (16 minute video)
Gerald of Wales by Siriol Animations (a 25 minute video) obtainable from Cadw, Brunel House, 2 Fitzalan Road, Cardiff CF2 1UY. Also three pamphlets for children, *Gerald and his Journey, Gerald Meets the Monks*, and *Gerald Travels North* and *A Mirror of Medieval Wales –Gerald of Wales and his Journey of 1188* by Charles Kightly.
Non-Theatrical Programmes, Geoff Foster, Yorkshire Television Enterprises Ltd., Leeds, LS3 1JS (videos of *How we used to Live* television programmes).
North West Film Archive, Minshull House, 47–9 Chorlton Street, Manchester, M1 3EU.
Scenes from History: the Woollen and Clothing Industries, (25 minute video) from Leeds University Audio Visual Service, The University, Leeds.
Wessex Educational Television Consortium, King Alfred's College, Winchester, SO22 4NR (35 minute video of the *Court Leet of 1566*).

Museums
Museum Education in London, Centre for Learning Resources, 275 Kennington Lane, London, SE11 5QZ (information about all museums in the London area).

Oral and Family History
Association of Teachers of Family History, c/o Thomas Nelson and Sons, Nelson House, Mayfield Road, Walton-on-Thames, Surrey, KT12 5PL.
Help the Aged, Education Department, St James Walk, London, EC1R 0BE.

Interaction Trust, Wilkin Street, London, W1.

E. McLaughlin, Varneys, Rudds Lane, Haddenham, nr. Aylesbury, Buckinghamshire (pamphlet on oral history).

Oral History Society, Department of Sociology, University of Essex, Wivenhoe Road, Colchester, Essex, CO4 3SQ.

The Age Reminiscence Centre, 11 Blackheath Village, London, SE3.

TV History Centre, 42 Queen Street, London, WC1N 3AJ.

Publications

Garnons Williams Publications, Hardwicke Stables, Hadnall, Shrewsbury, Shropshire, SY4 4AS. (county Domesday Maps).

Greater Manchester Primary Contact, Didsbury School of Education, Manchester Polytechnic, 799 Wilmslow Road, Manchester, M20 8RR.

Junior Education, Child Education, Junior Projects, Infant Projects, Bright Ideas, Scholastic Publications Ltd., Marlborough House, Holly Walk, Leamington Spa, Warwickshire, CV32 4LS.

Pictorial Charts Educational Trust, 23 Krichen Road, West Ealing, London, W13 0UD.

Primary Teaching Studies, Department of Teaching Studies, Polytechnic of North London, Prince of Wales Road, London, NW5 3LB.

School Curriculum Development Committee, Newcombe House, 45 Notting Hill Gate, London, W11 3JB.

Teacher Publishing Co. Ltd., Derbyshire House, Lower Street, Kettering, Northamptonshire, NN16 8BB.

The Tudors at Hampton Court Palace: A Pack for Teacher by Angela Cox, Department of the Environment, Royal Parks and Palaces series; HMSO 1987.

Teachers' Centres

Avon Resources, Resources for Learning Development Unit, Bishop Road, Bishopston, Bristol, BS7 8LS.

Centre for North West Regional Studies, University of Lancaster, Bailrigg, Lancaster (a university department, very helpful to teachers).

Heritage Project, The Oxford Story, 5 Broad Street, Oxford, OX1 3AJH.

I.L.E.A. Centre for Learning Resources, Thackeray Road, London, SW8 3TB.

I.L.E.A. History and Social Sciences Teachers' Centre, 377 Clapham Road, London, SW9 9BT.

School in the World, World Development Centre, S. Katherine's College, Stand Park Road, Liverpool, L16 9JD.

Teachers' Centre, Queen's University, Upper Crescent, University Road, Belfast, BT7 1NT.

The Canterbury Pilgrims Way, St Margaret's Street, Canterbury, CT1 2TC (teaching packs are available).

York Centre for School Visits, St William's College, 6 College Street, York, YO1 2TF.

Miscellaneous

The Mapograph Co. Ltd. Concordia Works, Department TES1, Carmichael Road, South Norwood, London, SE25 5LX (period costumes and maps).

Index